TEACHING CHILDREN WITH SPECIAL NEEDS

TEACHING CHILDREN WITH SPECIAL NEEDS

SONIA GROVER

2007

SBS Publishers & Distributors Pvt. Ltd.
New Delhi

ISBN 10 : 81-89741-56-X
ISBN 13 : 978-81-89741-56-3

Indian Price - Rs 795
Foreign Price - USD 39.95

First Published in India in 2007

Published by:
SBS PUBLISHERS & DISTRIBUTORS PVT. LTD.
2/9, Ground Floor, Ansari Road, Darya Ganj,
New Delhi - 110002, INDIA
Tel: 23289119, 41563911
Email: mail@sbspublishers.com
www.sbspublishers.com

Printed in India by SALASAR IMAGING SYSTEMS.

Preface

The field of special education is so diverse and complex that it overflows with unresolved issues. Although most individuals agree that special education is an aspect of education needed in today's society, they are unclear about how it should be defined or delivered. This has led to a number of books and articles examining various issues and raising questions to explore the outer limits of the field

This book is a general introduction to the characteristics of children with disabilities and their education. This book emphasized classroom practices as well as the psychological, sociological, and medical aspects of disabilities.

This text is written with three audiences in mind: those individuals who are preparing to be special educators and those who are preparing to be general educators, and the parents of disabled children. This book also is appropriate for professional in other fields who work with children's having disabilities.

I believe that text of this book reaches the heart as well as the mind. It is my conviction that persons working with disabled children need to develop not only a solid base of knowledge, but also a healthy attitude towards their need and the people whom they serve.

It is hoped that if those new to teaching students with disabilities accept some of these ideas, may be they can avoid the "sink or swim" mentality that many of us experienced when we first started. For teachers reading this book for the first time, there may be strategies that apparently don't apply. As in many new endeavors, there may be a tendency to "not know what you don't know." We ask that you come back and revisit this book from time to time throughout the year. What may not be applicable the first time you read it may be of help at a later date. The more resources teachers have at their fingertips to assist their practice along their educational journey, the better the outcome for us all. I hope all teachers will find this book useful and practical in defining and enhancing their teaching skills.

Contents

1 Introduction

Special Education: An Introduction

All students require support from teachers, classmates, family, and friends in order to thrive and to gain full benefit from their school experience. Some students have special needs that require additional supports beyond those ordinarily received in the school setting. Children who have behavioural or communication disorders, or intellectual, physical or multiple disabilities, or who are gifted, may require special education services or special education programmes in order to enable them to attend school and to benefit fully from their school experience. Such students may be formally identified as exceptional pupils. Definitions of exceptionalities that must be used by school boards after determining that a student is an "exceptional pupil".

Special education (also known as special ed, SPED or defectology) refers euphemistically to the teaching of students with a learning disability, a developmental disability or a behavioural problem, or to that of gifted children. This article will focus mainly on the teaching of students with disabilities.

Throughout the world, Children With Special Needs (CWSN) were a neglected lot till the 18th century, when the ideas of fraternity, equality and liberty sweeping France and America inspired political reformers and leaders in medicine and education to turn their attention towards the educational needs of such individuals. France played a pioneering role in the area of special education. It was in Paris that Valentine Huay started a School for the Blind in 1785 and Father De L'epee developed an early version of finger spelling for the deaf. Jean Marc Gaspard Itard's case study of 'The Wild Boy of Aveyron' is a pioneering work in the field of education for the mentally retarded.

History

Naturally, many students' challenges have historically driven their placement in classes which are specific to a particular. However, the goal is for all students to be placed in a learning environment that is the least restrictive for each individual learner. In the past 15 years, that has come to mean inclusive environments: all students learning together with each individual's specific learning needs being met within a typically occurring classroom environment. The fact that this has been less than successful may have more to do with the resources allotted such programmes, and the inability of an entrenched model of education to change to accommodate such an educational process, than with the legitimacy of such a model itself.

National Perspective

Along with other parts of the world, India too, witnessed the emergence of special schools for people with disabilities. The first school for the deaf was set up in Bombay in 1883, and the first school for the blind at Amritsar in 1887. There was rapid expansion in the number of such institutions. Today, there are more than 3200 special schools throughout India.

The emergence of the concept of integrated education in India during the mid 1950s was seen as a solution to these problems. Small experiments in this area were begun by the Royal Commonwealth Society for the Blind, and the Christopher Blind Mission. The Ministry of Education, launched a comprehensive scholarship scheme in 1952—a rudimentary beginning of the integrated education initiative by the Government.

However, these special schools have certain disadvantages which became evident as the number of these schools increased. These institutions reached out to a very limited number of children, largely urban and they were not cost effective. But most important of all, these special schools segregated CWSN from the mainstream, thus developing a specific disability culture.

International Perspective

The concept of integrating CWSN in regular schools was introduced in many countries in 1960's. 1970's witnessed new initiatives in the area of integrated education, with awareness and services for children with special needs becoming more accessible. Further thrust was given to this sector when the UN General Assembly declared 1981 as the International Year of Disabled Persons, with equalisation of opportunities and full participation of the disabled being the main goals. Subsequently, 1983-1992 was proclaimed as the Decade of the Disabled by UN. In this decade, UN standard rules on equalisation of opportunities for persons with disabilities were framed in which education of children with special needs in regular schools along with appropriate services was emphasized. This Decade also became memorable as the World Conference on EFA was held in March, 1990, which affirmed the ultimate goal of meeting the basic learning all children, youth and adults. This Decade was followed by the UNESCAP Decade of the Disabled Persons from 1993-2002. During the ESCAP Decade, the Government of Spain in cooperation with UNESCO organized the World Conference on Special Needs Education in Salamanca in June 1994, which caste responsibility on the general school system to find ways of successfully educating all children, including those who have serious disabilities. Thus, various Declarations and Decades promoted by organisations like UN have had a significant effect on the policies regarding persons with disabilities.

In United States

Special education programmes in the United States were made mandatory in 1975 when Congress passed the Education of the Handicapped Act (EHA) in response to discriminatory treatment by public educational agencies against students with disabilities. The EHA was later modified to strengthen protections to disabled pupils and renamed the Individuals with Disabilities Education Act (IDEA). The IDEA is found in Title 20 of the United States Code, starting at section 1400.

The two most basic rights ensured by the IDEA is that every disabled student is entitled to a free, appropriate public education (FAPE) in the least restrictive environment (LRE). To ensure a FAPE, a team of professionals and parents meet to develop an individuali zed educational programme to determine the student's unique educational needs, develop annual goals for the student, and determine the placement and special services the student needs. The educational agency is required to develop and implement an IEP that meets the standards of the state educational agency. The LRE mandate requires that the student be exposed to the maximum extent with non-disabled peers, while still providing a FAPE. The LRE requirement is intended to prevent unnecessary segregation of the disabled, and is based on Congress' finding that over twenty years of research and experience demonstrates that education of disabled students is more effective by having high expectations of such children and ensuring their access to the general curriculum to the maximum extent possible. Some special education services (such as speech and language therapy, occupational therapy, physical therapy, etc) may be provided within the mainstream class (i.e. inclusion) or in a separate classroom if this is decided to be the LRE. Students receive individualized services to meet their goals, and these services are outlined in each child's Individualized Education Plan (IEP). Federally, students who reach the age of 16 will also need an Individual Transition Plan (ITP). The ITP focuses on the learner's goals for the future, addressing living and employment.

United Kingdom

In schools in the United Kingdom, special education is referred to as SEN (Special Educational Needs). Each school is required to have a Special Educational Needs Co-Coordinator, or SENCO, whose responsibility it is to ensure all pupils in the school with SEN receive the appropriate support to facilitate their successful education. According to Teacher net, a UK government website set up to aid teaching staff. The current SEN Code of Practice came into force at the beginning of January 2002, replacing the original version dating to 1994.

To qualify as having SEN, a student must be assessed by a professional, usually an Educational Psychologist, Doctor or Psychiatrist. If a disability or difficulty is identified which it is considered, presents a significant challenge to what is considered normal learning patterns, and education, a recommendation or application can be made for the issue of a Statement of Educational Need, which entitles the student to the appropriate learning support. Disabilities that may merit the issue of a statement include, Physical disability, eg. the lack of functioning or loss of limbs or movement, Motor or fine motor disability, Learning difficulties or disabilities, developmental disorders, mental illness or incapacity, or behavioural difficulties. With the correct support, many students with SEN have the potential to develop into productive, successful and fully integrated members of society, as has been proved the case on numerous occasions

Criticism

While terms such as "normal" and "typical" can be debated endlessly, there is *research* that shows that students with the most significant disabilities benefit academically and socially in a *classroom* and a *curriculum* that is adapted and modified to help them be successful in school. Some learning activities may be best presented away from the chaos of a general education classroom, but any student can benefit from this type of intervention.

Disability

The term "disability", as it is applied to humans, refers to any condition that impedes the completion of daily tasks using traditional methods. National governments and global humanitarian agencies have narrowed this definition for their own purposes, only pledging aid to those with specific disabilities of a certain severity.

Types of Disability

"Disability" can be broken down into a number of broad sub-categories, which include the following:

- Physical impairments affecting movement, such as *muscular dystrophy post-polio syndrome*, *spina bifida* and *cerebral palsy*
- Sensory impairments, such as visual or hearing impairments.
- Cognitive impairments such as *Autism*or *Down Syndrome*
- Psychiatric conditions such as *Depression* and *Schizophrenia*

A list of disabilities can never be complete or finalized because individuals, organizations, and governments define disabilities differently.

Evolution of a Movement

Historically, disabilities have often been cast in a negative light. An individual thus a ffected was seen as being a "patient" subject either to cure or to ongoing medical care. His condition is seen as disabling; the social reactions to it are justified, and the barriers unavoidable. This position is known as the medical model of disability. Over the past 20 years, a competing view known as the social model of disability has come to the fore. In this model, disability is seen more as a social construction than a medical reality. Disabled activists, such as Tom Shakespeare (2002), argue that although their impairments may cause them pain or discomfort, what really disables people as members of society is a socio-cultural system which does not recognise their right to genuine equality

Both the medical and social models agree, to a point, that facilities and opportunities should be made as accessible as possible to individuals who require adaptations. Dismantling physical barriers, or setting up adaptations such as wheelchair ramps, is known as "fostering accessibility". The disability rights movement began in the 1970s and is largely responsible for the shift toward independent living and accessibility.

The Language and Terminology of Disability

Lately, the term disability has replaced the older designation handicapped. While these two designations can be used interchangeably, proponents of the social model of disability have appropriated the latter term to describe those social and economic consequences of the former. An individual with a physical or intellectual disability, then, is said to be "handicapped" by the lowered expectations of society. A person may also be "impaired" either by a correctable condition such as myopia, or by an uncorrectable one such as cerebral palsy. For those with mild conditions, related impairments disappear with the application of corrective devices. More serious impairments call for adaptive equipment.

In the United Kingdom, people within the disability rights movement commonly use the term "Disabled" to denote someone who is "disabled by society's inability to accommodate all of its inhabitants." The Person First Movement has added another layer to this discourse by asking that people with disabilities be identified first as individuals. "Person First Language"—referring, for example, to a "woman who is blind," rather than to "a blind woman"-is a form of political correctness-designed to further the aims of the social model by removing attitudinal barriers.

Some people with disabilities support the Person First Movement, while others do not. People who are Deaf in particular may see themselves as members of a specific community, properly called the Deaf culture, and so will reject efforts designed to distance them from the central fact of their identity. This is a view that is becoming increasingly prevalent within other disabled communities, that are becoming self-aware and self defining by seeing their impairments as a central part of their upbringing, education, personality and Lifestyle.

The American Psychological Association style guide devotes a large section to the discussion of individuals with disabilities, and states that in professional writing following this style, the person should come first, and nominal forms describing the disability should be used so that the disability is being described, but is not modifying the person. For instance, "people with autism," "man with schizophrenia," "girl with paraplegia." Similarly, a person's adaptive equipment should be described functionally as something that assists a person, not as something that limits a person. "A woman who uses a wheelchair"—she is not "in" it or "confined" to it, and she leaves it at the very least for sleeping and bathing. "A communication aid user." "A girl who uses a ventilator." "A man who takes antipsychotic medications to optimize his daily functioning." Many people with disabilities especially dislike "disabled person" or "the disabled," as this implies that one's overall "personness" is defective, while "person with a disability" acknowledges the disability without implying anything about the overall person. However, according to the "social model", as it is society that disables a person, the reality of being a "person with a disability" is not really possible because it is impossible for an individual to "have" a society, therefore the term "disabled person" does not signify the lack of one's own "person-ness" but points an accusing finger at society for excluding those with impairments.

A human rights based approach has been adopted by many organizations of and for people with disabilities. In 2000, for example, the United Nations Assembly decided to start working on a comprehensive convention for the rights of people with disabilities. Since 2002 the "UN Ad-Hoc meeting" gathers every six months to discuss the content of this UN convention. These meetings are open for Non-Government Organisations and

Disabled Peoples' Organisations. Unfortunately there has not been a lot of media attention for this event.

An approach that has led to tangible improvements in the lives of people with disabilities in many countries has been the *Independent Living* Movement. The term "Independent Living" was taken from 1959 California legislation that enabled people disabled by polio to leave hospital wards and move back into the community with the help of cash benefits for the purchase of personal assistance with the activities of daily living. With its origins in the US civil rights and consumer movements of the late 1960s, the movement and its philosophy have since spread to other continents influencing disabled people's self-perception, their ways of organizing themselves and their countries' social policy.

Handicapped

Handicapped is an adjective used to refer to a person or animal who is partially disabled or unable to use a limb or limbs. The use of this term is sometimes considered offensive, though it is preferable to the derogatory term "cripple" or "retard".

Prevalence and Incidence of Disabilities

Prevalence and incidence are different measures of a disease's occurrence. The "prevalence" of a condition means the number of people who currently have the condition, whereas "incidence" refers to the annual number of people who have a case of the condition. These two measures are very different. A chronic incurable disease like *diabetes* can have a low incidence but high prevalence, because the prevalence is the cumulative sum of past year incidence rates. A short-duration curable condition such as the *common cold* can have a high incidence but low prevalence, because many people get a cold each year, but few people actually have a cold at any given time (so prevalence is low and is not a very useful statistic).

The magnitude of disability is vast and its impact on the individual, family and community is severe. The most vulnerable groups among the persons with disabilities include very young children, children in general, women and senior citizens with disabilities. They require special measures and due emphasis has to be giver to their rehabilitation.

The community has a major role to play in the rehabilitation process. One of the major barriers to rehabilitation is the attitude of the community. The participation of the community will ensure that all attitudinal and social barriers to the rehabilitation process are minimised.

The role and inherent potential of the family to overcome problems of disability must be recognized as a basic building block of the rehabilitation process. The absence of a formal body to advocate the interests of persons with disabilities results in all efforts by and for them remaining fragmented. The inclusion of persons with disability in all developmental activities in the district will be facilitated with the formation of the District CBR Society. The Govt. has initiated many schemes and projects for persons with disabilities. The District CBR Society will function as a networking body and will access the funds available under the various schemes.

The absence of a formal proactive body to identify and address disability issues often means that PWDs remain as beneficiaries of a scheme, rather than as managers of interventions meant for them. The District CBR Society will function as a NGO. It will plan projects for PWDs and monitor the programmes in total partnership with the community. Govt. has taken many pioneering initiatives in the field of disability promoting horizontal inclusion of PWDs in all developmental programmes- Udisha Portage one among the programmes, trains all the Anganwadi workers to include children with disabilities and to ensure early stimulation for all children.

Disability in India

While there is no precise data on the incidence of disability in India, it is estimated that about 5 per cent of the population suffers from disability of some kind—visual, hearing, orthopedic or mental retardation based on sample survey done by the National Sample Survey Organisation in 1991. While the type and pattern of disability may change over the years, there is no indication of decline in the number of persons with disabilities. On the contrary, with life expectancy going up, geriatric disabilities are expected to rise.

1. 5 per cent of our population of 102 Crores is with disabilities. (Physical: 2% and Mental: 3%)
2. Estimated 5 million persons are disabled.
3. Incidence of Disability more in weaker/poorer sections of society/rural areas.

However, these figures are extremely conservative. The consensus among non official sources is that 10% of India's child population have special needs, and this is the assumption taken by the Rehabilitation Council of India.

Taking the UNICEF figure that there are 300 million children (age 0-14) in India, that means there are between 6 and 30 million disabled children in India, depending on how conservative your estimate is.

And yet the gap between even the smaller number and those actually given special education of some sort is enormous. The 2,500 special schools in India, include establishments where children with special needs are included in integrated and inclusive settings, or in non-formal education. These schools educate a total of 100,000 children with special needs.

Further, 15,000 schools have enrolled a total of 60,000 children under the IEDC of the Ministry of Human Resource Development. However, many Orthopaedically handicapped children or those with learning difficulties attend schools with no support services provided. Frequently, they drop out of education because of the lack of support.

Even assuming our most conservative figure, no more than 4 per cent of children with disabilities have access to education with appropriate support.

The RCI takes the figure of 30 million disabled children as the best estimate and aims to have 10 per cent of them given special education by 2020, an increase of 2.8 million. It will do this, in part, through the establishment of a further 1,000 schools with special support services.

Truly, the figures are staggering, and yet this is the problem which Amar Jyoti seeks and has always sought to address. Certainly, the RCI's recommendation of a multi-disciplinary team approach could almost have been modeled on Amar Jyoti, with its suggestion that a team should include a psychiatrist, a clinician, a speech therapist, an occupational therapist, a psychiatric social worker, a special educator and others.

During the last few years, high priority was given and concerted efforts made towards empowerment of persons with disabilities particularly in the area of outreach to ensure that appropriate rehabilitation services reach persons with disabilities living even in rural and remote areas. This is a daunting and challenging task in a country of the size and diversity of India.

A large number of preventable disabilities are occurring at present due to various life style factors including inadequate intake of nutrients including micro nutrients like iodine, vitamin A, iron etc.; unhygienic and insanitary living conditions leading to diseases and morbidity and conditions such as anemia as well as unscientific birth and rearing practices.

Disability and poverty are closely interlinked. The reach of rehabilitation services at present is far weaker in rural and far flung areas with a much lower estimated coverage compared to the national average.

Strategy

Along with the existing legislative framework for persons with disabilities enshrined in the Persons with Disabilities (Equal Opportunities, Protection of Rights and Full Participation) Act, 1995; the National Trust for Welfare of Persons with Autism, Cerebral Palsy, Mental Retardation and Multiple Disabilities Act 1999 and the Rehabilitation Council of India Act 1992 supportive legislation are envisioned to be adopted in the field of health, education, vocational training, employment to realize fully the provisions of the above three legislation especially those relating to education of persons with disabilities, their economic independence, care giving services to those who need them and their social integration. Other Acts and Rules which are relevant would be reviewed to bring them in consonance with the legislation in the disability sector.

Very few buildings, transportation services and other public facilities including roads, stations etc., are at present accessible. One of the critical aspects of provisions of equal opportunities is creation of non-handicapping physical environment. It is envisaged that through appropriate schemes and programmes, almost the entire built infrastructure both in rural and urban areas would be made barrier free and the guidelines and space standards prescribed by Ministry of Urban Development would be implemented in letter and spirit in all buildings and environment outside buildings. Persons with disabilities would be able to access all public facilities and most private building or built infrastructure easily.

A small percentage of the estimated 15 million children with disabilities are receiving educational services at present. One of the important areas of empowerment of persons with disabilities is their education. The strategy for achieving the vision of an equalization society would be universalization of education. An inclusive education system, which caters to the needs of most of children with special needs will be created. However, for a small proportion of children, special education arrangements (Special schools, home based learning, distant learning) appropriate to the needs of individual children with disabilities would be created. Supportive services like suitable teaching/learning materials, accessible hostels and schools would be provided.

These efforts would be supplemented by training of all teachers on disability and development of a large number of rehabilitation professionals through an appropriate infrastructure for it. A University of Rehabilitation Sciences with a large number of colleges and institutions affiliated to it spreading through out India and offering courses at different levels would be in place.

The ultimate aim of providing services to persons with disabilities is their socio-economic empowerment and integration. The desirable level of employing 5 per cent disabled persons both in the public sector and private sector through appropriate incentives, as per the provisions of the Persons with Disabilities (Equal Opportunities, Protection of Rights and Full Participation) Act has to be ensured.

The economic emancipation through wage or self-employment are a key to rehabilitation of persons with disabilities and promoting a life of dignity and responsibility. It is envisioned that through higher and technical education, vocational training, financial assistance, persons with disabilities in the employable age group would have appropriate and equal opportunities for placement. The work environment and the tools & instruments would be modified to meet the needs of the persons with disabilities. The private sector would be provided the incentives, concessions and facilities to provide employment to the extent of 5 per cent to the persons with disabilities.

Use of scientific methods and appropriate latest technology can make lives of persons with disabilities easier and more productive. Much greater incentives and support will be provided to public and private sector for developing and producing aids & appliances of international standard by utilizing advanced technology and innovative practices. It is also envisioned that a system of social audit and accountability on expenditure for empowerment of persons with disabilities would be in place and the social audit would be done through professionals, community and other knowledgeable people.

Information and communication technology will be utilized for establishing a network connecting all district rehabilitation centers with the national and regional level technical institutions which can provide correct information and guidance to persons with disabilities, their families, communities as well as local decision makes and influential persons without necessitating long journeys with consequent costs in terms of time, travel and mobility problems. This would be an effective example of using IT for impacting one of the most vulnerable sections of the population

Estimates of the number of disabled vary a great deal, depending on the definitions, the source, the methodology and the extent of use of scientific instruments in identifying and measuring the degree of disability. It is estimated that the population with disability in India is approximately over 90 million, of these 12 million are blind, 28.5 million are with low vision, 12 million are with speech and hearing defects, 6 million orthopaedically handicapped, 24 million mentally retarded, 7.5 million mentally ill, 1.1 million leprosy cured.

A comprehensive country-wide sample survey of persons with disabilities was undertaken by National Sample Survey Organisation (NSSO) in its 36th round in 1981 at the request of the Ministry of Welfare which indicated that 1.8 per cent of the total population of the country has physical and sensory disabilities. No survey on mentally retarded persons was done at that time. However, surveys done by various research organisations indicate that about 2-2.5 per cent of the total population of the country has mental retardation.

Findings of NSSO: Persons with Disabilities

Survey was conducted by NSSO in 1991 to estimate the magnitude of the persons with disabilities in India.

- 1.9 per cent of the total population of the country, i.e., 16.15 million persons have physical or sensory disabilities which include visual, speech, hearing and locomotors disabilities. There was thus a slight increase in disability over the previous decade both in terms of absolute numbers and percentage.
- Children's of age group from 0-14 years, with delayed mental development, it was found that 29 out of 1000 children in the rural areas had developmental delays which are usually associated with mental retardation. Approximately 3 per cent of the children between 0-14 years of age have developmental delays associated with mental retardation.
- As regards the State-wise distribution of physical disability, the States which have higher prevalence rate, than the national average, were Andhra Pradesh (24.98/1000), Himachal Pradesh (28.70/1000), Karnataka (21.31/1000), Madhya Pradesh (27/1000), Orissa (23.06/1000), Punjab (29.36/1000) and Tamil Nadu (23.72/1000). The national average is 19/1000.
- The rate of prevalence of physical disability in urban population was 16.75/1000 as compared to 19.75/1000 in rural areas.
- About 9.14 and 6.77 per cent of the total estimated households respectively in rural and urban India were reported to have at least one disabled person in the household. The average household size in urban and rural sectors was 5.8 persons.
- 12.3 per cent of the disabled people identified were multi-handicapped.
- The incidence of physical disability (number born or otherwise rendered disabled) in the rural areas of the country was on an average 90 persons per 1,00,000 population during the past one year.
- The incidence rate, as is the case with prevalence rate, is higher in the case of males than females. There were significant inter-state variations. The rates among males were 99 and 90 in rural and urban India respectively as against 81 and 75 among females in rural and urban areas respectively.

- Among the physically disabled 25 per cent of the disabled people in the rural areas and 20 per cent in urban areas suffered from such severe disabilities that they could not perform activities of self-care and daily living even with aids/ appliances.
- Estimated number of disabled persons in the country, on the basis of the survey is as follows:

Table 1.1: Estimated Number of Disabled Persons in India-1991 (in millions)

Type of Disability	*Rural*			*Urban*			*Total*
	Male (1)	*Female (2)*	*Persons (3)*	*Male (4)*	*Female (5)*	*Persons (6)*	*(3)+(6*
Visual	1.539 (46.15)	1.796 (53.85)	3.335 (83.27)	0.308 (45.97)	0.362 (54.03)	0.670 (16.73)	4.005
Hearing	1.409 (54.76)	1.164 (45.24)	2.573 (79.36)	0.339 (50.67)	0.330 (49.33)	0.669 (20.64)	3.242
Speech	0.942 (62.84)	0.557 (37.16)	1.499 (76.25)	0.298 (63.81)	0.169 (36.19)	0.467 (23.75)	1.966
Hearing and/or Speech	2.009 (57.42)	1.490 (42.58)	3.499 (78.07)	0.557 (56.66)	0.426 (43.34)	0.983 (21.93)	4.482
Locomotor	4.396 (64.58)	2.411 (35.42)	6.807 (76.15)	1.370 (64.26)	0.762 (35.74)	2.132 (23.85)	8.939
Physical (at least one of the above)	7.442 (58.82)	5.210 (41.18)	12.652 (78.32)	2.078 (59.34)	1.424 (40.66)	3.502 (21.68)	16.15

Notes: 1. Figures in brackets indicate percentages, and percentages shown in cols. (1) and (2), in cols (3) and (6), and in cols. (4) and (5) add up to 100.

2. Figures of hearing, speech and hearing and/or speech disability excludes the age-group below 5 years.

Source: Report No. 393. NSSO. A Report on Disabled Persons. 47th Round July-December 1991 & Report on Manpower Development. Rehabilitation Council of India, New Delhi, January 1996.

Amongst the visually handicapped, nearly 70 per cent are in the age-group 60+ and less than 3 per cent are in the age group of 0-

14. For speech disability, nearly 26 per cent are in 5-14 age group. Nearly 50 per cent of the locomotor disabled and the speech disabled are in the age group 15-59.

Table 1.2: Show the Age-wise Distribution Per Thousand Disabled

Age group (Years)	*Visual*		*Hearing*		*Speech*		*Locomotor*		*Disability*	
	Rur.	*Urb.*	*Rur.*	*Urb.*	*Rur.*	*Urb.*	*Rur.*	*Urb.*	*Rur.*	*Urb.*
0-4	4	5	N.A.	N.A.	47	47	27	30		
5-14	24	21	85	80	262	261	224	223	150	165
15-59	255	304	387	377	539	513	487	503	425	458
60 and above	717	670	526	541	197	225	240	227	398	346

Notes: Rur = Rural, Urb = Urban, N.A. = Not Available

Source: Report No. 393 NSSO A Report on Disabled Persons 47th Round July-December-1991.

The table below shows that after 45 years of age most of the people acquire all kinds of disabilities–visual, hearing, speech, locomotor.

Table 1.3: Per 1000 Distribution of Physically Disabled Persons of Age 60 Years and Above by Age at Onset of Disability for Each Type of Disability

(All India) *Age at onset (years)*

Type of disability	*0-4*	*5-9*	*10-14*	*15-19*	*20-24*	*25-29*	*30-34*	*35-44*	*45-59*	*60 & above*	*Total*
(1)	*(2)*	*(3)*	*(4)*	*(5)*	*(6)*	*(7)*	*(8)*	*(9)*	*(10)*	*(11)*	*(12)*
					Rural						
Visual	8	8	9	1	3	3	4	18	255	689	1000
Hearing	9	6	12	9	11	10	12	41	280	609	1000
Speech	42	23	24		10		12	25	262	594	1000
Locomotor	29	19	17	17	10	8	22	59	278	511	1000
					Urban						
Visual	12	15	7	3	6	5	5	18	236		1000
Hearing	7	13	10	11	9	14	13	55	215	651	1000
Speech	35	39	9		23		7	27	287	572	1000
Locomotor	21	16	15	9	12	8	13	41	280	586	1000

Source: Table (2.6.2) of Report No. 393. A Report on Disabled Persons, NSSO, 47th Round, July-December 1991.

The survey has also estimated the causes of various disabilities. The findings can be summarised in the following tables:

Per Thousand Distribution of Persons with a Particular Disability

Visual Disability

Causes of Disability	*Rural*	*Urban*
Sore eyes during first month of life	5	3
Sore eyes after the month	6	8
Severe diarrhea before 6 years of age	11	13
Cataract	236	280
Glaucoma	34	42
Corneal opacity	13	16
Other eye diseases	130	107
Smallpox	29	35
Burns	2	5
Injuries other than burns	32	35
Medical/surgical intervention	18	38
Old age	362	273
Other reasons	49	74
Not known	72	71
Total	**999**	**1000**

The major share of cataract, old age and injuries are among the causes of visual disability.

Hearing Disability

Causes	*Rural*	*Urban*
German measles/rubella	9	14
Noise induced hearing loss	17	18
Ear discharge	175	143

(*Contd.*)

(*Contd.*)

Other illnesses	186	197
Burns	2	2
Injury other than burns	35	52
Medical/surgical intervention	10	21
Old age	310	316
Other reasons	77	88
Not known	179	149
Total	*1000*	*1000*

For about 31 per cent, the cause is old age. For a large number, the reasons are unknown. Ear discharge, too, is an important reason for this disability.

Speech Disability

Causes	*Rural*	*Urban*
Hearing Impairment	36	32
Voice disorder	90	63
Cleft palate	26	14
Paralysis	191	240
Mental illness/retardation	91	90
Other illness	221	207
Burns	4	6
Injury other than burns	32	47
Medical/surgical intervention	15	29
Old age	25	27
Other reasons	72	81
Not known	197	164
Total 1000	*1000*	*1000*

Locomotor Disability

Causes	*Rural*	*Urban*
Cerebral Palsy	48	43
Polio	328	346
Leprosy	30	19
Stroke	29	41
Arthritis	20	19
Cardio-respiratory diseases	4	5
Other illnesses	112	115
Burns	22	15
Injury other than burns	211	225
Medical/surgical intervention	22	34
Old age	62	49
Not known	60	44
Total	*1002*	*999*

Source: Report No. 393, Report on Disabled Persons, NSSO, 47th Round, July-December 1991.

Estimates of the Disabled

In most populations all over the world approximately two to three per cent of the population is expected to be mentally handicapped, mental handicap being defined as a condition characterised by significantly sub-average general intellectual functioning existing concurrently with deficits in adaptive behaviour and manifested during the developmental period.

It can be estimated that there are nearly 24 million individuals in India with mental retardation, out of which approximately six million are moderately, severely or profoundly handicapped. Out of the 24 million, 0.8 million are adults over 20 years of age whereas 15 million are children below 10 years of age.

A National Survey on Blindness conducted during 1986–89 under the aegis of the Ministry of Health & Family Welfare by

Dr. Madan Mohan estimated that 11.92 million persons are blind as against 3.47 million estimated by the NSSO survey in 1981. The NSSO Survey conducted in 1991 reports that there has been marginal decline in the incidence of blindness. It has also been observed in the report (NSSO: 1991) "experts are of the opinion that with greater pace of development and urbanisation the disability prevalence rate is also likely to rise". On the other hand, owing to better health care and advancement of medical sciences during the decade (1981–91), the incidence of some types of disabilities may show a decreasing trend, although, as the survey reveals, the overall impact of these factors is a marginal rise in the prevalence rate of physical disability of all types, taken together, during the decade 1981–91.

According to the National Programme for Control of Blindness (WHO Report: 1989) about 28.56 million persons are with low vision. A study conducted by Indian Council for Medical Research (ICMR) estimated that 6.8 per cent in urban areas and 10.8 per cent in rural areas had significant hearing losses.

For policy formulation and provision of services it is imperative that reliable estimates of the incidence and prevalence of various disabilities be made in accordance with accepted definitions of various categories of disabilities.

With the strengthening of preventive measures and coordinated efforts at their universal application the rate of disability should get reduced. Incidence of violence—domestic, ethnic, communal etc. is on the rise and keeps adding to the numbers of disabled people.

The logical answer to this new trend for rights and dignity of disabled people can be responded to by planning and implementing a range of services aimed at making them independent in all respects. Together, these services must help disabled people to fully participate in all activities of the society.

It is an opportune time to avoid the wastage caused by excluding disabled people from the productive activities of the society and at the same time by making them dependent on existing resources.

Table 1.4: Distribution of the disabled by type of disability, sex, literacy status and residence – 2001 (India, States and Union Territories)

Type of disability	*Sex*	*Literate*			*Illiterate*		
		Total	*Rural*	*Urban*	*Total*	*Rural*	*Urban*
Total disabled population	Persons	10,801,232	7,276,755	3,524,477	11,105,537	9,111,627	1,993,910
	Males	7,330,091	5,091,686	2,238,405	5,275,544	4,318,499	957,045
	Females	3,471,141	2,185,069	1,286,072	5,829,993	4,793,128	1,036,865
In Seeing	Persons	5,301,316	3,429,812	1,871,504	5,333,565	4,443,571	889,994
	Males	3,414,027	2,287,732	1,126,295	2,318,311	1,934,985	383,326
	Females	1,887,289	1,142,080	745,209	3,015,254	2,508,586	506,668
In Speech	Persons	594,431	390,344	204,087	1,046,437	853,510	192,927
	Males	394,825	266,313	128,512	547,270	447,653	99,617
	Females	199,606	124,031	75,575	499,167	405,857	93,310
In Hearing	Persons	544,748	402,083	142,665	716,974	620,733	96,241
	Males	375,492	286,586	88,906	298,305	262,416	35,889
	Females	169,256	115,497	53,759	418,669	358,317	60,352
In Movement	Persons	3,502,924	2,501,178	1,001,746	2,602,553	2,153,374	449,179
	Males	2,554,053	1,860,193	693,860	1,348,699	1,114,934	233,765
	Females	948,871	640,985	307,886	1,253,854	1,038,440	215,414
Mental	Persons	857,813	553,338	304,475	1,406,008	1,040,439	365,569
	Males	591,694	390,862	200,832	762,959	558,511	204,448
	Females	266,119	162,476	103,643	643,049	481,928	161,121

Table 1.5: Distribution of the Disabled by Sex and Residence – 2001 (India, States and Union Territories)

Sl. No.	*India/State/Union Territory*	*Sex*	*Total*	*Rural*	*Urban*
00.	**INDIA**	**Persons**	**21,906,769**	**16,388,382**	**5,518,387**
		Males	**12,605,635**	**9,410,185**	**3,195,450**
		Females	**9,301,134**	**6,978,197**	**2,322,937**
01.	Jammu & Kashmir	Persons	302,670	229,718	72,952
		Males	171,816	129,443	42,373
		Females	130,854	100,275	30,579
02.	Himachal Pradesh	Persons	155,950	144,756	11,194
		Males	90,444	83,646	6,798
		Females	65,506	61,110	4,396
03.	Punjab	Persons	424,523	297,018	127,505
		Males	252,856	177,552	75,304
		Females	171,667	119,466	52,201
04.	Chandigarh	Persons	15,538	1,656	13,882
		Males	9,538	1,097	8,441
		Females	6,000	559	5,441
05.	Uttaranchal	Persons	194,769	154,829	39,940
		Males	113,209	88,961	24,248
		Females	81,560	65,868	15,692
06.	Haryana	Persons	455,040	339,792	115,248
		Males	273,837	204,908	68,929
		Females	181,203	134,884	46,319
07.	Delhi	Persons	235,886	13,432	222,454
		Males	144,872	8,424	136,448
		Females	91,014	5,008	86,006
08.	Rajasthan	Persons	1,411,979	1,109,383	302,596
		Males	840,650	657,600	183,050
		Females	571,329	451,783	119,546
09.	Uttar Pradesh	Persons	3,453,369	2,705,784	747,585
		Males	2,076,504	1,625,941	450,563
		Females	1,376,865	1,079,843	297,022
10.	Bihar	Persons	1,887,611	1,692,454	195,157
		Males	1,131,526	1,013,699	117,827
		Females	756,085	678,755	77,330
11.	Sikkim	Persons	20,367	18,571	1,796
		Males	11,409	10,365	1,044
		Females	8,958	8,206	752

(Contd.)

(*Contd.*)

12.	Arunachal Pradesh	Persons	33,315	27,456	5,859
		Males	22,175	17,848	4,327
		Females	11,140	9,608	1,532
13.	Nagaland	Persons	26,499	23,520	2,979
		Males	14,541	12,778	1,763
		Females	11,958	10,742	1,216
14.	Manipur	Persons	28,376	20,955	7,421
		Males	15,456	11,387	4,069
		Females	12,920	9,568	3,352
15.	Mizoram	Persons	16,011	9,691	6,320
		Males	8,763	5,228	3,535
		Females	7,248	4,463	2,785
16.	Tripura	Persons	58,940	48,800	10,140
		Males	33,461	27,638	5,823
		Females	25,479	21,162	4,317
17.	Meghalaya	Persons	28,803	22,740	6,063
		Males	15,317	12,052	3,265
		Females	13,486	10,688	2,798
18.	Assam	Persons	530,300	468,113	62,187
		Males	297,516	261,460	36,056
		Females	232,784	206,653	26,131
19.	West Bengal	Persons	1,847,174	1,354,253	492,921
		Males	1,058,685	774,521	284,164
		Females	788,489	579,732	208,757
20.	Jharkhand	Persons	448,377	348,928	99,449
		Males	264,229	203,463	60,766
		Females	184,148	145,465	38,683
21.	Orissa	Persons	1,021,335	877,709	143,626
		Males	568,914	485,418	83,496
		Females	452,421	392,291	60,130
22.	Chhattisgarh	Persons	419,887	344,993	74,894
		Males	231,768	188,571	43,197
		Females	188,119	156,422	31,697
23.	Madhya Pradesh	Persons	1,408,528	1,060,433	348,095
		Males	824,693	618,152	206,541
		Females	583,835	442,281	141,554
24.	Gujarat	Persons	1,045,465	719,367	326,098
		Males	604,964	415,093	189,871
		Females	440,501	304,274	136,227

(*Contd.*)

(*Contd.*)

25.	Daman & Diu	Persons	3,171	1,880	1,291
		Males	1,779	1,143	636
		Females	1,392	737	655
26.	Dadra & Nagar Haveli	Persons	4,048	3,269	779
		Males	2,329	1,843	486
		Females	1,719	1,426	293
27.	Maharashtra	Persons	1,569,582	1,020,371	549,211
		Males	933,867	600,603	333,264
		Females	635,715	419,768	215,947
28.	Andhra Pradesh	Persons	1,364,981	1,050,400	314,581
		Males	773,971	590,258	183,713
		Females	591,010	460,142	130,868
29.	Karnataka	Persons	940,643	661,139	279,504
		Males	537,730	375,809	161,921
		Females	402,913	285,330	117,583
30.	Goa	Persons	15,749	8,559	7,190
		Males	8,889	4,846	4,043
		Females	6,860	3,713	3,147
31.	Lakshadweep	Persons	1,678	989	689
		Males	901	520	381
		Females	777	469	308
32.	Kerala	Persons	860,794	647,782	213,012
		Males	458,350	344,491	113,859
		Females	402,444	303,291	99,153
33.	Tamil Nadu	Persons	1,642,497	945,019	697,478
		Males	791,685	446,948	344,737
		Females	850,812	498,071	352,741
34.	Pondicherry	Persons	25,857	9,541	16,316
		Males	14,765	5,420	9,345
		Females	11,092	4,121	6,971
35.	Andaman & Nicobar Islands	Persons	7,057	5,082	1,975
		Males	4,226	3,059	1,167
		Females	2,831	2,023	808

2 Policies and Programmes

Laws on Education for the Disabled

All children have the right to be educated regardless of their disability or learning difficulty, because education is a human right. Exclusionary policies and practices however, are widely prevalent all over the country. Many premier schools in the country deny admission to disabled children in violation of their right to education.

Educational Programmes for Children with Special Needs

The community at large is often unaware of the potential of children with special needs. In the popular mind/special needs are usually identified with very low expectations. Parents should believe in value of educating children with special needs. The higher the expectations, the higher will be their acceptance in the family—All the children with special needs. must be enrolled in primary schools—After the assessment of their disabilities by a team of a doctor, a psychologist, and a special educator in schools, the child will be placed in appropriate educational settings. Children with mild and moderate disabilities of any kind may be integrated in normal schools, severe in special schools/remedial schools, drop outs, who have problems in availing benefits of normal schools can join open school. All the children with learning disabilities are managed in normal schools. Open and special schools offer vocational courses also for children with disabilities.

Educational Programmes for Children with Special Needs

There is, however, no dearth of laws and schemes in the country to promote education of children with special needs. Central and State governments and local authorities are legally bound to provide access to free education to all the disabled children till the age of 18 years and also promote integration of disabled children in normal schools under the Persons with Disabilities (Equal Opportunities, Protection of Rights and Full Participation) Act, 1995, better known as PWD Act. The Government, as per the Act, should formulate schemes to conduct part-time classes, impart non-formal education, and provide education through open schools and open universities for children with special needs. The Act also envisages a comprehensive education scheme to provide transport facilities, remove architectural barriers, and supply free books, uniform and other materials, grant scholarship, restructure curriculum and modify the examination system for the benefit of children with special needs.

The National Policy on Education (NPE) 1986 advocates' integrated education in general school for locomotor impaired children and the mildly disabled children and special education to the severely handicapped children. It also recommends orientation and pre-service training for general teachers on disability management and provision of vocational training. The Policy document says that the objective should be to integrate the physically and the mentally handicapped with the general community as equal partners to prepare them to face life with courage and confidence.

Schemes for Disabled Children

In 1974, Integrated Education of Disabled Children (IEDC) launched and it revised by the Central Government in 1992 was one of the first schemes in this area. Its main aims to provide educational opportunities for the moderately disabled children in the general school system. The scope of the Scheme includes pre-school training, counselling for parents and community involvement. Besides providing allowances for books and stationary, uniform, transportation, attendant, reader and escort, hostel facilities and assistive devices, IEDC provides for one special teacher for every eight disabled children and resource room in every cluster of 8 to 10 schools. The scheme implemented in 15,000 schools of 26 States and Union Territories covering 65,000 disabled children.

UN agencies like UNDP and UNICEF have also initiated several interventions for these disadvantaged children in the country. The Ministry of Social Justice and Empowerment has several schemes, to assist these children in special schools. The most important among them are the scheme of assistance to voluntary organisations for the special schools for the handicapped and the scheme of assistance to the disabled persons for purchasing appliances. In addition, a large number of NGOs are working in this area.

Formal Schools

The Ministry of Human Resource Development Department of Secondary and Higher Education) has been implementing a scheme of 'Integrated Education for the Disabled Children' (IEDC) in formal schools since 1982. The main objective of the scheme is to provide educational opportunities for the disabled children in normal schools, to facilitate their retention in the school system—The disabled children who are placed in special schools should also be integrated in common schools once they acquire the communication and daily living skills at the functional level.

The following types of children with disabilities must be integrated in the normal school system-formal as well as in non-formal schools.

— Children with locomotor handicaps (OH).
— Mildly and moderately hearing impaired.
— Partially sighted children.
— Mentally handicapped educable group (IQ 50-70).
— Children with multiple handicaps (blind and orthopaedic, hearing impaired and orthopaedic, educable mentally retarded and orthopaedic, visual impaired and mild hearing impaired).

A three-member assessment team comprising of a doctor, a psychologist and a special educator is formed and their assessment report indicate whether the child can be put directly into school or should receive preparation in special school, special preparatory class in Early Childhood Education Centre (ECCE) specially equipped for the purpose. Under the scheme resource and itinerant teachers are provided. Children are also given certain incentive like book allowance, equipment allowance, transport allowance, etc.

Its aim cannot be achieved until and unless 10 percent of children with special needs are integrated in the education system. With this aim, since 1998, IEDC programme has been receiving special emphasis under DPEP and endeavouring to integrate children with disabilities in DPEP primary schools. DPEP supports for the activities like community mobilization and early detection, in-service teacher training, resource support, educational aids and appliances, architectural designs in schools, etc. Children with learning disabilities also get special care in primary schools in DPEP. In the other non, DPEP districts the same IEDC activities will be supported under the programme of Sarva Shiksha Abhiyan (SSA).

Earlier, there were no activities for children with learning disabilities under the programme of IEDC. Since, estimates of prevalence rate of children with learning disabilities seem to be very high, i.e., ranging from 1-30 percent of the school population depending on the criteria used to determine the disability. Some studies estimate the prevalence of learning disabilities to be 7-8 percent whereas others indicate a prevalence rate of 15 percent. Now under SSA and DPEP such children are being specially taken care of strategies of teaching such children have been developed.

Special Schools

This is a programme of Ministry of Social Justice and Empowerment. Children with severe multiple disabilities who have difficulty in coping in regular schools avail special schools. Most of these special schools are located in urban areas and are being run by voluntary organizations. Most of these are residential schools and boarding-lodging and other services are provided free of cost. At present more than 3,000 special schools for the disabled are functioning in the country. Among them approx- 900 institutions are for hearing impaired children, 400 for children with visual impairment, 1,000 for mentally retarded and the remaining 700 for children with physically disabilities. Forty percent disability is the benchmark for identification and certification for admission in special schools.

National Open School (NOS)

The NOS was established as an Autonomous Registered Society in 1989 with the mission to provide education through an open learning system at the school stage as an alternative to the formal system for school dropouts, girls, mentally/physically disabled, etc. It has also developed materials for teaching children with special needs in their own homes. At present there are 1,459 NOS study centres in the country. It offers courses like the foundation course, notionally equivalent to class VIII level, secondary education, senior secondary course and vocational courses. The NOS also provides the programme of Open Basic Education for Universal Elementary Education (UEE), which includes programme for disabled children. It offers Open Basic Education courses through the following:

Special Features

- NOS allows total freedom to learn at ones own speed. One will have a period of five years and nine chances to complete the course.
- Flexibility in choice of subjects.
- There is no age limit for admission to NOS programmes whether for lower or upper.

Open Basic Education (OBE)

This project is for out of school children in the age group 6-14 and for adult learners. This has three levels:

(i) Preparatory,

(ii) Primary, and

(iii) Elementary which are equivalent to formal school standard of III, V and VIII respectively. This is for general information.

Special Accredited Institutions for Education of the Disadvantaged (SAIED)

To cater to the needs of the people with physically and mentally disabilities, etc., the NOS has accredited institutions for education of the disadvantaged. Academic Courses like Open Basic Education, Secondary and Senior Secondary courses and vocational courses are being offered independently or in combination with academic subject through SAIED.

National Policy on Education (NPE)—1986

The NPE brought the fundamental issue of equality centre stage. Section 4.9 of the policy clearly focuses on the needs of the children with disabilities. "The objective should be to integrate the physically and mentally handicapped with the general community as equal partners, to prepare them for normal growth and to enable them to face life with courage and confidence. The following measures will be taken in this regard:

Wherever it is feasible, the education of children with motor handicaps and other mild handicaps will be common with that of others

Special schools with hostels will be provided, as far as possible at district headquarters, for the severely handicapped children

Adequate arrangements will be made to give vocational training to the disabled

Teachers' training programmes will be reoriented, in particular for teachers of primary classes, to deal with the special difficulties of the handicapped children; and

Voluntary effort for the education of the disabled will be encouraged in every possible manner."

Plan of Action (POA)—1992

The NPE was followed by POA (1992). The POA suggested a pragmatic placement principle for children with special needs. It postulated that a child with disability who can be educated in a general school should be educated in a general school only and not in a special school. Even those children who are initially admitted to special schools for training in plus curriculum skills should be transferred to general schools once they acquire daily living skills, communication skills and basic academic skills.

Project Integrated Education for the Disabled (PIED)

The Project Integrated Education for the Disabled (PIED) supported by UNICEF through UNICEF from 1987-93 came out with the report that the disabled children identified in these blocks were 530, of whom visually impaired were 778 (14.65%), hearing impaired 1236 (23.28%), mentally retarded 655 (12.34%) and locomotor disabled 2640 (49.73%). Nearly 2.5 per cent of the school-going children have disability of some kind or the other.

District Primary Education Programme (DPEP)

The DPEP has had a powerful impact on integrating disabled children. The scheme was launched in select clusters and blocks but now it has been expanded to more blocks and districts in the country. The advantage of this scheme is that it takes care of all areas from identification, assessment, enrolment and provision of appliances to total integration of disabled children in schools with resource support, teacher training and parental counselling. Many other schemes like Janshala, the joint programme of the Government of India and five U.N. agencies, have included the interventions of DPEP. The newly launched Sarva Shiksha Abhiyan (SSA) aims to universalise elementary education.

UN agencies like UNDP and UNICEF have initiated several interventions for the special children. The Ministry of Social Justice and Empowerment has several schemes to assist these children. The most important among them being, assistance to voluntary organisations for special schools for the handicapped, assistance to the disabled persons for purchasing appliances (ADIP scheme). A number of NGOs are working in this area.

Inclusive Education

For over a century, the prevalent model for offering education to children with special needs has been the special school. This system had major drawbacks—it is expensive and has only limited reach. Moreover, segregating children based on disability was discriminatory and violation of the human rights. Subsequently, the philosophy of 'integration' emerged which advocated education of children with mild and moderate disabilities in general schools along with others with adequate resource support. However, children under integration method were still treated separately in schools and integration or mainstreaming was only partial.

This led to the emergence of the new concept called Inclusive Education (IE), which argues that all children irrespective of the nature and degree of the disability should be educated, in general schools with normal children. More and more experts in special needs education are now advocating inclusive education not only on educational grounds but also on social and moral grounds. Inclusive education is all about making classrooms responsive to the needs of the learner. It stresses on child-cantered pedagogy using peer tutoring, co-operative learning and group learning.

Inclusive education has been introduced in the schools in the project areas of DPEP on a limited scale. Success of IE depends on teachers and good classroom practices. A beginning has been made in this area, but a lot more has to be done. Inclusive education may be the *mantra* to provide education to all children with special needs in the country. Then only the country will be able to achieve the elusive goal of Universal Elementary Education (UEE).

National Trust Act, 1999

Another landmark legislation is the National Trust Act. In 1999, the Indian Parliament passed an Act entitled "National Trust for the Welfare of Persons with Autism, Cerebral Palsy, Mental Retardation and Multiple Disability. This Act seeks to protect and promote the rights of persons who, within the disability sector, have been even more marginalized than others. Though the National Trust Act of 1999 does not directly deal with the education of children with special needs, one of its thrust areas is to promote programmes, which foster inclusion and independence by creating barrier free environment, developing functional skills of the disabled and promoting self-help groups.

These three landmark legislations have highlighted the enormous thrust that this area has received from the Ministry of Social Justice and Empowerment and the Ministry of Human Resource Development.

The Persons with Disabilities (Equal Opportunities, Protection of Rights and Full Participation) Act, 1995

"The Persons with Disabilities (Equal Opportunities, Protection of Rights and Full Participation) Act, 1995" has come into force on February 7, 1996. This law is an important landmark and is a significant step in the direction of ensuring equal opportunities for people with disabilities and their full participation in the nation building. The Act provides for both preventive and promotional aspects of rehabilitation like education, employment and vocational training, job reservation, research and work force development, creation of barrier-free environment, rehabilitation of persons with disability, unemployment allowance for the disabled, special insurance scheme for the disabled employees and establishment of homes for persons with severe disability etc.

Main Provisions of the Disabilities Act

- Preventions and Detections of Disabilities
- Education
- Employment
- Non-discrimination
- Research and Manpower Development
- Affirmative Action
- Social Security
- Grievance Redressed

Prevention and Early Detection of Disabilities

- Surveys, investigations and research shall be conducted to ascertain the cause of occurrence of disabilities.
- Various measures shall be taken to prevent disabilities, Staff at the Primary health Centre shall be trained to assist in this work.
- All the Children shall be screened once in a year for identifying 'at-risk' cases.
- Awareness campaigns shall be launched and sponsored to disseminate information.
- Measures shall be taken for pre-natal, prenatal, and post-natal care of the mother and child.

Education

- Every child with disability shall have the rights to free education until the age of 18 years in integrated schools or special schools.
- Appropriate transportation, removal of architectural barriers and restructuring of curriculum and modifications in the examination system shall be ensured for the benefit of children with disabilities.
- Children with disabilities shall have the right to free books, scholarships, uniforms and other learning material.
- Special School for children with disabilities shall be equipped with vocational training facilities.
- Non-formal education shall be promoted for children with disabilities.
- Teacher's Training Institutions shall be established to develop requisite work force.
- Parents may move to appropriate fora for the redressal of grievances regarding the placement of their children with disabilities.

Employment

1. 3 per cent of vacancies in government employment shall be reserved for people with disabilities, 1 per cent each for persons suffering from:
    - Blindness or Low vision
    - Hearing Impairment
    - Locomotor Disability & Cerebral Palsy
2. Suitable schemes shall be formulated for
    - The training and welfare of persons with disabilities
    - The relaxation of upper age limit
    - Regulating the employment
    - Health and safety measures and creation of a non-handicapping environment in places where persons with disabilities are employed.

3. Government Educational Institutes and other Educational Institutes receiving grant from Government shall reserve at least 3 per cent seats for people with disabilities.
4. All poverty alleviation schemes shall reserve at least 3 per cent for the benefit of people with disabilities.
5. No employee can be sacked or demoted if they become disabled during service, although they can be moved to another post with the same pay and condition. No promotion can be denied because of impairment.

Affirmative Action

1. Aids and Appliances shall be made available to people with disabilities.
2. Allotment of land shall be made at concessional rates to the people with disabilities for:
    - House
    - Business
    - Special Recreational Centres
    - Special Schools
    - Research Schools
    - Factories by Entrepreneurs with Disability

Non-Discrimination

- Public buildings, rail compartments, buses, ships and aircrafts will be designed to give easy access to disabled people.
- In all public places and in waiting rooms, toilets shall be wheel chair accessible. Braille and sound symbols are also to be provided in lifts.
- All the places of public utility shall be made barrier-free by providing ramps.

Research and Manpower Development

Research in the following areas shall be sponsored and promoted:

- Prevention of Disability
- Rehabilitation including CBR

- Development of Assistive Devices
- Job Identification
- On site Modifications of Offices and Factories

Financial assistance shall be made available to the universities, other institutions of higher learning, professional bodies and non-government research units or institutions, for undertaking research for special education, rehabilitation and work force development.

Social Security

- Financial assistance to non-government organisations for rehabilitation of persons with disabilities.
- Insurance coverage for the benefit of the government employees with disabilities
- Unemployment allowance to people with disabilities registered with the special employment exchange for more than a year and who could not be placed in any gainful occupation.

Grievances Redressal

In case of violation of rights as prescribed in that act, people with disabilities may move an application to:

- Chief Commissioner for Persons with Disabilities in the Centre, or
- Commissioner for Persons with Disabilities in the States.

Scheme of Integrated Education for the Disabled Children

The country has witnessed a phenomenal expansion of educational opportunities in the post-Independence period. The disabled children, however, have not benefited substantially from this growth in educational facilities. The Government of India, therefore, has brought the education of this group of children for special attention to achieve the goal of education for all. The objective is to integrate the handicapped with the general community at all levels as equal partners, to prepare them for normal growth and to enable them to face life with courage and confidence.

Aims and Objectives

The centrally sponsored scheme of Integrated Education for the Disabled Children (IEDC) purports to provide educational opportunities for the disabled children in common schools, to facilitate their retention in the school system. The disabled children who are placed in special schools should also be integrated in common schools once they acquire the communication and daily living skills at the functional level.

Type of Scheme

The Central Government will assist the States/Union Territories in its implementation because of the criteria laid down under this centrally sponsored scheme. Assistance for all the items covered in the scheme will be on 100 per cent basis but assistance for the programme would be conditional on provision of professionally qualified staff.

Implementing Agencies

The scheme shall be implemented through the State Governments/ UT Administrations/Autonomous Organisations of stature having experience in the field of education and/or rehabilitation of the disabled. Because this scheme has to be implemented in schools, the Education Department would be the implementing agency. The State Governments may take the assistance of voluntary organisations also for this purpose as may be feasible.

Scope

It is proposed to provide educational facilities under this scheme for children with disabilities that can be integrated in general schools. While rehabilitation assistance will be made available to all children with disabilities, student benefits will be extended on the recommendation by the Assessment Team.

The scope of the scheme includes pre-school training for the disabled children and counselling for the parents. This would be an activity preparatory to the child coming into the regular school system. It would include, among other things, special training for the hearing handicapped children, mobility and orientation training for the visually handicapped, daily living and communication skills training required by children with other disabilities, parent counselling and training in home management of these children.

The education of the disabled children under this scheme will continue up to the senior secondary school level and includes vocational courses equivalent to the senior secondary stage.

A disabled child in receipt of any scholarship/assistance under some other scheme relating to disability from State/Central Government will not be eligible for any of the benefits under this scheme unless he/she is willing to forego the other sources of assistance.

Procedure for Implementation

The implementing agency should set up an administrative cell under an officer not below the rank of Deputy Director to implement, monitor and evaluate the programme. These officials will be chosen for their special qualifications in this field, or if they are not so qualified, will be trained in a course conducted by the National Council of Educational Research and Training (NCERT) or some other designated organization. This cell will identify the areas and institutions for implementing the scheme.

It is preferable that in order to properly plan and supervise the implementation of the scheme a number of developmental blocks should be selected for operation of the scheme, rather than scattering the schools under this scheme all over the State. Within the area of a selected block all, the desired inputs should be provided to the schools covered.

To identify disabled children in the blocks/districts where the scheme is yet to be implemented, the first task should be to provide suitable orientation to all schoolteachers in the area for conducting a survey to identify disabled children in general schools. Teachers may be provided a small honorarium for conducting the survey. Each primary school may be provided Rs. 100 (to be shared by teachers) for conducting this survey. The IEDC cell should provide printed survey forms for identification of these children. Assistance up to Rs. 10,000 may be provided to the IEDC cell for this purpose. These efforts should be supplemented by publicity through mass media.

The State-level cell will arrange for equipment, learning materials, staff, etc. in order to provide education to disabled children. The cell will also set up the machinery for assessment of the disabled children. Wherever survey has been conducted by any other agency, it would be utilised and augmented with the survey of disabilities not covered by the earlier survey. Monitoring and evaluation of the scheme at the State level will be carried out by the cell. The cell will ensure that the information regarding the scheme is widely known.

Administrative Cell

The Administrative Cell to be set up by the State Education Department will have a Deputy Director (in the scale of pay applicable in the State Government). A Coordinator (who will be a psychologist) in the scale applicable to a university lecturer, a Special Educator in the pay scale applicable to a university lecturer, a Stenographer and a Lower Division Clerk in the pay scales applicable in the State/UT.

Assessment of the Disabled Children

The Coordinator of the programme will be responsible for arranging for the assessment of the children and monitoring their progress on ongoing basis. A three-member assessment team, comprising a doctor, a psychologist and a special educator will be formed. The State/UT assessment team would function under the Administrative Cell. Specialists will be drawn upon in consultation with the State Health Department. Wherever district rehabilitation centres have been established, its resources for assessment may be used. The non-government organisations (NGOs) with infrastructural facilities may also be used for assessment purposes.

The average cost of an assessment should not exceed Rs. 150 per disabled child. It will be necessary to examine a large number of children to select those considered suitable for placement in an integrated programme. Members of the assessment team would be given TA and DA as per State Government/UT Administration rules.

The assessment report should be comprehensive enough for educational programming; a profile of what a particular child can or cannot do during testing situations should be adequately reported. The report should specifically indicate whether the child can be put directly into school or should receive preparation in special school/special preparatory class in the Early Childhood Education Centre specially equipped for this purpose. Functional assessment can be carried out by the teacher if formal assessment is to take a long time so that the educational programme can be started for these children.

Linkages

Integrated education of disabled children requires inputs from different Departments like Education, Health, Labour, Welfare, etc. For effective linkages between these Departments and NGOs, working in this area, coordination committees will be formed at State, regional, district and block levels.

Facilities for Disabled Children

A disabled child may be given the following kinds of facilities at the rates prevalent in the State/UT concerned. The facilities should, as far as possible, be given in kind. In case similar incentives are not being offered by the State Government/UT Administration under any other scheme, the following rates could be adopted.

- Actual expenses on books and stationery up to Rs. 400 per annum.
- Actual expenses on uniform up to Rs. 200 per annum.
- Transport allowance up to Rs. 50 per month. If a disabled child admitted under the scheme resides in the school hostel within the school premises, no transportation charges would be admissible.
- Reader allowance of Rs. 50 per month in case of blind children after Class V.
- Escort allowance for severely handicapped, with lower extremity disability at the rate of Rs. 75 per month.
- Actual cost of equipment subject to a maximum of Rs. 2000 per student for a period of five years.

In the case of severely orthopaedically handicapped children, it may be necessary to allow one attendant for 10 children in a school. The attendant may be given the standard scale of pay prescribed for Class IV employees in the State/UT concerned.

Disabled children residing in school hostels within the same institution where they are studying may also be paid boarding and lodging charges as admissible under the State Government rules/schemes. Where there is no State scheme of scholarships to hostellers, the disabled children whose parental income does not exceed Rs. 5,000 per month may be paid actual boarding and lodging charges subject to a maximum of Rs. 200 per month. However, disabled children should generally not be placed in hostels unless the required educational facilities are not available in the nearby schools.

Severely orthopaedically handicapped children residing in school hostels may need the assistance of a helper or an *ayah*. A special pay of Rs. 50 per month is admissible to any employee of the hostel willing to extend such help to children in addition to his/her duties.

Special Teacher Support

Except for children with locomotor disabilities, special education teachers may be appointed in schools where the scheme is in operation to provide specific attention to the disabled children.

Appointment of Special Teachers

The teacher-pupil ratio for special education teachers envisaged under this scheme is 1:8. This ratio will be the same for normal classes as well as for preparatory pre-school classes. The same teachers will provide counselling to the parents. In accordance with this ratio the requisite number of special teachers may be appointed in schools (or for a cluster of schools) for children requiring special teacher support.

Qualifications

Special teachers so appointed should possess the following qualifications.

Primary: Academic qualifications as prevalent in the States and Union Territories with one-year course, preferably multi-category, in special education or with specialisation in teaching any type of disabled children depending upon the category of children enrolled in the IEDC Units. Such teachers can be oriented subsequently in the education of other categories of disability.

Secondary: Graduates with B.Ed. (Special Education) or any other equivalent professional training in special education.

In case qualified special teachers are not available, teachers with short training course may be appointed with the condition that they will complete the full course within three years of appointment. Special allowance for these teachers will be admissible only after completion of the full course. Teachers with single disability professional courses will be encouraged to take courses in other disabilities to improve viability in rural areas.

Since teachers with experience in Non-Formal Education (NFE) and Adult Education (AE) are likely to have a better understanding of local environment and need, they could also be identified for training under the scheme and appointed as special teachers.

Scales of Pay: The same scales of pay as available to the teachers of the corresponding category in that State/UT will be given to special teachers. Considering the special type of duties, these teachers will be given a special pay of Rs. 150 per month in urban areas and Rs. 200 per month in rural areas. The State Education Department may recruit such teachers for this purpose following the normal recruitment procedures.

Training of Special Teachers: The facilities for the training of special teachers are readily available in the Regional Colleges of Education (RCEs), Regional Training Centres being run by the National Institute for the Handicapped, Special Education Departments in the universities and selected Colleges for Education. The training facilities are being further expanded. The State Government may prepare an estimate of the requirements of teachers under each category of disability and send it to the Regional Colleges Education/*District Institutions of Education and Training* (DIETs), National Institutes for the Handicapped and the University Grants Commission under intimation to the NCERT. Since the appointment of fully trained, full-time resource teachers is an essential input for the successful implementation of the scheme, the State-Government/UT Administration must ensure appointment of such teachers on priority basis.

Under the scheme, grant is available through UGC for instituting full-time training courses for special teachers. The university/ training institutes are expected to utilise the existing infrastructural facilities and other resources to the extent possible. The cost of the additional aids/equipment/space, and the additional faculty members will be met from the funds under this scheme. DIETs should organise in-service training courses for general teachers and refresher courses for resource teachers.

Training of Other Staff: The successful implementation of the IED depends upon the responsiveness of the administrators and general teachers in the school. Short orientation courses for administrators, heads of the institutions and general teachers associated with the implementation of the scheme may be organised. Training of administrators/key persons will be organised by the NCERT. State Government/UT administration may organise orientation programmes of three days' duration for heads of the institutions and of five days' duration for general teachers of the institutions implementing the IED scheme with the help of RCEs, Regional raining Centres and DIETs for the handicapped. The modules for these orientation programmes will be provided by the NCERT. Expenditure on TA/DA of the participants will be borne by the State Government/UT Administrations concerned. The cost of honorarium and TA/DA of resource persons and contingencies, etc. will be met under this scheme.

Resource Room: A resource room having all the essential equipment, learning aids and materials may be provided for a cluster of schools implement ting the scheme of integrated education. The NCERT has prepared a handbook, which also indicates the type of facilities, which may be provided in the resource room. The average cost of such equipment is estimated at Rs. 30,000. The need for equipment would depend upon the disability types of the students enrolled in the associated schools. The resource room may be set up preferably in an existing room in the school. A new room may be built only where no accommodation is available to the satisfaction of the State Government. Grant shall be available for construction of a resource room in a school in such circumstances subject to a maximum of Rs. 50,000. NGOs/special schools wherever available should be used as resource centres for the IED programme in general schools.

Removal of Architectural Barriers: It may be necessary to remove architectural barriers or to modify existing architectural facilities, to provide easier access to orthopaedically disabled children to the school premises. Grant shall be available for this purpose for the schools where such handicapped children are enrolled.

Instructional Materials: At present sufficient facilities for production of instructional material for children with different disabilities, do not exist in the country. Availability of requisite teaching/learning material for the disabled is vital for successful implementation of the scheme. The requirement of such materials is bound to increase with the increased coverage of disabled children. Financial assistance under this scheme will be available for purchase/production of instructional materials for the disabled and for purchase of equipment required there of. Wherever necessary the available material may be translated and produced in regional languages.

Visually and hearing impaired children should be allowed to take only one language as already recommended. Provision for alternative modes of examination for blind and other children with physical disabilities coming in the way of writing should be considered and provided by the Boards of Examination.

Regulations for Relaxation of Rules: State Government/UT Administrations/other implementing agencies should also frame regulations for relaxation of rules relating to admissions, minimum or maximum age limit for admissions, promotions, examination procedures, etc. for improving access of the disabled children to education. Provision for admission of disabled children older than the normal eligibility (up to 8-9 years instead of 6 years) is essential in the transitional phase at least until the target of universal primary education (UPE) is achieved.

Pre-School and ECCE Facilities: Preparation of disabled children for education being essential, preference should be given to the blocks where the schemes of Integrated Child Development (ICD) and Early Childhood Centres of Education (ECCE) exist while selecting blocks for implementation of the scheme. Support for services for disabled children will be available for instructional materials and training of teachers.

Procedure for Grant to Voluntary Organisations: The voluntary organisations desirous of implementing the scheme should send their applications through the concerned State Government/UT Administration (with a copy endorsed directly to the Ministry). The State Government should give its views within a period of three months regarding the organisations' eligibility, suitability, relevance of the proposal and the capacity of the agency to implement it. Comments should be sent by the State Government even if the proposal is not recommended giving reasons there of.

In order to be eligible for financial assistance under these scheme voluntary organisations, public trusts and non-profit making companies should:

— have proper constitution of articles of association;
— have a properly constituted managing body with its powers and duties clearly defined in the constitution;
— be in a position to secure the involvement, on voluntary basis, of knowledgeable persons for furtherance of their programmes;
— not discriminate against any person or group of persons on ground of sex, religion, caste or creed;
— not be run for the profit of any individual or a body or individuals;
— not directly function for the furtherance of the interests of any political party; and
— not in any manner incite communal disharmony.

Only those eligible agencies, which have been in existence for three years, would be considered for assistance under this scheme. This requirement may be waived in respect of agencies with specially qualified workers or which can otherwise justify a special consideration.

If any agency is already receiving or expecting to receive grant from some other official source for a project for which application is made under this scheme, assistance under this scheme will be made after taking into consideration the grant received, or likely to be received from such other official source. It should also be ensured that an agency already in receipt of a grant from any other official source, Central or a State should not transfer any part of that liability to a grant to be sanctioned under this scheme.

The proposals of the voluntary organisations with the recommendation of the State Government/UT Administration should be sent to the Ministry of Human Resource Development (Department of Education), Government of India by the end of December every year for the following financial year. The proposals will be examined in the Ministry and 50 per cent of the approved grant for a year will be released as the first instalment and the remaining 50 per cent after the agency reports utilisation of at least 75 per cent of the grant sanctioned earlier. The request for release of the second instalment should be accompanied by a progress report and statement of expenditure. The grant will be remitted to the agency directly by Demand Draft/Cheque drawn in its favour by the Ministry of Human Resource Development, Department of Education.

Conditions of Grant to Voluntary Organisations: The grant-receiving agency will be required to execute a bond. The bond should be supported by two sureties if the agency is not a legal entity.

An agency in receipt of financial assistance shall be open to inspection by an officer of the Union Ministry of Human Resource Development or the State Education Department.

The accounts of the project shall be maintained properly and separately and submitted as and when required. They should be open to check by an officer deputed by the Government of India or the State Government. They shall also be open to a test-check by the Comptroller and Auditor General of India at his discretion.

The audited accounts together with the utilisation certificate in the prescribed form duly countersigned by the Chartered Accountant are required to be furnished within six months in respect of a preceding year or after expiry of the duration for which grant is approved.

The agency shall maintain a record of all assets acquired wholly or partially out of government grant and maintain a register of such assets in the prescribed preformed. Such assets shall not be disposed of, encumbered or utilised for the purposes other than those for which the grant was given, without prior sanction of the Government of India. Should the agency cease to exist at any time, such properties shall revert to the Government of India.

When the State Government/Government of India have reasons to believe that the sanctioned money is not being utilised for the approved purpose the payment of grant may be stopped and the earlier grants recovered.

The institution must exercise reasonable economy in the working of the approved project.

The grantee agency shall furnish to the Ministry of Human Resource Development reports as may be prescribed.

The decisions of the Secretary to the Government of India in the Ministry of Human Resource Development, Department of Education, on the question whether there has been breach of violation of any of the terms and conditions mentioned in the sanction letter shall be final and binding on the grantee.

Evaluation and Monitoring: State Governments/UT Administrations may identify institutions/agencies to take up concurrent evaluations of the programme in selected areas/schools. The cost of such evaluation studies would be reimbursable to the State Government under the scheme. The Central Government may also undertake a summarise evaluation of implementation of the scheme through the NCERT (or other institutions) at the end of the Plan period.

Scheme of Assistance to Disabled Persons for Purchase/ Fitting of Aids and Appliances (ADIP) Scheme

Education of CWSN cannot be successful until they are provided those essential aids and appliances that enhance their functional ability. Therefore, the Union Ministry of Social Welfare in 1981 launched the ADIP Scheme. The main objective of the scheme is to assist the needy disabled children in procuring durable, sophisticated and scientifically manufactured, modern, standard aids and appliances that can promote their physical, social and psychological well being by enhancing their educational potential. The scheme provides aids and appliances to locomotor disabled, visually disabled, hearing disabled, mentally disabled and multiple disabled.

Initial Experiments on Integrated Education in India

The early attempts to include CWSN in regular schools were through Project Integrated Education for the Disabled (PIED) and District Primary Education Programme (DPEP).

Project Integrated Education for the Disabled (PIED)

The first pilot project on integrated education in India came in the form of Project Integrated Education for the Disabled (PIED). PIED launched in 1987, was a joint venture of MHRD and UNICEF. This project was implemented in one administrative block each in Madhya Pradesh, Maharashtra, Nagaland, Orissa, Rajasthan, Tamil Nadu, Haryana, Mizoram, Delhi Municipal Corporation and Baroda Municipal Corporation. In these ten blocks, 6000 children with special needs were integrated in regular schools.

District Primary Education Programme (DPEP)

The success of PIED led to the inclusion of the component of Integrated Education of the Disabled (IED) in DPEP, a scheme launched by the Government of India for the development of elementary education. At present, IED in DPEP is going on in 242 districts of 18 states. In these states, approximately 6.21 lakh children with special needs have been enrolled in regular schools with adequate support services.

Sarva Shiksha Abhiyan (SSA)

A recent initiative of the Government of India to Universalise Elementary Education is Sarva Shiksha Abhiyan (SSA). SSA is a response to the demand for quality basic education all over the country. However, UEE cannot be achieved unless children with special needs are also provided access to education. Hence, education of CWSN is an essential part of the SSA framework.

CBSE Relaxation for Disabled Children

The facilities extended by the Board to the disabled candidates (Dyslexic, Blind, Spastic and Candidate with Visual Impairment) are as under:

- The persons with disabilities (Dyslexic, Blind, Spastic and Candidate with Visual Impairment) have the option of studying one compulsory language as against two. The language opted by them should be in consonance with the overall spirit of the Three Language Formula prescribed by the Board. Besides one language, they can offer any four of the following subjects: Mathematics, Science and Technology, Social Science, Another Language, Music, Painting, Home Science and Introductory Information Technology.
- From the 2002 Examination, alternate questions in lieu of questions requiring special skills based on visual inputs have been provided in Mathematics and Science for Sec. School Examination (Class X).
- Blind, Physically Handicapped and Dyslexic Students are permitted to use and amanuensis. The amanuensis must be a student of a class lower than the one for which the candidate is taking the examination.

- The visually handicapped students appearing from Delhi were provided Questions Papers with enlarged print for 2003 Examination.
- Disabled candidates are allowed additional one hour (60 minutes) for each paper of external examination.
- Board does not give relaxation in minimum marks prescribed by it.
- Exemption from Examination in the Third Language.
- The Board considers the Physiotherapic exercises as equivalent to Physical and Health Education course of the Board.
- Centre Superintendents have been instructed to make arrangements for the conduct of the examination of such candidates on the Ground Floor as far as possible.
- Physically challenged children will specifically indicate their category and state whether they have been provided with a Writer in the columns provided in the Main Answer Book.
- Answer books of such candidates are evaluated by the Regional Officers at one Nodal Centre.
- The Centre Superintendents have been requested to send the Answer books of such candidates in the separate envelope to the Regional Officer concerned.
- Separate question papers in Science & Mathematics at Secondary (Class X) level have been provided for blind students w.e.f. 2003 Examinations.
- Assistant Superintendents for the blinds are teachers from the schools where the blinds are studying. As far as possible, teachers of the same subject are not allowed to be appointed on the day of examination. One invigilator is from outside the school.
- Assistant Superintendents supervising the physically challenged children who have been granted 60 minutes extra time are paid remuneration @ Rs. 50/- + Rs. 20/
- Amanuensis is paid @ Rs. 100/- per day/paper daily by the Centre Superintendent from the centre charges amount.

Rehabilitation Council of India (RCI)

In 1983, the National Handicapped Council consisting of representatives of the Central Ministries, National Institutes prominent voluntary organizations concluded that one of the main reasons of the programmes on disability not making headway was lack of trained workers in the field of disability. The training programmes were going on in an isolated and *ad hoc* manner and the courses were not uniform and the institutes were awarding certificates, diplomas and degrees according to their own convenience. Therefore, the need was felt for having a central body in order to maintain uniformity in standards of training and examinations. Later on in 1984, the Conference of State Social Welfare Ministers recommended to the Government of India to set up the Rehabilitation Council, which will be responsible for standardization and monitoring of training programmes all over the country. Accordingly, Rehabilitation Council was set up by the Ministry of Welfare, Government of India in January, 1986 as a registered society. However, it was realized that the Rehabilitation Council could not effectively enforce uniform standards and norms all over the country due to lack of statutory powers.

Rehabilitation Council of India Act, 1992

Subsequently a Bill was introduced in the Parliament to make it a statutory body. The President of India gave his assent to the Rehabilitation Council of India Act, 1992 on September 1, 1992. As provided in the Rehabilitation Council of India Act, 1992, Rehabilitation Council was converted into a statutory body called "Rehabilitation Council of India" from June, 1993. The RCI Act was amended by the Parliament in 2000 to make it more broad based. The Act casts onerous responsibility on the Council and prescribes that any one delivering services to people with disability, who does not possess qualifications recognized by RCI, could be prosecuted. Thus, the Council has the twin responsibility of standardizing and regulating the training of professionals in the field of rehabilitation and special education. The Act also requires the Council to maintain a Central Rehabilitation Register for registration of trained professionals and personnel and promote research in rehabilitation and special education.

Objectives

1. To regulate the training policies and programmes in the field of rehabilitation of disabled persons.
2. To prescribe minimum standards of education and training for various categories of professionals dealing with disabled persons.
3. To regulate these standards in all training institutions to bring about uniformity throughout the country.
4. To recognize institutions/universities running degree/diploma/certificate courses in the field of rehabilitation of the disabled and to withdraw recognition, wherever facilities are not satisfactory.
5. To recognize foreign degrees/diplomas/certificates on reciprocal basis and to get Indian degrees/diplomas/certificates recognized abroad and to withdraw such recognition awarded by universities/institutions on a reciprocal basis.
6. To maintain Central Rehabilitation Register of persons possessing the recognized rehabilitation qualification.
7. To encourage Continuing Rehabilitation Education in collaboration with organizations working in the field of disability.
8. To promote research in rehabilitation and special education.

Categories of Rehabilitation Professionals

Under the Act, following categories of Professionals/Personnel have been notified under the purview of the Council:

(*i*) Audiologists and Speech Therapists.

(*ii*) Clinical Psychologists.

(*iii*) Hearing and Ear Mould Technicians.

(*iv*) Rehabilitation Engineers and Technicians.

(*v*) Special Teachers for Educating and Training the Handicapped.

(*vi*) Vocational Counsellors, Employment Officers and Placement Officers Dealing with Handicapped.

(*vii*) Multi-purpose Rehabilitation Therapists & Technicians.

(*viii*) Speech Pathologists.

(*ix*) Rehabilitation Psychologists.

(*x*) Rehabilitation Social Workers.

(*xi*) Rehabilitation Practitioners in Mental Retardation.

(*xii*) Orientation and Mobility Specialists.

(*xiii*) Community Based Rehabilitation Professionals.

(*xiv*) Rehabilitation Counsellors/Administrators.

(*xv*) Prosthetists and Orthotists.

(*xvi*) Rehabilitation Workshop Managers.

(*xvii*) Any other category of Professionals included from time to time.

Vision

In the post-independence era, India has been a pioneer in the fields of industrial development, agriculture, health, education, etc. However, the progress in social development has been below the desired standards. Therefore, time has come when the pace of social development needs to be accelerated. Rehabilitation of persons with disabilities is an important component of social development as making them contributing citizens of the country, which will immensely help in economic development. India has a large population of persons with disabilities. Each disability brings in its wake problems in education, training, employment and social participation. The approach to resolving the problems of each disability will vary according to the nature and extent of the disability as well as the socio-economic situation in which the individual is placed.

Persons with disabilities may have problems in undertaking education, work and participation in community activities expected of an individual of the same age and socio-economic status. Therefore, the purpose of rehabilitation will be to enhance the capacity of a person with disability to receive better education, vocational training and social skills so that he/she can be mainstreamed in the society. The vision document of RCI has set following specific objectives:

- To formulate broad strategies for universalizing special education in all forms like special schools, integrated schools, non-formal education, alternative schooling, distance education, home based education, etc.
- To achieve a better psychosocial environment for the rehabilitation of persons with disabilities.
- To promote and undertake research designed to ascertain the models of rehabilitation or special education that is most suitable for the people with disabilities in the Indian context.
- To develop and revise curricula for human resource development in the field of rehabilitation and special education adapted to Indian needs.
- To promote orientation training of medical and paramedical personnel with a view to give better understanding of the issues related to the disabled in general and rehabilitation in particular.
- To mould human resource development in such a way as to promote positive attitudes and community mobilization.
- To facilitate the provision of vocational training to such disabled persons as are capable of engaging in productive work.
- To establish National University of Rehabilitation Sciences.
- To achieve optimum human resource development in the field of geriatric rehabilitation and other neglected categories.
- To promote uniformity in the evaluation of candidates

appearing for various examinations by setting up a central examination board.

— To launch National Programme to accelerate the pace of human resource development.

— To launch foundation courses of short duration on disability management through conventional and distance modes for accelerating human resource development.

— Maintenance of Central Rehabilitation Register through computerization.

Various Institutes and Services Provided of Government for Disabled

Govt. of has setup Institutes to cater to the needs of various categories of the disabled population. In consonance with the policy of providing a complete package of welfare services to the physically and mentally disabled individuals and groups and in order to effectively deal with the multi dimensional problems of the disabled population, the following National Institutes/apex level institution have been setup in each major area of disability:

(*i*) National Institute for the Visually Handicapped, Dehradun

(*ii*) National Institute for the Orthopaedically Handicapped, Calcutta.

(*iii*) Ali Yavar Jung National Institute for the Hearing Handicapped, Mumbai

(*iv*) National Institute for Mentally Handicapped, Secunderabad.

(*v*) National Institute for Rehabilitation Training and Research, Cuttack.

(*vi*) Institute for the Physically Handicapped, New Delhi.

Main Functions of these Institutes

These Institutes are forerunners as well as trendsetters in their respective areas of specialization. They have been staffed with talented professionals and equipped with modern and scientific equipments. To develop manpower for delivery of services to the disabled persons, the Institutes run various specialized courses to train professionals in the different areas of disability like Degree courses in Physiotherapy, Occupational Therapy, Prosthetic and Orthotic Engineering, Bachelors Degree Courses in Mental Retardation, Diploma in Special Education (Mental Retardation), Diploma in Vocational Training and Employment (Mental Retardation), Bachelor and Master in Education (Hearing Impaired), Bachelors and Masters Degree in Hearing, Language and Speech Bachelors and Masters Degree in Audiology and Speech Rehabilitation, Primary and Secondary level Teachers Training Programme for Visually Handicapped and Training Course for Orientation and Mobility Instructors for Visually Handicapped, etc.

Composite Regional Centres

Government have decided to set up Regional Centres in the country to provide composite services for different kinds of disabilities. A scheme for setting up five Composite Regional Centres for persons with disabilities in the States of Uttar Pradesh, Madhya Pradesh, Himachal Pradesh, Assam, and Jammu & Kashmir has been approved recently with a total cost of Rs. 16.89 crores to provide composite rehabilitation services to the disabled and conduct training programmes to generate professionals in this field. The centre will also promote research & generate awareness. CRC at Srinagar and Lucknow have been inaugurated and have become functional.

Regional Rehabilitation Centres

Government propose to setup Regional Rehabilitation Centres for Spinal injuries and Orthopaedic disabilities; Four Regional Rehabilitation centres for are proposed to be setup these Centres would provide facilities for basic management and follow up of the spinally injured with focus on the rehabilitation services. The centres will be established as a centrally sponsored scheme with the centre, state ratio of 90:10 the centres will be run by agency identified by the respective State Govts.

Artificial Limbs Manufacturing Corporation of India (ALIMCO), Kanpur

To meet the growing needs of the physically handicapped population of country, ALIMCO will set up four auxiliary production centres to augment its manufacturing capacity of wheel chairs and tricycles. Besides the corporation has taken up a comprehensive modernization plan for improving production & Services

Indian Spinal Injury Centre (ISIC)

The Indian Spinal Injury Centre (ISIC) has been set up in collaboration with the Italian Government, to provide comprehensive treatment, rehabilitation services and vocational training and guidance to patients with spinal injury. It is the first centre of its kind in Asia. The centre also conducts research in multidimensional aspects of rehabilitation of such patients. The machinery and technical expertise were made available to the Centre under Indo-Italian cooperation. Further support to ISIC is provided for capital expenditure. Provision with an escalation of 10 per cent expenditure from 1997-98 towards maintenance has been made in order to sponsor 30 free beds to the poor patients.

Provision to Safeguard Rights and Facilities for Persons with Disabilities

The Persons with Disabilities (Equal Opportunities, Protection of Rights and Full Participation Act, 1995 safe-guards rights and facilities made available to persons with disabilities and also looks into complaints with respect to deprivation of rights of persons with disabilities. The Implementation of provisions of the Act require a multi-sectoral collaborative approach of all concerned Ministries of the Central Government, the State

Government and the Union Territories and other appropriate authorities. While in the area of prevention, early detection and intervention, Ministry of Health & Family Welfare and Department of Women & Child Development have to play a major role, in the area of education, the Department of Education has to initiate programmes such a transport facility, financial incentives, etc. to promote education among the children with disabilities. The department of Education has to integrate these programmes within their schemes/ programmes. For the creation of barrier free environment, the Ministries of Urban Area and Employment, Surface Transport, Railways and Civil Aviation have to take steps. In the area of employment and training, Ministry of Labour has an important role. The appropriate Governments have to ensure the implementation of Persons with Disabilities (Equal Opportunities, Protection of Rights and full Participation Act, 1995 by making necessary institutional arrangements and implementing various programmes economic capacity and development.

Science and Technology Mission Mode

Science and Technology Mission Mode is to coordinate, fund and direct application of technology in development and utilisation of-

1. Suitable and cost effective aids and appliances
2. Methods of education and skill development leading to enhancement of opportunities for:
   (*a*) Employment
   (*b*) Easier living and mobility
   (*c*) Communication
   (*d*) Recreation and
   (*e*) Integration in society

The Mission Mode covers all the areas of disability viz. speech & hearing, visual, mentally, orthopaedoically handicapped (includes cerebral palsy, leprosy, and spastic). It supports all aspects of rehabilitation-development of new assistive devices, enhancement of new employment opportunities, educational skills and recreation of persons with disabilities.

Approach to the Disability Sector in the X Five Year Plan

While there is no precise data on the incidence of disability in India, it is estimated that about 5% of the population suffers from disability of some kind—visual, hearing, orthopedic or mental retardation based on sample survey done by the National Sample Survey Organisation in 1991. While the type and pattern of disability may change over the years, there is no indication of decline in the number of persons with disabilities. On the contrary, with life expectancy going up, geriatric disabilities are expected to rise. Similarly, with a declining infant mortality rate, more babies at risk are likely to survive with morbidity and disability.

Accidents are also a major factor in the wake of industrialization and development. During the last few years, high priority was given and concerted efforts made towards empowerment of persons with disabilities particularly in the area of outreach to ensure that appropriate rehabilitation services reach persons with disabilities living even in rural and remote areas. During the X Plan period, it is necessary to strengthen and consolidate outreach and extension programmes through the National Programme for Rehabilitation of Persons with Disabilities (NPRPD) which was launched last year. The aim would be to reach every district in the country with a District Rehabilitation Centre which will work as a single window service delivery as well as facilitation centre for the entire range of requirements of PWDs including therapeutic services, assistive devices as well as information and guidance on education and placement services, rural development and poverty alleviation schemes, etc. This would promote convergence with other developmental programmes and ensure that persons with disabilities are able to access such benefits.

A large number of preventable disabilities are occurring at present due to various life style factors including inadequate intake of nutrients including micro nutrients like iodine, vitamin A, iron etc.; unhygienic and in sanitary living conditions leading to diseases, morbidity and disability as well as unscientific birth and rearing practices. During the Tenth Plan period, issues such as sanitation including potable drinking water, food security including micro nutrients, care of the girl child and proper birth and rearing practices need to be highlighted as these would have an inter-generational impact on prevention of mortality, morbidity and disability. The importance of providing barrier free access to public facilities and other services including recreation which are taken for granted by non-disabled citizens to persons with disabilities need emphasis during the 10th Plan. While awareness has to be promoted on these issues, all appropriate authorities providing public facilities have to undertake access audit and ensure that the environment is non-handicapping for persons with disabilities as well as aged persons. The ultimate aim of rehabilitation services is socio-economic empowerment and integration of persons with disabilities into the mainstream of society. The thrust in the Tenth Plan period has, therefore to be towards providing appropriate education, training and employment opportunities to such persons both within the Government for which there is a provision of 3 per cent reservation and also in the private sector which could be encouraged through suitable incentives and concessions for employment of persons with disabilities.

International Statements

There are several international statements and conventions, which proclaim the right of all disabled children to education. The UN World Programme of Action Concerning Disabled Persons (1983) was one of the earliest statements of the UN, which called up on all States to adopt policies that recognise the rights of the disabled to equal educational opportunities. It also recommended that the education of the disabled persons should as far as possible take place in the general school system. The UN convention on the Rights of the Child, adopted in 1989 and ratified by over 190 countries including India, which stressed on non-discrimination and universal access to basic education to all children. The World Declaration on Education For All (1990) exhorted States to provide equal access to education to every category of disabled person. Another important document of the UN on disability is the "Standard Rules" on equalisation of opportunities for persons with disabilities adopted in 1993.

The landmark International statement, however, is the UNESCO Salamanca statement and Framework for Action (1994). The statement proclaimed that every child has a fundamental right to education and children with special needs must have access to regular schools, which should accommodate them with in a child centred pedagogy. Other International documents include the World Summit for Social Development (1995) and UNDP's Inter-regional programme for the disabled people (1995).

International Treaties

The promotion and protection of human rights is one of the fundamental aims of the United Nations. Since its creation, the Organisation has made enormous progress in setting legal standards in the field of human rights and establishing mechanisms to monitor the implementation of these standards.

The State Parties to the six core human rights conventions are obliged to respect and to ensure the rights recognized in these instruments to all individuals, and to take the necessary steps to give effect to these rights. Each of these six core human rights treaties establishes a committee of independent experts—usually referred to as "treaty monitoring body" or "treaty body"—to monitor the domestic implementation of the human rights provisions contained in those treaties. Four treaties also establishes procedures which allow individuals who claim to be victims of a violation by a State party of the rights set out in the respective treaties may submit individual complaints to the treaty monitoring body.

There are no international human rights treaties, which apply solely to persons with disabilities. Rather, international human rights treaties apply to this category of individuals via the anti-discrimination clause, which is included in each treaty. Under these provisions, States Parties undertake to guarantee that the rights recognized in the treaty will be exercised without distinction of any kind, "such as race, colour, sex, language, religion, political or other opinion, national or social origin, property, birth or other status". Although disability is not expressly included among the prohibited grounds for discrimination, it is widely accepted that it falls under the heading "other status" and is thus treated as a ground in respect of which discrimination is prohibited.

The International Covenant on Economic, Social and Cultural Rights (ICESCR)

The 1966 International Covenant on Economic, Social and Cultural Rights (ICESCR) aims at the protection and promotion of a wide range of economic, social and cultural rights. Like ICCPR, it does not contain any explicit reference to persons with disabilities, but many of its provisions are undoubtedly of great importance for ensuring the full participation of, and equal opportunities for, disabled persons in their societies. Under Article 2, for example, States parties are required to respond appropriately, to the maximum extent of their available resources, to enable such persons to seek to overcome any disadvantages, in terms of the enjoyment of the rights specified in the Covenant, flowing from their disability. The right to education (Article 13) is violated whenever children with disabilities are denied access to public educational institutions (e.g. because buildings are not accessible) or when their special educational needs—including special communication needs (e.g. use of sign language or Braille)—are not taken into account in developing national educational programmes. According to Article 12 (Right to health), persons with disabilities must be provided with the same level of medical care as other members of society, and have the right to have access to, and to benefit from, those medical and social services—including orthopaedic devices—which enable them to become independent, prevent further disabilities and support their social integration. The right to work (Article 6) may be violated when the State fails to adopt adequate regulations and policies to make the workplace accessible to disabled persons, to provide persons with disabilities with adequate technical and vocational guidance to improve their capabilities and skills or to support the integration of the disabled in mainstream employment.

The International Covenant on Civil and Political Rights (ICCPR)

The 1966 International Covenant on Civil and Political Rights (ICCPR) provides protection for civil and political rights. It seeks to underpin the freedom of the individual and to ensure that he/she is enabled to exert influence over the political life of the community. Disabled persons are not explicitly mentioned by the ICCPR; however, many provisions of the Covenant are of direct relevance for persons with disabilities. For instance, Article 7 (right to freedom from torture and other cruel, inhuman or degrading treatment and punishment) may be violated when persons with disabilities are placed in an inappropriate environment or when a person with a mental or psychiatric disability is subject to medical or scientific experimentation without his/her prior informed consent. Involuntary or forced institutionalisation of a person with a mental or psychiatric disability may constitute, when carried out without strict procedural safeguards, a breach of the right to liberty and security of a person (Article 9). The right to be recognised as a person before the law (Article 16) may be violated when a person is deprived of his/her legal capacity on account of an actual or perceived disability without the safeguards to protect the rights of the person and/or periodical review by competent judicial authorities to verify the need for representation and the proper exercise of the function by the legal representative. Finally, the denial of the right to form a family (e.g. forced sterilisation), to live with one's own family or to experience sexuality and parenthood may constitute violations of the right to right to marry and found a family (Article 23) and/or the right to privacy and family life (Article 17).

Convention against Torture and Other Cruel, Inhuman or Degrading Treatment or Punishment (CAT)

Four other United Nations treaties are usually included among the "core" human rights instruments. One of them deals with the right to be free from torture: the Convention against Torture and Other Cruel, Inhuman or Degrading Treatment or Punishment (CAT). This Convention is of obvious importance to persons with disabilities. Torture is often the cause of severe physical or mental disability. Furthermore, persons with disabilities, and especially those who live in institutionalized settings, are particularly vulnerable to torture or other forms of inhuman or degrading treatment. A massive imbalance of power often exists in institutions between an inmate and those in authority. This imbalance is magnified many times over in institutional settings for persons with disabilities. Torture, and the less severe but equally abominable phenomena of cruel, inhuman or degrading treatment or punishment, are common in mental and physical disability institutions—whether public or private—and negatively affect the physical and emotional well-being of their residents. Legal protection against torture is therefore of the utmost importance in protecting the human rights and dignity of persons with disabilities and ensuring respect for their physical and psychic integrity wherever they reside.

The definition of torture contained in Article 1 of CAT covers those forms of ill-treatment that intentionally cause severe pain or suffering and are carried out by individuals exercising public functions, which renders it inapplicable in many cases involving the abuse of persons with disabilities in institutions and other settings. However, States parties to the Convention are also under a duty to prevent cruel, inhuman or degrading treatment or punishment (Article 16), and this provision may be of great relevance in cases of ill-treatment against persons with disabilities. A violation of this provision may occur, for example, when the State:

— fails to take positive action such as the provision of medical treatment or services to disabled persons living in institutionalised settings;
— fails to proceed to a prompt and impartial investigation, when there is reasonable ground to believe that torture or inhuman or degrading treatment has been inflicted on a disabled person living in a public or private institution;
— fails to provide a victim of cruel, inhuman or degrading treatment with appropriate means of redress and fair and adequate compensation, including the means for full rehabilitation.

The International Convention on the Elimination of All Forms of Racial Discrimination (CERD) and the Convention on the Elimination of All Forms of Discrimination against Women (CEDAW)

Other two treaties, the 1965 International Convention on the Elimination of All Forms of Racial Discrimination (CERD) and the 1979 Convention on the Elimination of All Forms of Discrimination against Women (CEDAW), deal with particular groups or categories of persons who are at risk of discrimination. These treaties generally serve two purposes. First, they establish the principle of non-discrimination with respect to the enjoyment of all human rights for the categories of persons covered. Secondly, and to the extent required, they add specificity to the general ICCPR and ICESCR rights, tailoring them more directly to the circumstances of the groups covered. These group-specific conventions are of obvious importance in the context of double discrimination. People with disabilities may suffer discrimination not only because they are disabled but also because they belong to other groupings or minorities such as ethnic groups or women.

CERD aims at the elimination of racial discrimination in all its forms. W hen people with disabilities happen to belong to a racial group or minority, they may face discrimination on the grounds of both race and disability. The Convention prohibits "any form of distinction, exclusion, restriction or preference based on race, colour, descent, or national or ethnic origin which has the purpose or effect of nullifying or impairing the recognition, enjoyment or exercise, on an equal footing, of human rights and fundamental freedoms in the political, economic, social, cultural or any other field of public life" (Article 1, paragraph 1). Special measures taken for the sole purpose of securing adequate advancement of certain groups or individuals requiring such protection as may be necessary in order to ensure such groups or individuals equal enjoyment or exercise of human rights and fundamental freedoms (i.e. affirmative action) shall not be deemed racial discrimination, provided that some conditions are respected (Article 1, paragraph 4).

The overarching goal of CEDAW is the achievement of *de iure* and *de facto* equality for women. The non-discrimination rights included in the Convention cover the whole spectrum of human rights, are they civil, cultural, economic, political or social. Women with disabilities may be vulnerable because of both disability and gender, and are more likely to suffer from discrimination than able-bodied women or men with disabilities. Although the Convention does not specifically refer to women with disabilities, it is clear that as the CEDAW provisions cover all women, they apply equally to women with disabilities and able-bodied women. With regard to disabled women, States are in particular required to take measures, including special measures to ensure that they have equal access to education and employment, health services and social security, and to ensure that they can participate in all areas of social and cultural life.

The Convention on the Rights of the Child (CRC)

The 1989 Convention on the Rights of the Child (CRC) is the first binding instrument in international law to deal with the rights of children. It contains 42 detailed provisions enshrining the rights of children in all areas of their lives and includes provisions on civil, cultural, economic, political and social rights. Unlike the other international human rights instruments, the CRC contains two provisions relating to disability. Article 2 expressly prohibits any discrimination in respect of the enjoyment of Convention rights on the ground of disability. Most importantly, the Convention includes a specific provision (Article 23) on the rights of children with disabilities, which reads as follows:

- States Parties recognize that a mentally or physically disabled child should enjoy a full and decent life, in conditions, which ensure dignity, promote self-reliance and facilitate the child's active participation in the community.
- States Parties recognize the right of the disabled child to special care and shall encourage and ensure the extension, subject to available resources, to the eligible child and those responsible for his or her care, of assistance for which application is made and which is appropriate to the child's condition and to the circumstances of the parents or others caring for the child.
- Recognizing the special needs of a disabled child, assistance extended in accordance with paragraph 2 of the present article shall be provided free of charge, whenever possible, taking into account the financial resources of the parents or others caring for the child, and shall be designed to ensure that the disabled child has effective access to and receives education, training, health care services, rehabilitation services, preparation for employment and recreation opportunities in a manner conducive to the child's achieving the fullest possible social integration and individual development, including his or her cultural and spiritual development
- States Parties shall promote, in the spirit of international cooperation, the exchange of appropriate information in

the field of preventive health care and of medical, psychological and functional treatment of disabled children, including dissemination of and access to information concerning methods of rehabilitation, education and vocational services, with the aim of enabling States Parties to improve their capabilities and skills and to widen their experience in these areas. In this regard, particular account shall be taken of the needs of developing countries.

The Convention also includes other provisions which are particularly relevant to children with disabilities, such as the right not to be separated from one's family (Article 9), the right to protection from abuse (Article 19), the right to an adequate standard of living (Article 27), the right to health care (Article 24), the right to education (Article s 28 and 29) and the right to physical and psychological recovery and social reintegration for victims of neglect, exploitation, abuse, torture or any other form of cruel, inhuman or degrading treatment or punishment, or armed conflicts (Article 39). The application of general rights provisions to disabled children is ensured by the prohibition of discrimination on the ground of disability contained in Article 2.

Other Treaties Addressing the Issue of Disability

In addition to human rights treaties, other United Nations instruments address the issue of disability. Article 1 of the UNESCO Convention against Discrimination in Education, for example, guarantees equal access to education of all types and levels and prohibits the limitation of any person or group of persons to education of an inferior standard. Persons with disabilities must therefore be provided with equal access to education, which is of a comparable standard to that available to non-disabled persons. The ILO Convention concerning Vocational Rehabilitation and Employment (Disabled Persons) recognises the rights of disabled persons to appropriate training and employment, not only in specialised institutions and sheltered workshops, but also in open labour markets, and stipulates that employers' and workers' organisations—together with Governments and organisations of disabled persons—share responsibility for helping disabled persons to realise their rights. The definition of discrimination in Article 1 of the ILO Convention concerning Discrimination in Respect of Employment and Occupation does not specifically include a distinction based on disability of a person; however, as under Article 1(2), the term discrimination includes "...such other distinction, exclusion or preference which has the effect of nullifying or impairing equality of opportunity or treatment in employment or occupation as may be determined by the Member concerned after consultation with representative employers' and workers' organisations...", discrimination on the ground of disability may come within the provisions of the Convention, if so determined by the Member.

At the regional level, the new Article 15 of the Revised European Social Charter recognises the "right of persons with disabilities to independence, social integration and participation in the life of the community", and commits Contracting Parties to: (1) take the necessary measures to provide persons with disabilities with guidance, education and vocational training, (2) to promote their access to employment through all measures tending to encourage employers to hire and keep in employment persons with disabilities in the ordinary working environment and to adjust the working conditions to the needs of the disabled, and (3) to promote their full social integration and participation in the life of the community in particular through measures, including technical aids, aiming to overcome barriers to communication and mobility and enabling access to transport, housing, cultural activities and leisure."

The Additional Protocol to the American Convention on Human Rights in the Area of Economic, Social, and Cultural Rights specifically refers to the rights of persons with disabilities.

According to Article 18, "everyone affected by a diminution of his physical or mental capacities is entitled to special attention to help him to achieve the greatest possible development of their personality". States Parties agree to undertake programmes aimed at providing persons with disabilities with the resources and environment needed for attaining this goal, to provide special training to the families of the handicapped.

The Inter-American Convention on the Elimination of all Forms of Discrimination against People with Disabilities is aims at the prevention and elimination of all forms of discrimination against persons with disabilities and the promotion of their full integration into society. States parties undertake to adopt the legislative, social, educational, labour-related, or any other measures needed to achieve the goals of the Convention, and to co-operate with one another in helping to prevent and eliminate discrimination against persons with disabilities.

United Nations: Rights of Persons with Disability

Declaration on the Rights of Mentally Retarded Persons

Declaration on the Rights of Mentally Retarded Persons and calls for national and international action to ensure that it will be used as a common basis and frame of reference for the protection of these rights:

1. The mentally retarded person has, to the maximum degree of feasibility, the same rights as other human beings.
2. The mentally retarded person has a right to proper medical care and physical therapy and to such education, training, rehabilitation and guidance as will enable him to develop his ability and maximum potential.
3. The mentally retarded person has a right to economic security and to a decent standard of living. He has a right to perform productive work or to engage in any other meaningful occupation fully of his capabilities.
4. Whenever possible, the mentally retarded person should

live with his own family or with foster parents and participate in different forms of community life. The family with which he lives should receive assistance. If care in an institution becomes necessary, it should be provided in surroundings and other circumstances as close as possible to those of normal life.

5. The mentally retarded person has a right to a qualified guardian when this is required to protect his personal well-being and interests.

6. The mentally retarded person has a right to protection from exploitation, abuse and degrading treatment. If prosecuted for any offence, he shall have a right to due process of law with full recognition being given to his degree of mental responsibility.

7. Whenever mentally retarded persons are unable, because of the severity of their handicap, to exercise all their rights in a meaningful way or it should become necessary to restrict or deny some or all of these rights, the procedure used for that restriction or denial of rights must contain proper legal safeguards against every form of abuse. This procedure must be based on an evaluation of the social capability of the mentally retarded person by qualified experts and must be subject to periodic review and to the right of appeal to higher authorities.

Declaration on the Rights of Disabled Persons

Declaration on the Rights of Disabled Persons and calls for national and international action to ensure that it will be used as a common basis and frame of reference for the protection of these rights:

1. The term "disabled person" means any person unable to ensure by himself or herself, wholly or partly, the necessities of a normal individual and/or social life, as a result of deficiency, either congenital or not, in his or her physical or mental capabilities.

2. Disabled persons shall enjoy all the rights set forth in this Declaration. These rights shall be granted to all disabled persons without any exception whatsoever and without distinction or discrimination on the basis of race, colour, sex, language, religion, political or other opinions, national or social origin, state of wealth, birth or any other situation applying either to the disabled person himself or herself or to his or her family.
3. Disabled persons have the inherent right to respect for their human dignity. Disabled persons, whatever the origin, nature and seriousness of their handicaps and disabilities, have the same fundamental rights as their fellow-citizens of the same age, which implies primarily the right to enjoy a decent life, as normal and full as possible.
4. Disabled persons have the same civil and political rights as other human beings; paragraph 7 of the Declaration on the Rights of Mentally Retarded Persons applies to any possible limitation or suppression of those rights for mentally disabled persons.
5. Disabled persons are entitled to the measures designed to enable them to become as self-reliant as possible.
6. Disabled persons have the right to medical, psychological and functional treatment, including prosthetic and orthetic appliances, to medical and social rehabilitation, education, vocational training and rehabilitation, aid, counselling, placement services and other services, which will enable them to develop their capabilities and skills to the maximum and will hasten the processes of their social integration or reintegration.
7. Disabled persons have the right to economic and social security and to a decent level of living. They have the right, according to their capabilities, to secure and retain employment or to engage in a useful, productive and remunerative occupation and to join trade unions.
8. Disabled persons are entitled to have their special needs

taken into consideration at all stages of economic and social planning.

9. Disabled persons have the right to live with their families or with foster parents and to participate in all social, creative or recreational activities. No disabled person shall be subjected, as far as his or her residence is concerned, to differential treatment other than that required by his or her condition or by the improvement, which he or she may derive there from. If the stay of a disabled person in a specialized establishment is indispensable, the environment and living conditions therein shall be as close as possible to those of the normal life of a person of his or her age.

10. Disabled persons shall be protected against all exploitation, all regulations and all treatment of a discriminatory, abusive or degrading nature.

11. Disabled persons shall be able to avail themselves of qualified legal aid when such aid proves indispensable for the protection of their persons and property. If judicial proceedings are instituted against them, the legal procedure applied shall consider their physical and mental condition.

12. Organizations of disabled persons may be usefully consulted in all matters regarding the rights of disabled persons.

13. Disabled persons, their families and communities shall be fully informed, by all appropriate means, of the rights contained in this Declaration.

3 Education of Children with Visual Impairments

Characteristics and Identification

It is very necessary to identify each category of children with visual impairments. Medical treatment may become necessary in some cases. Parents also need to be informed.

Children with visual impairment may be identified from the following:

1. Having watery eyes.
2. Rubbing eyes frequently.
3. Reddening of eyes frequently.
4. Covering one eye and tining the head forward.
5. Holding objects and books close to the eyes.
6. Asking help from others when taking notes from the blackboard.
7. Blinking frequently—squinting eyelids together.
8. Complaining about headache following close eye work.
9. Bumping into people or objects.
10. Skipping words or lines while reading.
11. Having poor eye-hand coordination.
12. Moving head forward and backward while looking at distant objects.

Blindness

Blindness can be defined physiologically as the condition of lacking *visual perception*. The definition as it applies to people thus legally classified is, however, more complex.

"Blindness" also applies to partial visual impairment: In *North America* and most of *Europe*, legal blindness is defined as *visual acuity* (vision) of 20/200 (6/60) or less in the better eye with best correction possible. This means that a legally blind individual would have to stand 20 feet from an object to see it with the same degree of clarity as a normally sighted person could from 200 feet. In many areas, people with average acuity who nonetheless have a visual field of less than 20 degrees (the norm being 180 degrees) are also classified as being legally blind.

Approximately ten percent of those deemed legally blind, by any measure, are fully sightless. The rest have some vision, from light perception alone to relatively good acuity. Those who are not legally blind, but nonetheless have serious visual impairments, possess *low vision* By the 10th Revision of the *WHO*. International Statistical Classification of Diseases, Injuries and Causes of Death, *low vision* is defined as visual acuity of less then 6/18, but equal to or better than 3/60, or corresponding visual field loss to less than 20 degrees, in the better eye with best possible correction. *Blindness* is defined as visual acuity of less than 3/60, or corresponding visual field loss to less than 10 degrees, in the better eye with best possible correction. Visual impairment includes low vision as well as blindness.

Causes of Blindness

Most visual impairment is caused by *disease*. According to WHO, the most common causes of blindness around the world are:

- *Cataracts*: A cataract is a large waterfall or place where the flow of a river changes dramatically. The term comes from the Greek word *kataraktes*, whose meaning "to dash down" or "downrush" describes rapidly running water, and the Latin *cataracta*, whose meaning describes "a waterfall", "a floodgate", or "a portcullis". As rapidly running water turns white, the term was later used metaphorically to describe the similar appearance of mature ocular opacities.

- *Glaucoma*: pink rim of disc contains nerve fibers. The white cup is a pit with no nerve fibers. As glaucoma advances, the cup enlarges until it occupies most of the disc area. Glaucoma is a group of diseases of the optic nerve involving loss of retinal ganglion cells in a characteristic pattern of optic neuropathy.
- *Age-Related Macular Degeneration*: Macular degeneration is a medical condition where the light sensing cells in the macula malfunction and over time cease to work. According to the American Academy of Ophthalmology, it is the leading cause of central vision loss (blindness) in the United States today for those over the age of fifty. There are two basic types of the disease: Standard Macular Degeneration (MD) and Age Related Macular Degeneration (ARMD), with ARMD being the most common form of the condition.
- *Trachoma:* An eye disease which may result in blindness, is caused by the bacteria Chlamydia trachomatis. Derived from the Ancient Greek, "Trachoma" means "rough eye." The blindness is caused by ulceration and consequent scarring of the cornea.
- *Corneal:* The cornea is the curved, transparent layer that covers the front part of the eye and protects its inner structures. Together with the lens, the cornea refracts light and consequently helps the eye to focus. The cornea gives a larger contribution to the total refraction than the lens, but whereas the curvature of the lens can be adjusted to "tune" the focus, the curvature of the cornea is fixed.
- *Diabetic Retinopathy:* Diabetic retinopathy is retinopathy (damage to the retina) caused by complications of diabetes mellitus, which could eventually lead to blindness. It is an ocular manifestation of systemic disease which affects up to

80 per cent of all diabetics who have had diabetes for 15 years or more.

People in developing countries are significantly more likely to experience visual impairment as a consequence of treatable or preventable conditions than are their counterparts in the developed world. While vision impairment is most common in people over age 60 across all regions, children in poorer communities are more likely to be affected by blinding diseases than are their more affluent peers.

The link between *poverty* and treatable visual impairment is most obvious when conducting regional comparisons of cause. Most adult visual impairment in North America and Western Europe is related to age-related macular degeneration and diabetic retinopathy. While both of these conditions are subject to treatment, neither can be cured.

In developing countries, wherein people have shorter life expectancies, cataracts and water-borne parasites—both of which can be treated effectively—are most often the culprits. Of the estimated 40 million blind people located around the world, 70–80 per cent can have some or all of their sight restored through treatment.

Genetic Defects

People with *albinism* often suffer from visually impairment to the extent that many are legally blind, though few of them are actually sightless.

Colour blindness

Color blindness is usually classed as a *disability*; however, in select situations color blind people have advantages over people with normal color vision. Colour blind hunters are better at picking out prey against a confusing background, and the *military* have found that color blind soldiers can sometimes see through *camouflage* that fools everyone else. Monochromats may have a minor advantage in dark vision, but only in the first five minutes of dark adaptation.

Classification of Color Deficiencies

- Acquired
- Congenital

Simple Test for Colour Blindness

To the right are four pictures with 2-digit numbers designed to test for different kinds of color blindness. Note that monitor or lighting differences may affect whether or not the images can be seen.

Causes of Colour Blindness

There are many types of color blindness. The most common varieties are hereditary (genetic) photoreceptor disorders, but it is also possible to acquire color blindness through damage to the retina, optic nerve, or higher brain areas. Higher brain areas implicated in color processing include the parvocellular pathway of the *lateral geniculate nucleus* of the *thalamus*, and visual area V4 of the *visual cortex*. Acquired color blindness is generally unlike the more typical genetic disorders. For example, it is possible to acquire color blindness only in a portion of the visual field but maintain normal color vision elsewhere. Some forms of acquired color blindness are reversible. Transient color blindness also occurs (very rarely) in the *aura* of some *migraine*

The different kinds of color blindness result from one or more of the different cone systems either not functioning at all, or functioning in an unusual way. When one cone system is compromised, *dichromacy* results. The most frequent forms of human color blindness result from problems with either the middle or long wavelength sensitive cone systems, and involve difficulties in discriminating reds, yellows, and greens from one another. They are collectively referred to as "red-green color blindness", though the term is an over-simplification and somewhat misleading. Other forms of color blindness are much rarer. They include problems in discriminating blues from yellows, and the rarest forms of all, complete color blindness or *monochromacy*, where one cannot distinguish any color from grey, as in a *black-and-white* movie or photograph.

Red-Green Color Blindness

Types of red-green color blindness

There are several types of red-green color blindness:

- *Protanopia*: Lacking the long-wavelength sensitive retinal cones, those with this condition are unable to distinguish between colors in the green-yellow-red section of the spectrum. They have a neutral point at a wavelength of 492 *nm*—that is, they cannot discriminate light of this wavelength from white. Their sensitivity to light in the orange and red part of the spectrum is also reduced. Very few people have been found who have one normal eye and one protanopic eye. These *unilateral dichromats* report that with only their protanopic eye open, they see wavelengths below the neutral point as blue and those above it as yellow. This is a rare form of color blindness.
- *Deuteranopia*: Lacking the medium-wavelength cones, those affected are again unable to distinguish between colors in the green-yellow-red section of the spectrum. Their neutral point is at a slightly longer wavelength, 498 nm. This is one of the rarer forms of colorblindness making up about 1 per cent of the male population, also known as *Daltonism* after Dalton. (Dalton's diagnosis was confirmed as deuteranopia in 1995, some 150 years after his death, by *DNA* analysis of his preserved eyeball.) Deuteranopic unilateral dichromats report that with only their deuteranopic eye open, they see wavelengths below the neutral point as blue and those above it as yellow.
- *Protanomaly*: Having a mutated form of the long-wavelength

pigment, whose peak sensitivity is at a shorter wavelength than in the normal retina, protanomalous individuals are less sensitive to red light than normal. This means that they are less able to discriminate colors, and they do not see mixed lights as having the same colors as normal observers. They also suffer from a darkening of the red end of the spectrum. This causes reds to reduce in intensity to the point where they can be mistaken for black. Protanomaly is a fairly rare form of color blindness, making up about 1 per cent of the male population.

- *Deuteranomaly*: Having a mutated form of the medium-wavelength pigment. The medium-wavelength pigment is shifted towards the red end of the spectrum resulting in a reduction in sensitivity to the green area of the spectrum. Unlike protanomaly the intensity of colors is unchanged. This is the most common form of color blindness, making up about 6 per cent of the male population.

Genetics of Red-Green Colour Blindness

Genetic red-green color blindness affects men much more often than women, because the *genes* for the red and green color receptors are located on the X *chromosome*, of which men have only one and women have two. Such a trait is called sex-linked. Genetic females (46, XX) are red-green color blind only if *both* their X chromosomes are defective with a similar deficiency, whereas genetic males (46, XY) are color blind if their only X chromosome is defective.

The gene for red-green color blindness is transmitted from a color blind male to all his daughters who are *heterozygote* carriers and are perceptually unaffected. In turn, a carrier woman passes on a mutated X chromosome region to only half her male offspring. The sons of an affected male will not inherit the trait, since they receive his Y chromosome and not his (defective) X chromosome.

Because one X chromosome is *inactivated* at random in each cell during a woman's development, it is possible for her to have four different cone types, if, for example, a carrier of protanomaly has a child with a deuteranomalic man. The deficiencies can combine to form a fourth receptor whose absorption spectrum peaks in the yellow-green area. Denoting the normal vision alleles by P and D and the anomalous by p and d, the carrier is PD pD and the man is Pd. The daughter is either PD Pd or pD Pd. Suppose she is pD Pd. The cells in her body express her mother's chromosome pD and her father's Pd. Thus some of the cones are anomalous with both deficiencies and some are normal. As a result she has the normal short, medium and long wavelength-sensitive types of cone, with an additional category of receptor that combines the deficiencies. Such women are *tetrachromats*, since with their four-cone systems, they require a mixture of four spectral lights to match an arbitrary light.

Blue-Yellow Color Blindness

Color blindness involving the inactivation of the short-wavelength sensitive cone system (whose absorption spectrum peaks in the bluish-violet) is called tritanopia or, loosely, blue-yellow color blindness. Mutation of the short-wavelength sensitive cones is called tritanomaly. Tritanopia is equally distributed among males and females, because the gene coding for the short-wavelength receptor is located on chromosome 7 and therefore not sex-linked, but since mutations in both copies are required, it is less frequently apparent.

Monochromacy

Complete inability to distinguish any colors is called *monochromacy*. It occurs in two forms: *cone monochromacy*, where only a single cone system appears to be functioning, so that no colors can be distinguished, but vision is otherwise more or less normal; and *achromatopsia* or *rod monochromacy*, where the retina contains no cone cells, so that in addition to the absence of color discrimination, vision in lights of normal intensity is difficult.

While normally rare, achromatopsia is very common on the island of Pingelap, a part of the *Pohnpei* state, where it is called *maskun*: about 1/12 of the population there has it. The island was devastated by a storm in the eighteenth century, and one of the few male survivors carried a gene for achromatopsia; the population is now several thousand, of whom about 30 per cent carry this gene.

Diagnosis of Colour Blindness

Color blindness is most often tested using the *Ishihara color test*, which consists of a series of pictures of colored spots. A figure (usually a number) is embedded in the picture as a number of spots in a slightly different color, and can be seen with normal color vision, but not with a particular color defect. The full set of tests has a variety of figure/background color combinations, and enable diagnosis of which particular visual defect is present.

However, the Ishihara color test is criticized for containing only numbers and thus not being useful for young children. It is often stated that it is important to identify these problems as soon as possible and explain them to the children to prevent possible problems and psychological traumas. For this reason, alternative color vision tests were developed using only symbols (square, circle, car).

Most clinical tests are designed to be fast, simple, and effective at identifying broad categories of color blindness. In academic studies of color blindness, on the other hand, there is more interest in developing flexible tests to collect thorough datasets, identify *countable points*, and measure *just noticeable differences*.

Design Implications of Color Blindness

Color codes present particular problems for color blind people as they are often difficult or impossible for color blind people to understand. Good *graphic design* avoids using color coding or color contrasts alone to express information, as this not only helps color blind people, but also aids understanding by normally sighted people. The use of *Cascading Style Sheets* on the *world wide web* allows pages to be given an alternative color scheme for color-blind readers. *This color scheme generator* helps a graphic designer see color schemes as seen by eight types of color blindness.

It is sometimes claimed that in extreme emergencies everyone is color blind. When the need to process visual information as rapidly as possible arises, for example in a train or aircraft crash, the visual system may operate only in shades of grey, with the extra information load in adding color being dropped. This is an important possibility to consider when designing, for example, emergency brake handles or emergency phones.

Tools

Designers, both visually impaired and sighted, have developed a number of tools for use by blind people.

Mobility

People with serious visual impairments can travel independently using a *white cane*, the international symbol of blindness.

A long cane is used to extend the user's range of touch sensation, swung in a low sweeping motion across the intended path of travel to detect obstacles. However, some visually impaired persons do not carry these kinds of canes, opting instead for the shorter, lighter identification (ID) cane. Still others require a support cane.

Each of these is painted white for maximum visibility, and to denote visual impairment on the part of the user. In addition to making rules about who can and cannot use a cane, some governments mandate the *right-of-way* be given to users of white canes or guide dogs.

A small number of people, about one percent, employ *guide dogs*. These companions are trained to lead blind individuals around obstacles on the ground and overhead. Though highly intelligent, guide dogs neither interpret street signs nor determine when the team ought to cross a street. Visually impaired people who employ these animals must already be competent travelers.

Drawings of the Eye

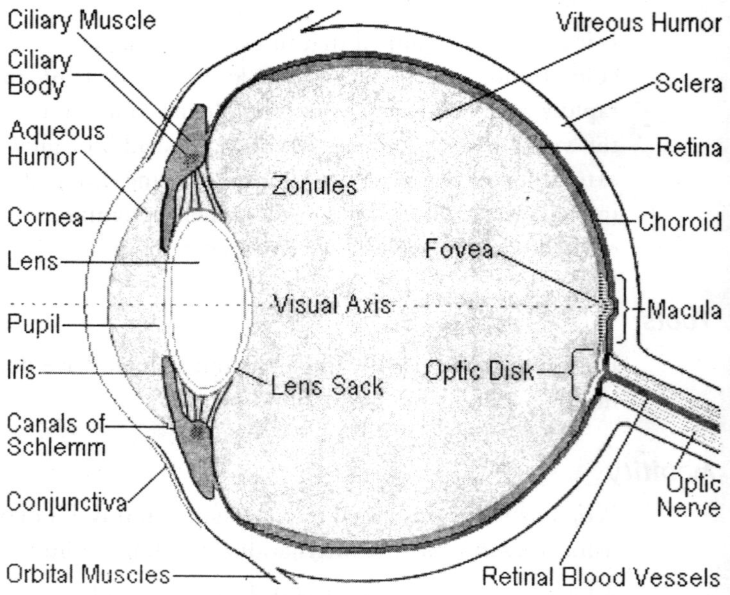

Cross section drawing of the eye—(side view) with major parts labeled.

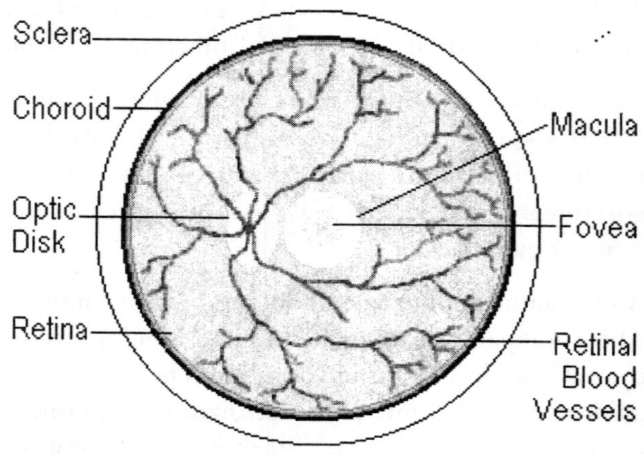

Cross section drawing of the eye—(rear view).

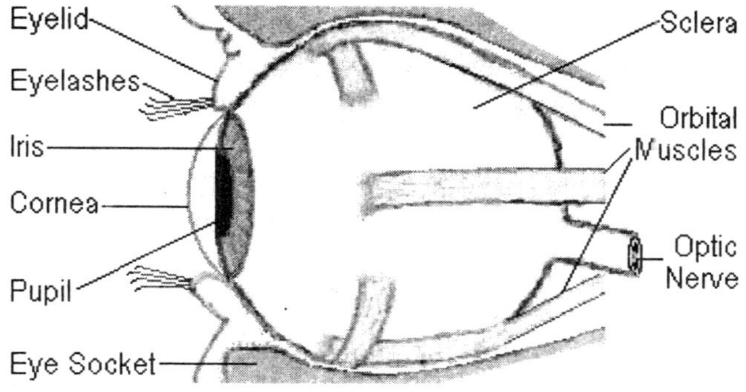

Cut-away view of the eye in its socket showing the: bony socket, orbital muscles, eyelids and eyelashes.

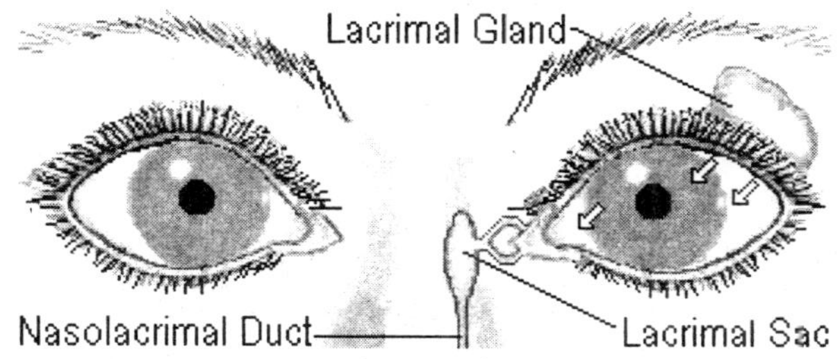

The lacrimal system—(tear ducts) produce tears to clean, moisten and lubricate the eyes and then drains the excess fluid into the nose.

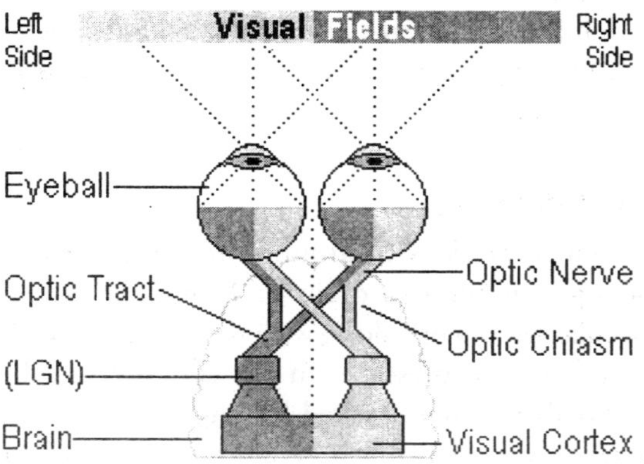

Our Eyes and brain divide what we see into a right and left half. In the drawing above, light gray represents the left half; dark gray represents the right half. The eyes invert the image and the left side of what we see ends up in the right side of our brain and visa versa. This all works out because the right side of our brain controls the left side of our bodies and visa versa.

Anterior Chamber

The space between the cornea and iris filled with Aqueous Humor.

Aqueous Humor

A water like fluid, produced by the ciliary body, it fills the front of the eye between the lens and cornea and provides the cornea and lens with oxygen and nutrients. It drains back into the blood stream through the canals of schlemm.

Brain

The brain is where the electrical signals sent from our eyes are processed into vision. Damage to the brain can lead to vision loss if the visual cortex or optic pathways are damaged. The majority of nerve fibers in the optic tract connect to the LGN. Several nerve fibers leave the optic tract before the LGN to connect to sub cortical structures through out the brain. These parts of the brain regulate things like: eye and head movements, pupillary light reflex—(pupil size), and circadian rhythms—(light/dark cycle). Damage to these parts of the brain often leads to vision disorders too.

Canals of Schlemm

These canals are located around the perimeter of the iris. They allow aqueous fluid to drain back into the blood stream. The Trabecular Meshwork along with the Canals of Schlemm regulate the eyes internal pressure. In the eye disease called glaucoma, these canals become blocked leading to increased pressure. The increased pressure, from this condition, destroys the optic nerve.

Choroid

The choroid is a layer of blood vessels between the retina and sclera; it supplies blood to the retina. In the disease called Macular Degeneration, abnormal blood vessels grow into the space between the retina and choroid damaging the macula.

Ciliary Body

This is where the Aqueous Humor is produced.

Ciliary Muscle

The eye can bring the fine print in a phone book into focus, or focus in on the moon over ¼ million miles away. The ciliary muscle changes the shape of the lens—(this is called accommodation). It relaxes to flatten the lens for distance vision; for close work it contracts rounding out the lens. Everyone will develop an eye condition called presbyopia. As we age, the ciliary muscle and crystalline lens lose their elasticity. This is why most people need reading glasses by their 40's.

Conjunctiva

The conjunctiva is a thin, clear membrane covering the front of the eye and inner eyelids. Cells in this lining produce mucous that helps to lubricate the eye. This is the eyes first layer of protection against infection. Inflammation of this membrane is called conjunctivitis, or pink eye.

Cornea

The cornea is a clear, dome-shaped surface that covers the front of the eye. It is the first and most powerful lens in the eye's optical system. To keep it transparent the cornea contains no blood vessels. Tears that flow over it and aqueous humor in the chamber behind it keep it nourished. When you hear of eye banks and eye transplants, it is the cornea that is being replaced. The cornea can be damaged from: accidents, infections, and genetic defects.

Crystalline Lens

The eye's crystalline lens works like the adjustable lens in a camera. Positioned just behind the cornea; it is responsible for keeping images in focus on the retina. It is adjustable for distance and close work. A cataract is the lens clouding up. This happens to most people as they age. A few people are even born with cataracts. Modern surgery has all but eliminated cataracts as a cause of blindness in the developed world.

Eyeball

The eye is like a little video camera measuring about 1 inch or 2.5 cm. in diameter. If someone's eyeball is larger then this, they will be nearsighted (myopic); if it is smaller then this, they will be farsighted (hyperopic). Having two eyes gives us binocular vision—(depth perception). This is due to the fusing of both images in the visual cortex.

Eyelashes and Eyebrows

These specialized hairs protect the eyes from particles that may injure them. They form a screen to keep dust and insects out. Anything touching them triggers the eyelids to blink.

Eyelids

Our eyelids protect and lubricate our eyes. Small oil-producing glands line the inner edge of our eyelids. These oils mix with tears when we blink, keeping the eye moist and clean.

Eye Socket

The orbit or eye socket is a cone-shaped bony cavity that protects the eye. The socket is padded with fatty tissue that allows the eye to move easily.

Fovea—(small pit)

The fovea is an indentation in the center of the macula. Its diameter is only 1.5 mm or about 1/16 inch. This small part of our retina is responsible for our highest visual acuity. It is the center of our central vision.

Lacrimal Gland—(Tear Duct)

This gland continually releases tears and other protective fluids onto the surface of the eye. It lubricates and keeps the cornea from becoming dehydrated.

Lacrimal Sac

The lacrimal sac is a tiny pump that drains tears and other debris from the eye. The fluids flow down the nasolacrimal duct into the nose where they help keep the nasal linings moist. This is why your nose runs when you cry.

Lateral Geniculate Nucleus—(LGN)

This part of the brain acts as a relay station; it decodes visual information from the optic tract before sending it to the visual cortex for final processing.

Lens Sack or Capsule

During modern cataract surgery the outer membrane of the lens is left in place. The artificial intraocular lens is placed in this sack.

Iris

This is the colored part of the eye: brown, green, blue, etc. It is a ring of muscle fibers located behind the cornea and in front of the lens. It contracts and expands, opening and closing the pupil, in response to the brightness of surrounding light. Just as the aperture in a camera protects the film from over exposure, the iris of the eye helps protect the sensitive retina.

Macula—(yellow spot)

This part of the retina is the most sensitive. Its diameter is only 7 mm or about 1/4 inch. It is responsible for our central, or reading vision. This part of the retina gives us 20/20 vision. Without the macula, you would be blind—Legally Blind that is. People with eye diseases like Macular Degeneration have vision from 20/200 to 20/800.

Optic Chiasm

This is the first part of the brain to receive visual input. Each eye takes a slightly different picture of the world. At the optic chiasm each picture is divided in half. The outer left and right halves continue back toward the visual cortex. The inner left and right halves cross over to the other side of the brain then continue back toward the visual cortex. See Drawing of optic pathways.

Optic Disk

The optic disk is the spot on the retina where the optic nerve leaves the eye. There are no sensory cells here, creating a blind spot. Each eye covers for the blind spot of the other eye and the brain fills in the missing information.

Optic Nerve

Each optic nerve has about 1.2 million nerve fibers. This is the cable connecting the eye to the brain.

Optic Tract

The nerves that connect the optic chiasm to the LGN are called the optic tract. If one of these tracts is damaged, vision will be lost in one side of each eye.

Orbital Muscles

Six muscles are in charge of eye movement. Four of these move the eye up, down, left and right. The other two control the twisting motion of the eye when we tilt our head. Defects in these muscles and the nerves that control them lead to conditions like Nystagmus and Amblyopia (Lazy Eye).

Photoreceptor Cells

The retina is composed of two types of photoreceptor cells. When light falls on one of these cells, it causes a chemical reaction that sends an electrical signal to the brain. Cone cells give us our detailed color daytime vision. There are 6 million of them in each human eye. Most of them are located in the central retina—macula fovea area. There are three types of cone cells: one sensitive to red light, another to green light, and the third sensitive to blue light. Rod cells are about 500 times more sensitive to light then cone cells; they give us our dim light or night vision. They are also more sensitive to motion then cone cells. There are 120 million rod cells in the human eye. Most rod cells are located in our peripheral or side vision.

The space between the iris and the front of the lens filled with Aqueous Humor.

Pupil

The pupil is the hole in the center of the iris that light passes through. The iris muscles control its size.

Retina

The retina is the film of the eye. It converts light rays into electrical signals and sends them to the brain through the optic nerve. The sides of the retina are responsible for our peripheral vision. The center area, called the macula, is used for our fine central vision and color vision. The retina is where most the problems leading to vision loss Occur. Three of the leading causes of blindness, from retina damage, are Retinitis Pigmentosa, Macular Degeneration and Diabetic Retinopathy.

Retinal Blood Vessels

A doctor can see the blood vessels that supply the retina when he looks into your eyes. These vessels are in the choroid just beneath the retina. Abnormal blood vessel growth and leaking blood vessels are the cause of vision loss in eye conditions like, Diabetic Retinopathy, ROP, and Macular Degeneration.

Retinal Pigment Epithelium—(RPE)

The RPE is a layer of cells between the retina and choroid. The inside of a camera is panted black to absorb scattered and reflected light. The black pigment known as melanin in the RPE dose the same job for the eye. The RPE gets rid of waste products produced by the photoreceptor cells. As we age, the RPE can sometimes lose its ability to process this waste. Deposits of this waste, called drusen, can distort and damage the retina leading to an eye condition called dry macular degeneration.

Sclera

The sclera is the white, tough wall of the eye. It along with internal fluid pressure keeps the eyes shape and protects its delicate internal parts.

Uvea

The uvea is the middle Vascular layer of the eye. It is made up of three parts: the iris, ciliary body and chorid. Uveitis is the inflammation (or swelling) of these parts of the eye.

Visual Axis

The Visual Axis is an imaginary line drawn through the center of the pupil to the center of the Fovea. The orbital muscles keep the visual axis of both eyes aligned on the center of what you are looking at (fixation point). An eye condition called Strabismus—(misaligned eyes) results when the orbital muscles fail to keep the eyes in alignment. Any damage to eye structures along this axis leads to severe vision loss.

Visual Cortex

The part of the brain that processes and combines visual

information from both eyes and converts it into sight. Damage to the visual cortex results in a condition called cortical blindness.

Visual Fields

The retina of each eye has two sections the nasal retina—(nose side) and temporal retina—(ear side). For example with your right eye, you see the right half of the world with your nasal retina; you see the left half of the world with your temporal retina. The picture your eye takes is flipped left for right and upside down; its up to the brain to sort things out.

Vitreous Cavity

The space between the lens and retina filled with the gel like Vitreous Humor.

Vitreous Humor

The vitreous humor is a jelly like liquid that fills most of the eye (from the lens back). As we age it changes from a gel to a liquid and gradually shrinks separating from the retina. This is when people start seeing floaters, dark specs in their vision. This is a normal sign of aging, but in a few cases the retina can become detached as the vitreous separates.

Zonules

Zonules are hundreds of string like fibers that hold the lens suspended in position and enable it to change shape for near or distant vision.

Four of the Most Common Eye Conditions

Myopia—(nearsightedness)

People with Myopic vision usually have eyeballs that are too large for their lens and cornea to focus light properly on their retina. Eyeglasses and contact lenses can usually correct this problem.

Hyperopia—(farsightedness)

Hyperopia vision is caused by the eyeball being too small for the lens and cornea to focus light properly on the retina. Eyeglasses and contact lenses can usually correct this problem.

Presbyopia—(aging eyes)

As people age, they often begin to have difficulty focusing their eyes for reading or close work. It is usually corrected with reading glasses. Some people may need bifocal of trifocal lenses.

Astigmatism—(distorted vision)

People with Astigmatism have irregularly shaped corneas. It is usually corrected with eyeglasses or contact lenses.

Most Common Causes of Vision Loss

Cataracts

There are over 1 million Cataract operations performed annually in the USA. Cataract surgery is an outpatient procedure with a very high success rate. Due to the lack of modern medical technology in the developing world, it is also the world's leading cause of blindness. Over 16 million people are blind from cataracts.

Age-Related Macular Degeneration—(AMD)

This is a degenerative disease of the macula; the macula is the part of the retina responsible for central vision. There is no way yet of repairing the vision that has been lost, but if detected early laser surgery can help slow the progression of the disease. (AMD) is the leading cause of vision loss in people over age 65. Eight million people are legally blind from macular degeneration worldwide and as the population ages this number is expected to grow.

Glaucoma

This disease increases the fluid pressure inside the eye, leading to loss of side vision and eventually total blindness. The increased pressure destroys the optic nerve. With early detection, it can be kept under control with pressure reducing eye drops and surgery. Chances of developing it increase with age. There are over five million people blind from glaucoma worldwide.

Diabetic Retinopathy

This complication of diabetes is a leading cause of blindness among middle-aged Americans. The longer a person has had diabetes the more apt they are to develop diabetic retinopathy. Laser surgery can slow the progression of this disease along with management of blood glucose levels. There are 2.4 million people blind from retinopathy worldwide.

Retinitis Pigmentosa—(RP)

This rare inherited degenerative disease slowly destroys the retina. Signs of (RP) first show up in early childhood. The side vision is lost first. The Disease progresses over many years leaving the person with only a small portion of their central vision. There is on cure for (RP) yet. There are 1.6 million people blind from (RP) worldwide.

Eye Injuries

Over 1 million people are blind worldwide from *eye injuries.* 90per cent of injuries can be avoided by using proper eye protection. If you are reading this page now because you or a loved one has an eye injury, turn your computer off and get medical attention. Any eye injury is a medical emergency.

Optic Nerve Hypoplasia

With this birth defect the optic nerve that connects the eye to the brain has not developed properly, it is underdeveloped. This happens before birth leaving the child with mild to sever vision loss. In most cases, there is no known cause.

Retinopathy of Prematurity—(ROP)

This is an eye disease of premature babies. Soon after birth, abnormal blood vessels start to grow on the retina eventually destroying it. No one is quite sure what causes this disease, but premature birth and low birth weight are thought to be the main causes. With modern medical procedures, only 400 babies a year go blind from this condition. In the 1950's the number of babies blind from (ROP) reached epidemic proportions.

Neurological Visual Impairment (NVI)

Children with (NVI) have normal eyes, but a part of the brain responsible for seeing is damaged. It can be caused from a lack of oxygen before, during, and after birth. Diseases like meningitis or traumatic brain injury can also cause it. Many of the children with (NVI) are multihandicapped. Vision loss can be temporary or last a lifetime.

Ocular Albinism

With this inherited birth defect, people have no pigment or reduced pigment in their eyes, skin and hair. This pigment called melanin is needed for the full development of the retina. Children with this condition have mild to sever vision loss and are very light sensitive.

Coloboma

Coloboma is a Greek word, which means mutilation. People with Coloboma are missing a portion of the structure of the eye. The human eye develops between the fourth and fifteenth week of pregnancy. As the eye starts to develop, a gap opens on the underside of each eye bud. This gap provides a way for the developing eye to be nourished. This gap, called the optic fissure, has to close before the eye is fully developed. Coloboma is the incomplete closer of the optic fissure. Gaps can occur in the eyelid, iris, ciliary body, lens, retina, macula, choroid and optic disc. It can cause from mild to sever vision loss. Coloboma occurs in about 1 in 10,000 births.

Preventable Vision Loss

Over 90% of the world's blind people live in developing countries. Many diseases can be prevented with education in basic hygiene, proper nutrition and medical care. Conditions unheard of in the modern world like: Trachoma, Onchocerciasis (river blindness) and nutritional blindness (vitamin A deficiency), are the leading causes of vision loss in these countries.

Role of the School and the Teacher in the Education of Students with Visual Impairment

1. Children with visual impairment may be seated in the front rows so that they can read and writing on the blackboard without any difficulty or pressure.
2. Such children may be given training in listening with comprehension.
3. Books with bold letters may be provided to such children.
4. Radio and T.V. broadcasts may be arranged for such children.
5. Efforts may be made to procure cassettes in different curricular areas. State Institutes of Education or State Councils of Educational Research and Training or District Institutes of Education and Training or Centres or Institutes of Educational Technology may be approached for this purpose
6. Blind children need Braille script books.
7. School doctor may be consulted from time to time.
8. Cooperation of the parents be sought in the follow-up work.

Education of the Blind Children

Children whose vision is so impaired that they can see objects at a distance of 20 ft. which a normal eye can see at a distance of 200 ft. are legally blind. The totally blind children read Braille. Blindness affects the life of the individual in the physical, mental, social, educational and vocational aspects.

Usually for blind children, going to school implies admission to a residential school for the blind (Braille classes). Of late some attempts have been made to integrate them with the normal children by admitting them to normal schools but the coverage of blind population of the students in this respect is not significant.

A blind school aims at assisting the blind child, through the use of special methods and aids, in his adjustment to the world in which he has to live as an adult.

Schools for the blind usually provide for activities such as dancing, scouting, and dramatics. Special equipment and methods of teaching are employed for the education of the blind. Particular attention is given to practice on typewriter because it permits written communication with the seeing.

Methods of Teaching the Blind

(*i*) As many as concrete experiences as possible, either by letting them observe the object as such or by providing replicas to the blind students.

(*ii*) Blind children at least during the primary classes, should be taught by a unit plan of instruction.

(*iii*) Topics of the units may consist of everyday experiences, such as, provision shops, post offices, etc.

(*iv*) Self-activity should be made an integral part of the education of the blind.

Social Attitudes Towards Blindness

Historically, blind and visually impaired people have either been treated as if their lack of sight were an outward manifestation of some internal lack of reason, or as if they possessed extrasensory abilities. Stories such as *The Cricket on the Hearth* by *Charles Dickens* provided yet another view of blindness, wherein those affected by it were ignorant of their surroundings and easily deceived.

The authors of modern educational materials, as well as those treating *blindness in literature*, have worked to paint a truer picture of blind people as three-dimensional individuals with a range of abilities, talents, and even character flaws. Certain individuals are gifted, and others licentious, but nothing definitive can be said of the blind as a class but that they cannot see well.

Adaptive Technology

Descriptions and links to the companies that produce and or sell adaptive technology for the blind and visually impaired.

Braille Embosser

A Braille printer.

Braille Translation Software

Software used to convert text to Braille using a computer and Braille embosser.

Braille Keyboard

The overlay measures approximately 15 by 4 inches and wraps snugly around the sides of the keyboard and can be secured with adhesive tape. Comes with five sets of overlays (along with a regular print and Braille guide). recommended for 6 years and older. Picture Braille software enables the user to create pictures in Braille format using a simple drawing programme. The user can draw free hand using the mouse supplied. Will work with most IBM-compatible computers. Speaqualizer A hardware attachment for some IBM PCs and compatibles. Enables the user to hear data being displayed on the video monitor. Requires no additional text-to-speech software so computer's memory is free for application programmes.

Braille Printer

Braille printers do the actual embossing of Braille onto paper. The first step in converting computer files into a Braille document is to choose the type of Braille. Grade 1 Braille consists of letters, numbers and punctuation marks while grade 2 Braille includes contractions of common combinations of letters and words. To print Grade 2 a Braille translation programme must be used to take the computer file, insert the contractions, and format the document for the Braille page.

Braille Translator

Blind or visually impaired people who read Braille can use the following specialized equipment: The first step in converting a computer programme into a Braille document is to chose the type of Braille. Grade 1 Braille consists of letters, numbers and punctuation marks while grade 2 Braille includes contractions of common combinations of letters and words. To print Grade 2 a Braille translation programme must be used to take the computer file, insert the contractions, and format the document for the Braille page. Braille translators are available in hardware and software.

3M Braille Labeler

Embosses braille on 3/8" or 1/2" labeling tape. Upper rim of the dial is Braille; lower rim has standard print alphabet. Symbols include small words, contractions, and punctuations marks.

Refreshable Braille Display

A device used to produce Braille output the way computer monitors produce print output. They are especially useful for deaf blind people that cannot use speech output.

CCTV (Closed Circuit Television)

A television video camera combination used by people who are visually impaired to magnify the print in books and newspapers. It can also be used to write letters, and checks, and do different types of crafts like needlepoint.

Large Print Printers

Any ink jet, dot matrix or laser jet printer can produce large print all you need to do is set the font size larger before printing.

Screen Magnification Software

Software used by people with poor eyesight to enlarge the text on the computer screen.

Screen Reading Software or Text to Speech

Software used to convert Text on the computer screen into spoken words. Used by the totally blind and others that have trouble reading even magnified text.

Reading and Magnification

Most blind and visually impaired people read print, either of a regular size or enlarged through the use of magnification devices. A variety of *magnifying glasses*, some of which are handheld while others rest on desktops, can make reading easier for those with decreased visual acuity.

The rest read *Braille* and *Moon type* or rely on talking books and readers. They use computers with special hardware such as scanners and refreshable Braille displays as well as software written specifically for the blind, like optical character recognition applications and screen reading software.

Some people access these materials through agencies for the blind, such as the National Library Service for the Blind and Physically Handicapped in the United States, the *National Library for the Blind* or the RNIB in the United Kingdom.

Closed-Circuit Televisions, equipment that enlarge and contrast textual items, are a more high-tech alternative to traditional magnification devices. So too are modern *web browsers*, which can increase the size of text on some web pages through browser controls or through user-controlled *style sheets.*

Computers

Access technology such as *Freedom Scientific*'s JAWS for Windows screen reading software enable the blind to use mainstream computer applications. Most legally blind people (70 per cent of them across all ages, according to the Lighthouse for the Blind) do not use computers. Only a small fraction of this population, when compared to the sighted community, have *internet* access.

This bleak outlook is changing, however, as availability of assistive technology increases, accompanied by concerted efforts to insure the accessibility of information technology to all potential users, including the blind.

The movement towards greater *web accessibility* is opening a far wider number of websites to adaptive technology, making the web a more inviting place for visually impaired surfers.

Experimental approaches such as the *seeing with sound* project are beginning to provide access to arbitrary live views from a *camera*.

Low Vision Projection Screen

This low vision projection system allows inspection of images which can be magnified up to 720X. A video camera is used with closed circuit television or CCD camera and monitor. Working distances range from 37 mm to 177 mm

Other aids

People may use talking *thermometers*, enlarged or marked oven dials, talking watches, talking clocks, talking *scales*, talking *calculators*, talking *compasses* and other talking equipment.

Myths About Vision Loss

- *Myth*: Safety goggles are more trouble than they are worth.
- *Fact*: There are 500,000 eye injuries every year in the USA. 50% of these accidents occur at home. The leading cause of blindness in children is eye injury. 90% of injuries can be avoided by using proper eye protection.
- *Myth*: There is no need to have your vision checked before you turn 40.
- *Fact*: There are treatable eye diseases; glaucoma is one of them, which can show up before you turn 40.
- *Myth*: Wearing poorly fit glasses damages your eyes.

- *Fact*: The right eyeglass prescription is required for good vision. Poor fitting glasses do not damage your eyes.
- *Myth*: Poorly fit contacts do not harm your eyes.
- *Fact*: Poorly fit contact lenses can damage your cornea. If you use contact lenses, have them checked regularly.
- *Myth*: Eating carrots will improve your vision.
- *Fact*: Carrots are high in Vitamin A, which is important for a balanced diet. Eating carrots or other foods high in Vitamin A will not improve your vision. Taking large amounts of Vitamin A can be very harmful. People that do not eat a balanced diet can develop vision problems along with other problems as they age.
- *Myth*: Sitting close to the television will harm your eyes.
- *Fact*: There is no evidence that sitting close to the television will damage your eyes. If this were true, office workers that sit 8 hours a day 17 inches from their computer screens, would all be blind. Sit wherever you are most comfortable when watching TV.
- *Myth*: Doctors can transplant eyes.
- *Fact*: Doctors can transplant the cornea, but not the eye its self. The retina and optic nerve are part of the brain. When doctors figure out how to transplant the brain, they will be able to transplant the eye.
- *Myth*: Scientists have created a Bionic Eye.
- *Fact*: Scientists have been working on a microchip to replace damaged retina cells in a person's central vision. Other scientists have been trying to figure out a way to connect a camera directly to the brain. The eye and the brain do not work the same way a camera and computer do. Even after someone figures out how to make a bionic eye, they still have to figure out how to connect it to the neural circuitry of the brain. What they have created so far is a crude form of vision consisting of several dots of light.

- *Myth*: Reading in dim light will damage your vision.
- *Fact*: Reading in dim light can make your eyes feel tired. It is not harmful and cannot damage your vision.
- *Myth*: Eye exercises will improve your vision.
- *Fact*: Eye exercises will not improve your vision. This myth has made many people wealthy. Rolling your eyes around has no effect on your vision.
- *Myth*: It is not harmful to look at the sun if you squint or use dark glasses.
- *Fact*: The sun's ultra-violet light will still get to your eyes, damaging the cornea, lens and retina. Never look directly at a solar eclipse. The direct light from the sun can blind a person in less then a minute.
- *Myth*: You can cure a black eye by putting a raw steak on it.
- *Fact*: Putting a steak on your eye will do nothing except expose your eye to any organisms living on the raw meat. Get immediate medical attention, a black can be a sign of serious eye injury.
- *Myth*: You can weir your eyes out by using them too much.
- *Fact*: You cannot wear your eyes out by using them. Cutting down on reading or close work, will not help or harm your eyesight.
- *Myth*: Doctors can only remove cataracts after they ripen.
- *Fact*: Cataracts, unlike fruit, do not "ripen." It is up to you, and your doctor, to decide when to remove a cataract. Most people have them removed when the decrease in vision starts bothering them.
- *Myth*: Too much sex, especially masturbation, can make you go blind.
- *Fact*: Syphilis, a sexually transmitted disease, if left untreated can lead to blindness, dementia and death. This is where this myth came from.
- *Myth*: Blind people have a sixth sense or extra ordinary talents.

- *Fact*: Most People with (20/20) vision do not pay much attention to their other senses. Blind people have worked hard to develop their other senses to compensate for their vision loss. There is no sixth sense.
- *Myth*: Blind people live in a world of total darkness.
- *Fact*: Only a small percentage of Legally Blind people see nothing at all. Darkness is the eye telling you that there is no light on. People who are (totally blind) do not have the ability to see light, or darkness. They see nothing at all.
- *Myth*: Strong enough glasses will help anyone who is visually impaired.
- *Fact*: Refractive lenses (glasses) cannot correct all visual impairments. Glasses cannot fix eye conditions that involve the retina, optic nerve, or brain.
- *Myth*: A dog-guide knows how to get its master where he wants to go.
- *Fact*: The blind person knows where they are going, and how to get there, not the dog. The dog's trainer teaches it to respond to traffic, street travel, and the commands their master will give them. A blind person goes through a month long training program to learn how to use the dog.
- *Myth*: All blind people read Braille.
- *Fact*: Only 10% of Legally Blind people read Braille. Developing the sense of touch it takes to read Braille is difficult for older people who make up 66% of the blind population. Ninety percent of Legally Blind people have some usable vision and most of them can read print or magnified print.
- *Myth*: You need to speak louder when talking to a blind person.
- *Fact*: Blind people have poor eyes not ears. Talk to them as you would to anyone else. When in a room with several other people use their name so they know you are speaking to them and not someone else.

- *Myth*: Blind people can always identify you by your voice.
- *Fact*: When answering your phone, do you know everyone by voice? It is a good idea to identify your self when meeting a blind person.
- *Myth*: In order to travel independently, a blind person needs a guide dog.
- *Fact*: To travel independently most Legally Blind people do not even need to use a White Cane. Very few use dog guides. Approximately 1,300,000 Americans are (Legally Blind); 109,000 of them use white canes; 7,000 use dog guides.
- *Myth*: All blind people are alike.
- *Fact*: "The Blind" is a term used by groups with political and social agendas. People with poor or no vision come from all races and ethnic groups, rich and poor alike. Being Legally Blind is a bit more then a nuisance for the 76-year-old women loosing vision from Macular Degeneration. A college student, who has had 18 years of training in how to function without vision, and knows no other way, may think of it differently. A 45-year-old truck driver going blind from glaucoma may go back to school and get an office job, or he may retire early and collect disability. A 39-year-old lawyer loosing his vision will get training in Braille, find readers and learn to rely on public transit to do his job. The 52-year-old stock clerk, that rides a bike to work every day, has been legally blind all his life. Everyone finds there own answers in life its no different for people that have poor or no eye sight.
- *Myth*: Blind people, to maintain secrecy and security, staff the snack bars at the CIA.
- *Fact*: Under the Randolph-Sheppard Act, blind people are allowed to operate all food service and vending facilities in government buildings. This act was one the first government programs to help employ the blind. The program has nothing to do with secrecy or security in government buildings.

Identification and Assessment of Student with Visual Impairment

School districts should co-operate with Ministry of Health personnel to ensure all students participate in a vision screening programme for the identification and prevention of visual impairments. Schools should also request a vision and hearing screening whenever they suspect a student is experiencing difficulties or is having trouble learning. The school district should develop and implement referral procedures to ensure that every visually impaired student is identified, and receives an appropriate educational programme.

In order to plan the educational programme the teacher of the visually impaired should conduct a functional vision assessment to identify the educational implications of the student's vision loss. In the case of students with a severe visual impairment, a qualified orientation and mobility instructor should also assess the students' skills in orientation and mobility.

Planning and Implementation

A component essential to the establishment of an effective system of delivery of services to students with visual impairment is the availability of qualified, experienced teachers who have regular classroom experience and in addition are competent to adapt materials, teach Braille, use visual aids and technological devices and plan, develop, deliver, and monitor all aspects of schooling affected by visual impairment.

With appropriate support services, many students can follow the curriculum with adaptation of learning resources or instructional methods. When necessary, however, the curriculum should be modified to reflect individual needs. The student's educational requirements and any special measures that are to be taken in order to help meet those requirements. The following needs should be considered:

- orientation and mobility skills;

- visual skills;
- specialized skills in reading (e.g., Braille, taped books, enhanced print, CCTV);
- specialized skills in mathematics (e.g., abacus, Nemeth Code);
- access to technology (e.g., Braille 'n Speak, tape recorders, computers);
- daily living skills;
- social skills;
- vocational planning and skill development;
- study skills and note-taking strategies; and
- concept development.

Orientation and mobility (O&M) is an essential component of the curriculum for students with severe visual impairments. It provides students with the skills necessary to know where they are in the school or community, where they want to go and how to get there in a safe and efficient manner with as much independence as possible. Orientation and mobility training should not be restricted to the school environment but should include other environments in which the student is required to function at different times of the day.

At the secondary level, school districts may develop and approve orientation and mobility programmes or Brailling programmes for visually impaired students as locally developed or independent study courses for credit toward graduation.

Most students with visual impairment require specialized equipment (e.g., Braillers, closed-circuit televisions, cassette recorders, optical aids) and adapted learning resources (e.g., Braille texts, enlarged print books, tapes). These tend to be very bulky. Schools should ensure there is adequate, accessible storage available to the student.

A working or instructional area for instruction in specific skill development by the itinerant or resource teacher should also be provided. This instructional area should be conducive to effective instruction (i.e., in compliance with health and safety codes, quiet, adequately lit, ventilated and free from distractions).

Who Invented Braille?

Louis Braille didn't invent Braille. As a boy he attended a school for the Blind in Paris, He learned how to read but not to write. Back then Blind People learned how to read raised letters with their fingertips. This form of writing was very difficult to read. In 1821 a soldier named Charles Barbier came to visit the school. He bought with him a system he had invented called 'night writing'. Barbier had designed it for Napoleon; who wanted a secret code that could be used at night. It proved to be too complex for soldiers to learn and was rejected by the army. Louis Braille realized how useful this system of raised dots could be for the Blind. He set to work simplifying it. His system used six dots instead of the 12 used in Barbier's code. Now Blind people could learn to read as well as write.

How Dose It Works?

Perkins Brailler-slate & stylist-electronic Braille note taker

Before computer technology, the devices people used to produce Braille were as old as Braille its self. The Perkins Brailler works like an old fashion typewriter. Its six keys produce the six dots of the Braille cell. The slate is a simple device used to punch out the dots using a stylist. These devices are still in use today. Computer technology has begun to replace these devices with electronic Braille note takers, refreshable Braille displays and Braille embossers; but the old ways of producing Braille will still be around as long as sighted people keep using pens.

Braille Alphabet (English Braille America Edition)

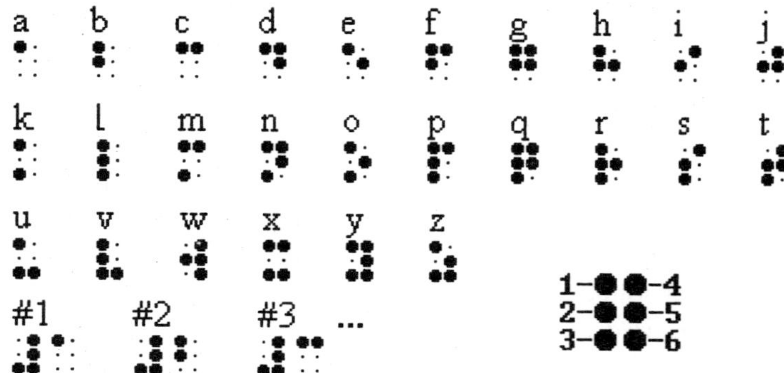

Punctuation Signs

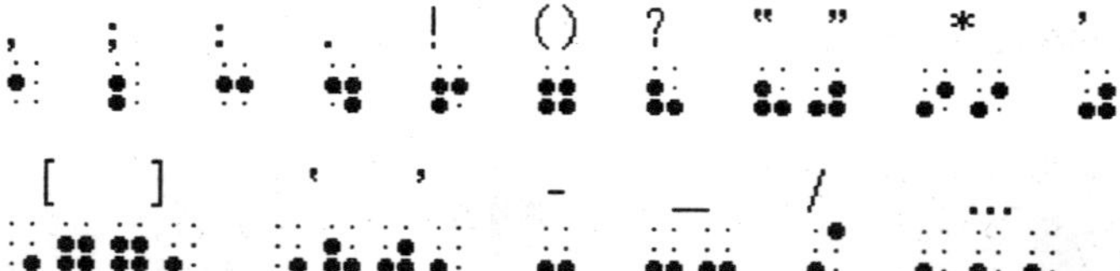

The Braille cell consists of six dots, two wide and three high. The dots are numbered one through six: the letter (a) is known as (dot 1), (b) — (dot 1 2), (c) — (dot 1 4), etc. Grade One Braille, used in some children's books, uses just the alphabet and punctuation marks. Grade Two Braille, used for almost everything produced in Braille, is a form of shorthand. Grade Three Braille, used for talking notes, is super shorthand. There is also a code used for music and one for math and science.

Evaluation and Reporting

Due to factors such as visual fatigue, slow reading and writing speed, and the visual components of evaluation tools such as video or maps the student may require adaptations to the usual classroom testing situation. Such adaptations could involve additional time, the use of a reader or scribe, the use of specialized equipment, reduction in the volume of work to be completed while retaining the same learning outcomes, the provision of a description of the visual components, such as a video, and the use of an alternate setting for completing the work. These adaptations should be documented in the student's IEP and monitored for their appropriateness and effectiveness.

For students writing provincial examinations, Braille, large print, computer disk and audio tape copies of the examinations can be provided if applied for well in advance.

Personnel

Teacher of the Visually Impaired

Where supplemental funding is requested by districts for students with visual impair.ff and get medical attention. Any eye injury is a medical emergency.

Protective eyewear should be made of polycarbonate plastic. If working with liquids they should be splash proof goggles. Use only high-quality sunglasses with (UV) ultraviolet light protection. If your eyewear came from your local dollar-mart, you should ask yourself how much your eyes are worth.

- Keep all household chemicals, paints, pesticides, fertilizers tools, etc. locked up away from children.
- Almost anything that can splash into the eye can damage it. Wear protective eyewear when working with: detergents, cleaning solvents, etc. Never mix cleaning agents.
- Car batteries contain sulfuric acid and produce hydrogen gas while being charged. This is one of the gasses used to send rockets into space. Always wear protective eyewear when working with batteries. Know the proper procedures for handling batteries and jump-starting cars .
- Never remove Safety guards from power equipment. Wear protective eyewear to protect against flying particles.

- Pick up all yard debris before using lawn equipment and wear protective eyewear while operating it. Children should not play in areas where lawn equipment is being used.
- Children and adults should use sports-specific eyewear to avoid sports related accidents.
- Consumer fireworks cause 2,000 eye injuries per year. The best protection is to leave fireworks to professionals.
- Ultraviolet and infrared light from the sun, welding arcs and tanning beds can damage your eyes; it may also contribute to age-related macular degeneration. Use proper eye protection and never look directly at a solar eclipse
- Never allow children to play with Laser pointers they are not toys. The light from a laser pointer aimed into the eye can be more damaging than staring directly into the sun.
- In the car, use infant and child safety seats, safety belts and shoulder harnesses. Keep children in the back seat away from air bags.
- Keep older children's toys away from younger children. Do not let children of any age use flying toys and projectile-firing toys with out adult supervision. Three out of four of children's eye injuries happen when no adult is present.
- To avoid eye infection do not share eye makeup or eye drops with anyone. Many bacteria, including the cold sore viruse (Herpes), can spread to your eyes and damage your vision.
- Do not let children play in areas where cats and dogs go to the bathroom. Roundworm (Toxocara) larvae in cat and dog droppings can cause blindness and other health problems. Wash your hands good after working in the yard, cleaning litter boxes, or handling animals. Have your pets dewormed.

4 Children with Hearing and Speech Impairment

Children with Hearing and Speech Impairment

Listening plays an important role in academic learning. Hearing problems interfere with the achievement of the students. It is, therefore, desirable to identify such children and take steps to meet their educational needs. Such children may be identified as under:

- Some observable deformity of the ear or ears.
- Frequent complaints of pain in ears.
- Frequent scratching of ears.
- Frequent discharge from ears.
- Turning head on one side to hear better.
- Frequent requests to teachers to repeat questions and directions etc.
- Making errors in taking dictation or notes.
- Displaying speech difficulty.

A picture of the human ear and it's important parts:

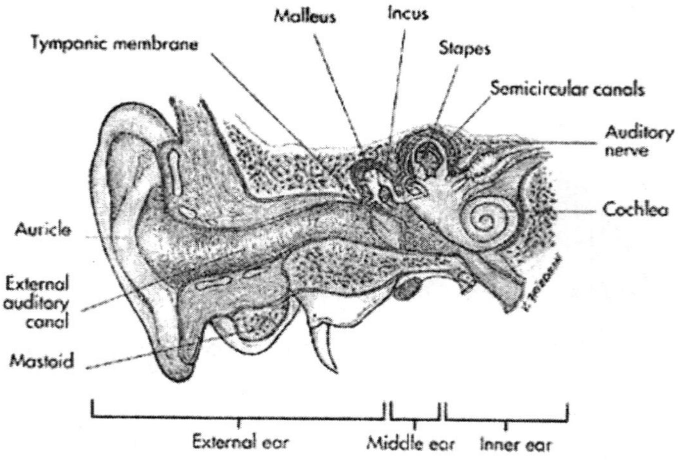

Sound is caused by very rapid changes in the air or other medium, alternating between what are called "condensation" and "rarefaction", with the disturbance spreading through the medium, or what is called "propagation". The rate of change, or frequency, is measured in cycles per second, the units being referred to as Hertz, after the discoverer of the process. Sound frequencies audible to the human ear fall in the range 20 Hz to 20000 Hz. Sound travels through the air at about 343 meters per second. Sound waves are transmitted from the passage way of the external ear to the structures of the middle ear and inner ear shown in the chart above, and finally transmitted as nerve impulses from the cochlea through the auditory nerve to the brain, where the impulses are interpreted and understood.

Hearing loss is of three broad types:

(*a*) Conductive hearing loss, which results from injury or other problems with the structures that transmit sound from the external and middle ear to the inner ear. These are generally remedied by medicine or surgery.

(*b*) Sensor neural hearing loss resulting from damage to or deterioration of the inner ear or auditory nerves, and hearing aids may be the main solution.

(*c*) Mixed hearing loss caused by a combination of both the above types.

Types of Hearing Impairments

Conductive Hearing Loss

Hearing loss caused by obstructions in the outer or middle ear or malformations that interfere with the conduction of sound waves to the inner ear. Can often be corrected surgically or medically. Conductive hearing impairment can often be corrected through surgical or medical treatment. Ex: excessive wax in the auditory canal, a disease that leaves fluid or debris.

Sensory Neutral Hearing Loss

A hearing loss caused by damage to the auditory nerve or the inner ear. Most sensory neutral hearing impairment cannot be corrected by surgery or medication.

Mixed hearing loss: combination of both conductive and sensory neutral impairments.

Hearing impairment can also occur unilateral (present in one ear only) or bilateral (present in both ears).

Causes of Hearing and Impairments

The causes of hearing impairments are usually classified as exogenous or endogenous.

Exogenous: Causes stem from factors outside the body (disease, toxicity, injury) and reduced the auditory system's ability to receive and transmit sounds.

Endogenous: Are inherited from the parents' genes.

Maternal rubella

Rubella (German measles) has relative mild symptoms, is know to cause deafness, visual impairment, heart disorders, and a variety of other serious disabilities in the developing child when it affects a pregnant woman, particular during the first trimester.

Heredity

Is the leading cause of deafness and more than 200 types of hereditary or genetic deafness have been identified.

Pre-maturity and Complications of Pregnancy

Increase the risk of deafness and other disabilities, difficult to precisely evaluate the effects of pre-maturity on hearing impairment

Meningitis

Is the leading cause of hearing impairment, it is a bacterial or viral infection that can destroy the sensitive acoustic apparatus of the inner ear. Children whose deafness is caused by meningitis generally have profound hearing losses but are not likely to have additional disabilities.

Ottis Media

Is an infection or inflammation of the middle ear, if untreated, it can result in a buildup of fluid and a ruptured eardrum, which cause permanent conductive hearing impairment.

Education of Children with Hearing and Speech Impairment

1. Children with hearing problems may be given front seats.
2. While speaking, the teacher may use a reasonable level of pitch.
3. The teacher should avoid mumbling.
4. The teacher should avoid speaking too fast.
5. Students should be encouraged to speak gradually and steadily.

6. Other students of the class may be asked to give due consideration to such students.
7. A lot of visual aids may be used in the classroom.
8. Some of the hearing problems can be corrected through drill and practice.

Medical help may be needed if speech disorder is due to an organic defect in speech mechanism.

Identification and Assessment of Children with Hearing and Speech Impairment

Most children with significant hearing loss will have been identified through an audiological assessment prior to entering the school system. A few children, however, particularly those with less severe hearing loss, may not have been identified prior to school entry. Under the audiological services protocol agreement between the Ministries of Health and Education, all students in the initial school entry year receive a hearing screening. Any student who fails the screening should be referred to the nearest health unit or audiology clinic for a complete hearing assessment. Indeed, any student referred for special education services during his or her school career should be referred for a hearing assessment in order to determine whether an intermittent or chronic hearing loss is the primary cause of any exhibited learning or behavioural problem.

Hearing loss is generally measured in terms of decibel loss using standards agreed on internationally. However, decibel losses do not always correlate with educational implications and are therefore not a sole criterion for determination of need for educational intervention. Any degree of hearing loss has educational implications, so following the identification of a student's hearing loss an assessment to determine the strengths and weaknesses of the student in the areas of language development and communication skills may be required. This assessment, usually administered by a teacher of the deaf and hard of hearing, may include the administration of standardized tests in the areas of ability and achievement, as well as curriculum-based assessment and observation and teacher reports. Programme planning decisions and recommendations for placement of the student in a specific programme should occur only once a full assessment has been completed.

A critical part of the assessment process is determining the method of communication to be used in the educational setting. While the majority of students who are hard of hearing will develop English language skills through the use of appropriate amplification and oral instruction, some students, often with more severe hearing losses, will require either an English-based sign system or American Sign Language. School districts are responsible for assessing the most enabling language(s) to allow a student who is deaf or hard of hearing to fully access the curriculum, and for providing staff with the qualifications to meet the specific communication needs of individual students.

Listening plays an important role in academic learning. Hearing problems interfere with the achievement of the students. It is, therefore, desirable to identify such children and take steps to meet their educational needs. Such children may be identified as under:

— Some observable deformity of the ear or ears.

— Frequent complaints of pain in ears.

— Frequent scratching of ears.

— Frequent discharge from ears.

— Turning head on one side to hear better.

— Frequent requests to teachers to repeat questions and directions etc.

— Making errors in taking dictation or notes.

— Displaying speech difficulty.

- Formal hearing test generates and audiogram, which

graphically shows the intensity of the faintest sound an individual can hear at various frequencies.

- Hearing impairments are classified as slight, mild, moderate, sever, or profound, depending on the degree of hearing loss.
- For education placement purposes, only children with hearing losses greater than 90 dB are considered deaf.

Prevalence

- Students with hearing impairments represent just over 1 per cent of all school-age students receiving special education.
- About 5 per cent of all school-age children have some form of hearing impairment, but most do not require special education.
- Only 20 per cent of hard-of-hearing children receive special services.

Assistive Aids

Assistive Listening Devices (ALD's), or Hearing Aids as they are more commonly called, are of four broad types : Acoustic, FM, Induction and Infrared. Acoustic Devices use a microphone to amplify the sound which the listener hears directly – typically public address systems. FMs utilise Radio Frequenciy patterns corresponding to sound patterns from a radio transmitter with the speaker to a radio receiver with the listener. This technique eliminates ambient noise which would otherwise muffle or drown the sound. The Induction type and the Infrared devices use magnetic fields or infra red waves to carry the sound form the source to the destination.

Hearing Aids must be selected and fitted, after testing by a qualified audiologist. They are available in a wide range of prices, depending on the technical features that are provided in them. The least expensive provide volume control only, while the more expensive models are adjustable for the frequency levels at which the user hears best and for filtering out background noise that interferes with the hearing.

The Cochlear implant is an advanced and expensive surgical technique to help in cases of total hearing loss. Here a special device inplanted by surgery takes the place of the cochlea and performs it's function of conversion of incoming sound energy into nerve impulses which are transmitted to the brain.

Devices are also available to enable the Hearing Impaired to communicate with others. These devices are generally a keyboard where a message can be typed to be sent over a telephone line or over a computer net work. On a telephone line the typed message is sent as a sound tone or code which is decoded at the other end into and displayed as a text message – these are called TTY devices. Now hardware or software based technology is available where the typed message itself can be rendered into speech or vice-versa.

Speech Impairment

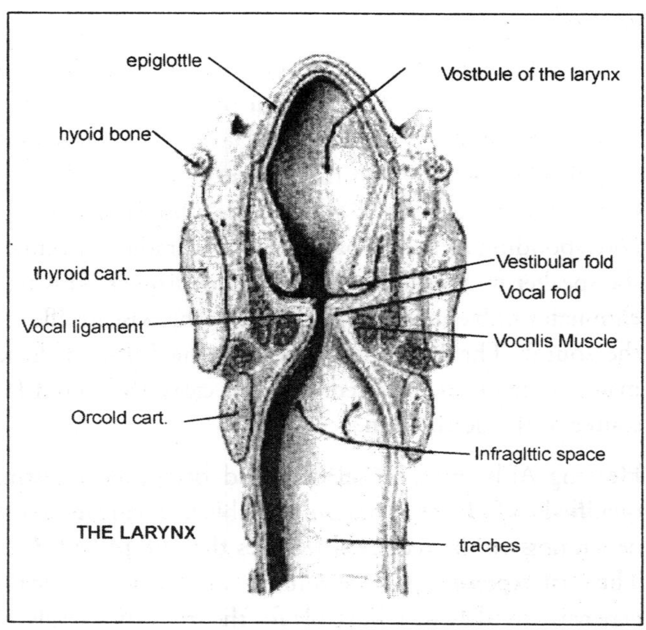

The human voice originates in the larynx, commonly called the voice box, illustrated above. It sits at the point of the neck, where the air passage to the lungs called the trachea, and the food passage to stomach called the oesophagus, separate into their separate pathways. The larynx has a critical role in swallowing, breathing and production of the voice, all controlled by it's cartilage and muscle structures shown above as "folds". Contraction and expansion and vibration of the vocal folds with the exhalation of air generates sound of varying volume, tone and quality and these sounds get clearly shaped into speech by alterations in the air space of the vocal tract—the space of the mouth between the throat and the lips, caused by changes in the position and shape of the throat, tongue and lips.

The development of speech and it's refinement with language is a process of intense training of these muscular structures of the vocal tract, right from early infancy. This is a process which is seriously impeded if the child has a hearing impairment, where it does not know how the words sound, and therefore it does not know how to manipulate the structures of it's vocal tract in order to produce them. Over a period of time, the related muscular controls may get totally lost due to not being exercised correctly, and the child may become a permanent mute, capable of producing only meaningless sounds. It is therefore vital that hearing disability should be detected at the earliest point of time possible, and action be initiated with provision of hearing aids and with intense training to preserve and build on whatever hearing levels are available, to establish voice and language skills.

When the voice is lost due to accident, infection, surgery or other cause, a device called an artificial larynx can be used, with appropriate training, to generate voice and speech. This device can be attached externally to the throat or implanted within the throat. A more indirect solution for enabling communication, is of course, to enter text into a computer and have the computer convert the text into speech using a hardware or software based speech synthesiser—the sort of device that is used by Stephen Hawking.

Speech Reading

The term "lipreading" conveyed the idea that one can understand speech by focusing only on the movements of the lips. While some comprehension of speech is possible with just a lip focus, in reality good lipreaders observe much more than just the lip movements. They observe, maybe not consciously, all aspects of non-verbal communication (facial expressions, body-stance, etc.) and they process (again, probably not consciously) all the available linguistic, situational, and auditory cues. There are lots of these cues and we'll be reviewing the basic ones in this paper.

The term "speech reading", on the other hand, recognizes that speech comprehension is a global process, in which a listener, hearing-impaired or not, employs all of this information to comprehend a message. This is the goal, and to reach this goal, it is not necessary for a "listener" to consciously identify any specific lip movement, or indeed any other element present in a communication exchange. In speech reading, one focuses on the meaning of the message and not its details (though, of course, the more "details" that can be rapidly and automatically processed, the greater the likelihood the message will be comprehended.

Over the years, there has been a great deal of research focused on speech reading. While we still don't really understand why some people are "stars", some just mediocre, and some few people unable to go beyond the most basic identifications, we can make some valid generalities about the speech reading process that should help us understand both its promise and limitations. I should begin this discussion with a word of comfort for the real "duds" out there; there has never been any research that has shown a correlation between intelligence and speech reading ability! In other words, in this skill area you're not stupid if you don't quite "get it". (But neither would you be showing much intelligence if you just gave up when you were capable of doing better!)

Cued Speech

Cued Speech is a sound-based visual communication system which, in English, uses eight handshapes in four different locations ("cues") in combination with the natural mouth movements of speech, to make all the sounds of spoken language look different. Cued Speech was devised by Dr. R. Orin Cornett and Professor of Emeritus of Audiology of Gallaudet University, USA in 1966. It has been adapted into 59 languages and dialects so far.

Even with hearing aids or a cochlear implant it is hard for some deaf people to understand spoken language.

Lipreading is of limited help because it is estimated that we lipread as little as 30 per cent of what is said—the rest we guess.

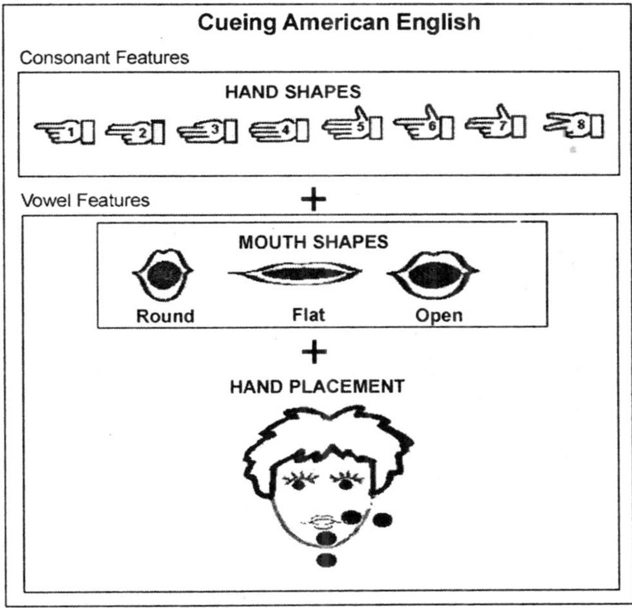

This makes it very difficult for born-deaf children to understand or think in English. With an incomplete understanding of spoken language it is hard to use spoken language, lipread, or read and write. Yet literacy is especially important because deaf people must use written language to access information, use a textphone, understand television subtitles, etc.

When a deaf child is born into a hearing family there is no immediately available, easy method of communication. Often there is a delay in the development of deaf children's language.

The visual components of the Cued Speech System include:

— *eight (8) handshapes* to distinguish consonant features

— *four (4) hand placements* combined with

— three (3) mouth shapes to distinguish the vowel features of American English

Benefits

Cued speech has quite a number of benefits. It can be learned in a relatively short period of time. Most parents can learn the system in a weekend. It takes about three to twelve months of consistent cueing to achieve fluency.

Most of the professional respondents felt that both deaf children and their parents would benefit from learning both ASL and Cued Speech. Professionals and parents expressed concern that parents who do not have a native grasp of ASL will be poor language models for their deaf children. Cued speech buys valuable time for the parents. They can begin the process of learning ASL while literally pouring the language they do know into their children during the critical language learning years. "The great majority of children learn language passively through exposure. Deaf children are able to do the same, but only with clear unambiguous access to language."

Cued speech positively affects literacy. "Hearing children become literate because they have a strong language base and an internal understanding of the syntax of spoken language long before they ever see the written word." Cued speech can enable the deaf child to internalize the target language. The step of internalizing a language is critical to the process of learning how to read and write. "We learn to read and write by decoding and encoding a language we already know."

Cued speech prevents parents from over-simplifying their English because they are communicating in a language they are intimately familiar with. "Hearing people, especially parents, who live with deaf children often 'dumb down' their language to make themselves more easily understood." When parents 'dumb down' language they use fewer idioms, adjectives, and synonyms. The language they use is anemic. Children need to be exposed to the orchestra of vocabulary and expressions that is within a language to gain native fluency. "A child with good verbal skills and a solid foundation of vocabulary will have a solid foundation for learning to read. This child will be more apt to develop higher level thinking skills and to understand advanced abstract concepts in later years."

Children that use Cued Speech speechread more accurately. There is improvement in auditory discrimination. Children who use Cued Speech generally read at or above grade level. Hearing families who use Cued Speech have better communication and fewer behavioural problems. Cued Speech makes it possible to learn to speak a foreign language in a clear and accessible manner.

Disadvantages

Cued speech users do confront some frustrations. One of the greatest frustrations is that it is not used as commonly as other methods. Deaf Cuers are dispersed geographically. Many individuals who cue also sign for companionship with other deaf individuals. They find this association to be really important. "No one but another deaf person can really understand what it's like to be deaf, and the social support and role models within the deaf community are very important to the deaf child."

There are not enough Cued Speech transliterators. Cuers are encouraging interpreter training programmes to help meet this need by including Cued Speech in their curricula.

For some families, "a very young hearing impaired child may have trouble expressing himself clearly until his speech skills (or expressive Cueing skills) have caught up with his receptive language abilities. Professionals and parents may opt to provide some children with basic signs to assist them with early expressive communication." There is absolutely no reason that a child exposed to Cued Speech should not also be exposed to ASL concurrently. "Choose a formal communication method based on the information you have and don't hesitate to add a second—just as you would a second language. Communication is too important to be compartmentalized and inhibited by external rules forced on you by one "camp" or another ASL and Cued Speech look entirely different and they convey two or more different languages. Early childhood is the optimal language learning period and children aren't easily confused—adults are!"

Cued Speech can be somewhat tiring to the adults and it is very important to stay in good physical form to prevent repetitive motion injuries. Other professionals are suspect of Cued Speech and are not familiar with the method, often making unfounded negative statements. Cued Speech provides something unique—sensory integrated visible spoken phonemes. Parents must determine whether this is appropriate for their child. It is not right for every parent/child pair. However, "Cued Speech seems to be an awfully good way to establish the language base with a young child

Finger Spelling

Fingerspelling is the process of spelling out words by using signs that correspond to the letters of the word. An ASL user would use the American Fingerspelled Alphabet, (also called the American Manual Alphabet). There are many different manual alphabets throughout the world.

The American Fingerspelled Alphabet consists of 22 handshapes that—when held in certain positions and/or are produced with certain movements—represent the 26 letters of the American alphabet.

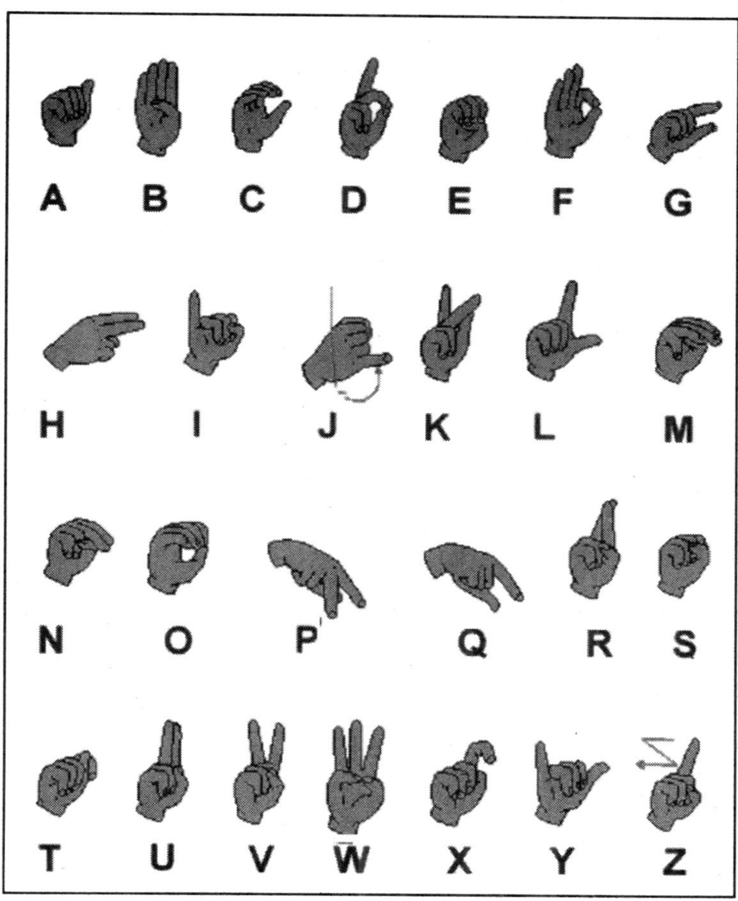

Sign Language

A sign language (also signed language) is a *language* which uses *manual communication* instead of *sound* to convey meaning—simultaneously combining handshapes, orientation and movement of the hands, arms or body, and facial expressions to fluidly express a speaker's thoughts. Sign languages develop in *deaf communities*, which can include interpreters and friends and families of deaf people as well as people who are *deaf* or *hearing-impaired* themselves.

When people using different signed languages meet communication is significantly easier than when people of different spoken languages meet. Sign language in this respect gives access to an international deaf community.

However, contrary to popular belief, sign language is not universal. Wherever communities of deaf people exist, sign languages develop, but as with spoken languages, these vary from region to region. They are not based on the spoken language in the country of origin; in fact their complex spatial grammars are markedly different. However, various signed "modes" of spoken languages have been developed, such as *Signed English* and *Walpiri Sign Language*. Hundreds of sign languages are in use around the world and are at the core of local *Deaf cultures*. Some sign languages have obtained some form of *legal recognition*, while others have no status at all.

Guidelines for Education of Children with Hearing and Speech Impairment

1. Children with hearing problems may be given front seats.
2. While speaking, the teacher may use a reasonable level of pitch.
3. The teacher should avoid mumbling.
4. The teacher should avoid speaking too fast.
5. Students should be encouraged to speak gradually and steadily.
6. Other students of the class may be asked to give due consideration to such students.
7. A lot of visual aids may be used in the classroom.
8. Some of the hearing problems can be corrected through drill and practice.
9. Medical help may be needed if speech disorder is due to an organic defect in speech mechanism.

Planning and Implementation

The educational programme for a student who is deaf or hard of hearing should not be confined to the regular programme but should also include specific instruction in:

- language development;
- auditory management;
- speech development;
- speech reading;
- sign language as required; and
- deaf culture when appropriate.

Most students who are deaf or hard of hearing can and should be educated in their local school district. Typically, programming for students with hearing loss involves one or more of the following services:

- a regular class with direct, frequent support from a qualified itinerant teacher of the deaf and hard of hearing;
- a resource room staffed by a teacher of the deaf and hard of hearing;
- a self-contained class staffed by a teacher of the deaf and hard of hearing who has access to the appropriate support services; and/or
- an individual programme for students with hearing loss and additional special needs.

The prevalence of hearing loss is low. Therefore, the provision of a full range of services within a single school district is not always feasible. In such cases, school districts are encouraged to collaborate to provide regional programmes that serve the needs of students in several districts. In particular, the social and emotional needs of adolescent students who are deaf or hard of hearing may require more than itinerant services. Where there are a sufficient number of students, local or regional school programmes for the deaf and hard of hearing should be developed to launch a flexible and comprehensive programme complete with qualified staff and the appropriate support services.

When the needs of a particular deaf or hard of hearing student cannot be met locally or regionally, or where special circumstances prevail, the student may be referred to the Provincial Educational Review Committee for Deaf and Hard of Hearing students for recommendations for programming and/or determination of eligibility for Provincial Resource Programmes designed for students with hearing loss.

Evaluation and Reporting

School districts are responsible for developing clearly defined policies and procedures which include a mechanism for:

- assessing the effectiveness of local programmes for deaf and hard of hearing students;
- monitoring the educational programme of a student placed in a regional or provincial setting to ensure continued appropriateness; and

evaluating student progress specific to the additional service provided by a teacher of the deaf and hard of hearing. Such evaluation may result in adjustment of communication methodology, recommendations for either additional or reduced service, recommendation for alternate placement, etc.

5 Childrens with Physical Disabilities

Meaning of a Physically Handicapped Child

Physically handicapped child is one who is exaggerated with a physical impairment that in any way limits or inhibits his involvement in normal activities. Impairment implies abnormalities of body structure and appearance. It represents trouble at the organ level. The impairment may be of a serious type or it may be slight in degree. For instance, a person hit by polio may be having only 15 per cent impairment on a certain part of the body or may have a total loss of mobility. Similarly, the visual defect may be total and it may not be restored. Other visual impairments may not pose serious problems and may be overcome with some aids.

Types of Physically Handicapped Children

Generally speaking, the physically handicapped may be classified as:

- The deaf or hard of hearing.
- The blind or near blind or partially blind.
- The language handicapped.
- Orthopaedically handicapped.

Characteristics and Problems of Physically Handicapped Children

A physical handicap may directly or indirectly create the following types of problems for the children and their parents:

1. Social Relationships or Emotional Reactions

(*i*) They also suffer from feelings of failures.

(*ii*) Quite a large number of physically handicapped children suffer from feelings of inferiority

(*iii*) Normal children are at times not only indifferent to the handicapped but also make fun of them. Thus the handicapped children are withdrawn.

(*v*) Sometimes parents', teachers' and students' attitudes may make a physically handicapped child feel 'unwanted' or 'rejected'.

(*vi*) Handicapped children are more prone to accident and injury. Thus, they are not in a position to participate in several co-curricular activities. This also creates a feeling of disgust and inferiority in them.

(*iv*) Aggressive feelings and tensions get accumulated in the handicapped as they have fewer opportunities for expressing their feelings.

2. Academic Performance

Some of the physically handicapped children find it difficult to deal with abstract concepts.

(*i*) Physically handicapped children generally work below their capacity in several areas

(*ii*) *Pattern of Education of the Physically Handicapped Children.* Following are the usual patterns of education of the handicapped:

(a) *Integration or Normal Schools.* Integration implies that the education of the handicapped should be so organised that they freely mix up with normal children. This can be achieved in various ways:

(*i*) Having regular classes for all children.

(*ii*) Deliberate architectural planning to allot space for regular classes and special classes separately but in the same building.

(*b*). *Partial Integration*: The brightest and the handicapped children join with regular groups for carefully selected experiences, games and play.

(*c*) *Total Segregation*. Under this system, the handicapped children are completely separated from other children. They are taught in special schools.

Children with Orthopaedic and Locomotor Impairment/Disability

Identification: Such children can be easily identified as their impairment is usually observable.

1. Deformity may be observable in fingers, hands, legs, neck or waist, etc.
2. Showing difficulty in sitting, standing and walking.
3. Showing difficulty in picking up and holding objects and putting them on the ground.
4. Frequently complaining of pains in the joints.
5. Experiencing difficulty in holding the pen to write.
6. Walking with jerks.
7. Experiencing difficulty in the movement of limbs.
8. Amputated limbs.

Children with Orthopaedic and Locomotor Impairment Disability

1. The teacher should accept such children as he accepts other children.

2. The teacher should avoid sarcasm for the disability of the child.
3. Other children should be advised to appreciate the disability and show due regard to such children. They should be made to understand the disability.
4. Seating arrangement in the class may be adjusted to the specific needs of such students.
5. Reasonable opportunities for participation in recreational activities, sports and games should be provided to these children.
6. Remedial teaching may also be arranged for them.

Student's with Multiple Disabilities: Identification and Assessment

A student who has been formally identified and assessed as having dependent needs is considered by the Ministry of Education for special education funding beyond that provided for low-incidence conditions.

Assessments should integrate current, relevant information related to their intellectual, social/emotional, sensory, physical and communicative abilities, as well as their ability to perform activities of daily living at school. There must be an Individual Education Plan that recognizes the broad range of intellectual abilities of the student, and that addresses the specific educational, health and personal care needs as well as the strategies to address those needs.

Developing an appropriate plan for a student with multiple needs frequently requires input from a number of specialists who are not typically part of a school-based team. These might include medical professionals, representatives of the Ministry of Social Services and the Ministry of Health, and individuals with expertise in augmentative/alternative communication. However, for ongoing management the team should include only key personnel.

Careful documentation and clear procedures are required to address the health needs of these students while in school. Therefore, the following should be incorporated into the planning:

- available medical assessments;
- health care plans; and
- special emergency procedures.

Planning and Implementation

In providing services to a student with dependent needs, unique issues around seating, lifting, positioning, movement, feeding, medication, hygiene and safety will have to be addressed by the school-based team. Many of these can be carried out in a classroom environment, but others, for reasons of privacy and dignity, require a more secluded space. The student will also require adaptations to the learning environment to participate in aspects of school life and to maximize independence. The student should have access to as many parts of the school as possible, to increase opportunities for participation. Equipment accessibility in these areas will also have to be addressed. Adaptations to facilities or equipment to allow access to school areas and programmes should be made as quickly as possible where physical barriers exist. Recent and ongoing technological advances in adaptive devices related to computer access, environmental controls and augmented communication have greatly enhanced learning opportunities for students with dependent needs. It is expected that specialist staff will stay informed about current developments and introduce new technology as appropriate.

A student with a degenerative and/or terminal condition who is or becomes dependent should have normal routines maintained as long as possible. Health care plans will need regular updating and will need to include emergency procedures to meet individual needs and circumstances.

Evaluation and Reporting

It is expected that districts and schools will include students with dependent needs in regular evaluation and reporting. Some students with dependent needs are of average or above average intellectual ability and can meet the learning outcomes identified in the prescribed curriculum if appropriate adaptations are made to instruction and assessment methods. Some students may require extensive modifications to parts or all of their programme so that the learning outcomes will be substantially different from the regular curriculum. Reports to parents should be provided on the same schedule used for all students. Progress should be reported with respect to all components of the programme and with reference to progress. Reports should indicate the adaptations and modifications made to the student's educational programme. All personnel directly involved in the ongoing educational programme (e.g., classroom teacher, specialist teacher, speech-language pathologist) should report on student progress.

Student Progress should be evaluated using a range of assessment techniques. These may include criterion-based measures, curriculum-based assessments, teacher observations, samples of student work.

Poliomyelitis (Polio)

The words polio (grey) and myelon (marrow, indicating the spinal cord) are derived from the Greek. It is the effect of poliomyelitis virus on the spinal cord that leads to the classic manifestation of paralysis. Records from antiquity mention crippling diseases compatible with poliomyelitis. Michael Underwood first described debility of the lower extremities in children that was recognizable as poliomyelitis in England in 1789. The first outbreaks in Europe were reported in the early 19th century, and outbreaks were first reported in the United States in1843. For the next hundred years, epidemics of polio were reported from developed countries in the Northern Hemisphere each summer and fall. These epidemics became increasingly severe, and the average age of persons affected rose. The increasingly older age of persons with primary infection increased both the disease severity and number of deaths from polio. Polio reached a peak in the United State sin 1952, with more than 21,000 paralytic cases. However, following introduction of effective vaccines, polio incidence declined rapidly. The last case of wild-virus polio acquired in the United States was in 1979, and global polio eradication may be achieved within the next decade. Poliovirus Polio-virus is a member of the enter virus subgroup, family Picornaviridae. Entero viruses are transient inhabitants of the gastrointestinal tract, and are stable at acid pH. Picornaviruses are small, ether-insensitive viruses with an RNA genome. There are three poliovirus serotypes (P1, P2, and P3). There is minimal heterotypic immunity between the three serotypes. That is, immunity to one serotype does not produce significant immunity to the other serotypes. The poliovirus is rapidly inactivated by heat, formaldehyde, chlorine, and ultraviolet light.

Pathogenesis

The virus enters through the mouth, and primary multiplication of the virus occurs at the site of implantation in the pharynx and gastrointestinal tract. The virus is usually present in the throat and in the stool before the onset of illness. One week after onset there is less virus of the throat, but virus continues to be excreted in the stool for several weeks. The virus invades local lymphoid tissue, enters the blood-stream, and then may infect cells of the central nervous system. Replication of poliovirus in motor neurons of the anterior horn and brain stem results in cell destruction and causes the typical manifestations of poliomyelitis.

Clinical Features

The incubation period for poliomyelitis is commonly 6–20days with a range of 3–35 days. The response to poliovirus infection is highly variable and has been categorized on the basis of the severity of clinical presentation. Up to 95 per cent of all polio infections are in apparent or asymptomatic. Estimates of the ratio of in apparent to paralytic illness vary from 50:1 to 1,000:1 (usually 200:1). Infected persons without symptoms shed virus in the stool and are able to transmit the virus to others. Approximately 4 to 8 per cent of polio infections consist of a minor, nonspecific illness without clinical or laboratory evidence of central nervous system invasion. This clinical presentation is known as abortive poliomyelitis, and is characterized by complete recovery in less than a week. Three syndromes observed with this form of polio virus infection are upper respiratory tract infection (sore throat and fever), gastrointestinal disturbances (nausea, vomiting, abdominal pain, constipation or, rarely, diarrhea), and influenza—like illness. These syndromes are indistinguishable from other viral illnesses. No paralytic aseptic meningitis (symptoms of stiffness of the neck, back, and/ or legs), usually following several days after a prodrome similar to that of minor illness, occurs in1 to 2 per cent of polio infections. Increased or abnormal sensations can also occur. Typically these symptoms will last from 2 to10 days, followed by complete recovery. Fewer than 1 per cent of all polio infections result in flaccid paralysis. Paralytic symptoms generally begin 1 to 10 days after prodromal symptoms and progress for 2 to 3 days. Generally, no further paralysis occurs after the temperature returns to normal. The prodrome may be biphasic, especially in children, with initial minor symptoms separated by a 1- to 7-day period from more major symptoms. Additional prodromal signs and symptoms can include a loss of superficial reflexes, initially increased deep tendon reflexes and severe muscle aches and spasms in the limbs or back. The illness progresses to flaccid paralysis with diminished deep tendon reflexes, reaches a plateau without change for days to weeks, and is usually asymmetrical. Strength then begins to return. Patients do not experience sensory losses or changes in cognition. Many persons with paralytic poliomyelitis recover completely and, in most, muscle function returns to some degree. Weakness or paralysis still present 12 months after onset is usually permanent.

Paralytic polio is classified into three types, depending on the level of involvement. Spinal polio is most common, and during 1969–79, accounted for 79 per cent of paralytic cases. It is characterized by asymmetric paralysis that most often involves the legs. Bulbar polio leads to weakness of muscles innervated by cranial nerves and accounted for 2 per cent of cases during this period. Bulb spinal polio, a combination of bulbar and spinal paralysis, accounted for 19 per cent of cases. The death-to-case ratio for paralytic polio is generally 2 to 5 per cent among children and up to 15 to 30 per cent for adults (depending on age). It increases to 25 to 75 per cent with bulbar involvement.

Laboratory Diagnosis

Viral Isolation

Poliovirus may be recovered from the stool or pharynx of a person with poliomyelitis. Isolation of virus from the cerebrospinal fluid (CSF) is diagnostic, but is rarely accomplished. If poliovirus is isolated from a person with acute flaccid paralysis, it must be tested further, using oligonucleotide mapping (fingerprinting) or genomic sequencing, to determine if the virus is "wild type" (that is, the virus that causes polio disease) or vaccine type (virus that could derive from a vaccine strain).

Serology

Neutralizing antibodies appear early and may be at high levels by the time the patient is hospitalized; therefore, a fourfold rise in antibody titer may not be demonstrated.

Cerebrospinal Fluid

In poliovirus infection, the CSF usually contains an increased number of white blood cells (10–200 cells/mm^3, primarily lymphocytes) and a mildly elevated protein (40–50 mg/100 ml).

Epidemiology

Occurrence

At one time poliovirus infection occurred throughout the world. Transmission of wild poliovirus was interrupted in the United States in 1979, or possibly earlier. A polio eradication program conducted by the Pan American Health Organization led to elimination of polio in the Western Hemisphere in 1991. The Global Polio Eradication Programme has dramatically reduced poliovirus transmission throughout the world. In 2003, only 784 confirmed cases of polio were reported globally and polio was endemic in six countries.

Reservoir

Humans are the only known reservoir of poliovirus, which is transmitted most frequently by persons with in apparent infections. There is no asymptomatic carrier state except in immune deficient persons.

Transmission

Person-to-person spread of poliovirus via the fecal-oral route is the most important route of transmission, although the oral-oral route may account for some cases. Temporal Pattern Poliovirus infection typically peaks in the summer months in temperate climates. There is no seasonal pattern in tropical climates.

Communicability

Poliovirus is highly infectious, with seroconversion rates among susceptible household contacts of children nearly 100%, and greater than 90% among susceptible household contacts of adults. Persons infected with poliovirus are most infectious from 7 to 10 days before and after the onset of symptoms, but poliovirus may be present in the stool from 3 to 6 weeks.

Secular Trends in the United States

Before the 18th century, polioviruses probably circulated widely. Initial infections with at least one type probably occurred in early infancy, when translucently acquired maternal antibodies were high. Exposure throughout life probably provided continual boosting of immunity, and paralytic infections were probably rare.

In the immediate pre-vaccine era, improved sanitation allowed less frequent exposure and increased the age of primary infection. Boosting of immunity from natural exposure became more infrequent and the number of susceptible persons accumulated, ultimately resulting in the occurrence of epidemics, with 13,000 to 20,000 paralytic cases reported annually.

In the early vaccine era, the incidence dramatically decreased after the introduction of inactivated polio vaccine (IPV) 1955. The decline continued following oral polio vaccine (OPV) introduction in 1961. In 1960, a total of 2,525 paralytic cases were reported, compared with 61 in 1965.

The last cases of paralytic poliomyelitis caused by endemic transmission of wild virus in the United States were in 1979, when an outbreak occurred among the Amish in several Midwest states. The virus was imported from the Netherlands.

From 1980 through 1999, a total of 152 confirmed cases of paralytic poliomyelitis were reported, an average of 8 cases per-year. Six cases were acquired outside the United States and imported. The last imported case was reported in 1993.Two cases were classified as in determinant (no poliovirus isolated from samples obtained from the patients, and patients had no history of recent vaccination or direct contact with a vaccine recipient). The remaining 144 (95%) cases were vaccine-associated paralytic polio (VAPP) caused by live oral polio vaccine.

In order to eliminate VAPP from the United States, ACIP recommended in 2000 that IPV be used exclusively in the United

States. The last case of VAPP acquired in the United States was reported in 1999. In 2005, an unvaccinated U.S. resident was infected with polio vaccine virus in Costa Rica and subsequently developed VAPP. Also in 2005, several asymptomatic infections with a vaccine-derived poliovirus were detected in unvaccinated children in Minnesota. The source of the vaccine virus has not been determined, but it appeared to have been circulating among humans for at least 2 years based on genetic changes in the virus. No VAPP has been reported from this virus.

Poliovirus Vaccines

Inactivated poliovirus vaccine (IPV) was licensed in 1955and was used extensively from that time until the early 1960s. In 1961, type 1 and 2 monovalent oral poliovirus vaccine (MOPV) was licensed, and in 1962, type 3 MOPV was licensed. In 1963, trivalent OPV was licensed and largely replaced IPV use. Trivalent OPV was the vaccine of choice in the United States and most other countries of the world after its introduction in 1963. An enhanced-potency IPV was licensed in November 1987 and first became available in 1988. Use of OPV was discontinued in the United States in 2000.

Characteristics

Inactivated Poliovirus Vaccine

Two enhanced forms of inactivated poliovirus vaccine are currently licensed in the United States, but only one vaccine (IPOL, Sanofi Pasteur) is actually distributed. This vaccine contains all three serotypes of polio vaccine virus. The viruses are grown in a type of monkey kidney tissue culture (Verocell line) and inactivated with formaldehyde. The vaccine contains 2-phenoxyethanol as a preservative, and trace amounts of neomycin, streptomycin, and polymyxin B. It is supplied in a single-dose prefilled syringe and should be administered by either subcutaneous or intramuscular injection.

Oral Poliovirus Vaccine

Trivalent OPV contains live attenuated strains of all three serotypes of poliovirus in a 10:1:3 ratio. The vaccine viruses are grown in monkey kidney tissue culture (Vero cell line).The vaccine is supplied as a single 0.5-mL dose in a plastic dispenser. The vaccine contains trace amounts of neomycin and streptomycin. OPV does not contain a preservative.

Live attenuated polioviruses replicate in the intestinal mucosa and lymphoid cells and in lymph nodes that drain the intestine. Vaccine viruses are excreted in the stool of the vaccinated person for up to 6 weeks after a dose. Maximum viral shedding occurs in the first 1–2 weeks after vaccination, particularly after the first dose.

Vaccine viruses may spread from the recipient to contacts. Persons coming in contact with fecal material of a vaccinated person may be exposed and infected with vaccine virus.

Immunogenicity and Vaccine Efficacy

Inactivated Poliovirus Vaccine

IPV is highly effective in producing immunity to poliovirus and protection from paralytic poliomyelitis. Ninety percent or more of vaccine recipients develop protective antibody to all three poliovirus types after two doses, and at least 99% are immune following three doses. Protection against paralytic disease correlates with the presence of antibody.

IPV appears to produce less local gastrointestinal immunity than does OPV, so persons who receive IPV are more readily infected with wild poliovirus than OPV recipients.

The duration of immunity with IPV is not known with certainty, although it probably provides protection for many years after a complete series.

Oral Poliovirus Vaccine

OPV is highly effective in producing immunity to poliovirus. A single dose of OPV produces immunity to all three vaccine viruses in approximately 50% of recipients. Three doses produce immunity to all three poliovirus types in more than 95% of recipients. As with other live-virus vaccines, immunity from oral poliovirus vaccine is probably life long. OPV produces excellent intestinal immunity, which helps prevent infection with wild virus.

Serologic studies have shown that seroconversion following three doses of either IPV or OPV is nearly 100% to all three vaccine viruses. However, seroconversion rates after three doses of a combination of IPV and OPV are lower, particularly to type 3 vaccine virus (as low as 85% in one study). A fourth dose (most studies used OPV as the fourth dose) usually produces seroconversion rates similar to three doses of either IPV or OPV.

Vaccination Schedule and Use

Trivalent OPV was the vaccine of choice in the United States (and most other countries of the world) since it was licensed in 1963. The nearly exclusive use of OPV led to elimination of wild-type poliovirus from the United States in less than 20 years. However, one case of VAPP occurred for every 2 to 3 million doses of OPV administered, which resulted in 8 to 10 cases of VAPP each year in the United States. From 1980 through 1999, VAPP accounted for 95% of all cases of paralytic poliomyelitis reported in the United States.

In 1996, ACIP recommended an increase in use of IPV through a sequential schedule of IPV followed by OPV. This recommendation was intended to reduce the occurrence of vaccine-associated paralytic polio. The sequential schedule was expected to eliminate VAPP among vaccine recipients by producing humeral immunity to polio vaccine viruses with inactivated polio vaccine prior to exposure to live vaccine virus. Since OPV was still used for the third and fourth doses of the polio vaccination schedule, a risk of VAPP would continue to exist among contacts of vaccinees, who were exposed to live vaccine virus in the stool of vaccine recipients. The sequential

IPV–OPV polio vaccination schedule was widely accepted by both providers and parents. Fewer cases of VAPP were reported in 1998 and 1999, suggesting an impact of the increased use of IPV. However, only the complete discontinuation of use of OPV would lead to complete elimination of VAPP. To further the goal of complete elimination of paralytic polio in the United States, ACIP recommended in July 1999 that inactivated polio vaccine be used exclusively in the United States beginning in 2000. OPV is no longer routinely available in the United States. Exclusive use of IPV eliminated the shedding of live vaccine virus, and eliminated any indigenous VAPP. A primary series of IPV consists of three doses. In infancy, these primary doses are integrated with the administration of other routinely administered vaccines. The first dose maybe given as early as 6 weeks of age but is usually given at 2months of age, with a second dose at 4 months of age. The third dose should be given at 6–18 months of age.

The first and second doses of IPV are necessary to induce a primary immune response, and the third dose of IPV ensures "boosting" of antibody titers to high levels. The preferred interval between the second and third doses of IPV is 2–8months. However, if accelerated protection is needed, the minimum interval between all doses of IPV is 4 weeks, and the minimum age for the fourth dose is 18 weeks. Children who receive three doses of IPV before the fourth birthday should receive a fourth dose before or at school entry. The fourth dose is not needed if the third dose is given on or after the fourth birthday. If all four IPV doses are administered after 6 weeks of age and are all separated by at least 4weeks, a fifth dose is not needed, even if the fourth dose was administered before 4 years of age (except if a specific state school entry requirement mandates a dose of polio vaccine on or after the fourth birthday). It is not necessary to repeat or add doses if the interval between doses is prolonged. Only IPV is available for routine polio vaccination of children in the United States. A polio vaccination schedule begun with OPV should be completed with IPV. If a child receives both types of vaccine, four doses of any combination of IPV or OPV by 4–6 years of age is considered a complete poliovirus vaccination series. A minimum interval of 4 weeks should separate all doses of the series.

In 2002, a pentavalent (5-component) combination vaccine (Pediarix) containing IPV was approved for use in the United States. The vaccine also contains DTaP and a pediatric dose of hepatitis B vaccine. The minimum age for the first dose of Pediarix is 6 weeks (as it is for IPV and DTaP). Pediarix is approved only for the first three doses of the DTaP and IPV series, which are usually given at about 2, 4, and 6 months of age. However, Pediarix is approved for use through 6 years of age, the same as the DTaP component. A child who is behind schedule can receive Pediarix as long as it is given for doses 1, 2, or 3 of the series, and the child is younger than7 years of age. Pediarix is not approved for fourth dose ofthe IPV series, or the fourth or fifth (booster) doses of the DTaP series.

Polio Vaccination of Adults

Routine vaccination of adults (18 years of age and older) who reside in the United States is not necessary or recommended because most adults are already immune and have a very small risk of exposure to wild poliovirus in the United States.

Some adults, however, are at increased risk of infection with poliovirus. These include travelers to areas where poliomyelitis is endemic or epidemic (currently limited to South Asia, the eastern Mediterranean, and Africa), laboratory workers handling specimens that may contain polioviruses, and healthcare workers in close contact with patients who maybe excreting wild polioviruses. In addition, members of specific population groups with a current disease caused by wild polioviruses (e.g., during an outbreak) are also at increased risk.

Recommendations for poliovirus vaccination of adults in the above categories depend upon the previous vaccination history and the time available before protection is required.

For unvaccinated adults (including adults without a written record of prior polio vaccination) at increased risk of exposure to poliomyelitis, primary immunization with IPV is recommended.

The recommended schedule is two doses separated by 1–2 months, and a third dose given 6–12 months after the second dose.

In some circumstances time will not allow completion of this schedule. If 8 weeks or more are available before protection is needed, three doses of IPV should be given at least 4 weeks apart. If 4–8 weeks are available before protection is needed, two doses of IPV should be given at least 4 weeks apart. If less than 4 weeks are available before protection is needed, a single dose of IPV is recommended. In all instances, the remaining doses of vaccine should be given later, at the recommended intervals, if the person remains at increased risk.

Adults who have previously completed a primary series of 3 or more doses and who are at increased risk of exposure to poliomyelitis should be given one dose of IPV. The need for further supplementary doses has not been established. Only one supplemental dose of poliovaccine is recommended for adults who have received a complete series (i.e., it is not necessary to administer additional doses for subsequent travel to a polio endemic country).

Adults who have previously received less than a full primary course of OPV or IPV and who are at increased risk of exposure to poliomyelitis should be given the remaining doses of IPV, regardless of the interval since the last dose and type of vaccine previously received. It is not necessary to restart the series of either vaccine if the schedule has been interrupted. Adverse Reactions Following:

Vaccination

Minor local reactions (pain, redness) may occur following IPV. No serious adverse reactions to IPV have been documented. Because IPV contains trace amounts of streptomycin, polymyxin B, and neomycin, allergic reactions may occur in persons sensitive to these antibiotics.

Vaccine-Associated Paralytic Poliomyelitis

Vaccine-associated paralytic polio is a rare adverse reaction following live oral poliovirus vaccine. Inactivated poliovirus vaccine does not contain live virus, so it cannot cause VAPP. The mechanism of VAPP is believed to be a mutation, or reversion, of the vaccine virus to a more neurotropic form. These mutated viruses are called revertants. Reversion is believed to occur in almost all vaccine recipients, but it only rarely results in paralytic disease. The paralysis that results is identical to that caused by wild virus, and may be permanent.

VAPP is more likely to occur in persons 18 years of age and older than in children, and is much more likely to occur in immunodeficient children than in those who are immunologically normal. Compared with immunocompetent children, the risk of VAPP is almost 7,000 times higher for persons with certain types of immunodeficiencies, particularly B-lymphocyte disorders (e.g., agammaglobulinemia and hypogammaglobulinemia), which reduce the synthesis of immune globulins. There is no procedure available for identifying persons at risk of paralytic disease, except excluding older persons and screening for immunodeficiency.

From 1980 through 1998, 152 cases of paralytic polio were reported in the United States; 144 (95%) of these cases were VAPP, and the remaining eight were in persons who acquired documented or presumed wild-virus polio outside the United States. Of the 144 VAPP cases, 59 (41%) occurred in healthy vaccine recipients (average age 3 months). Forty-four (31%) occurred in healthy contacts of vaccine recipients (average age 26 years), and 7 (5%) were community acquired (i.e., vaccine virus was recovered but there was no known contact with a vaccine recipient). Thirty-four (24%) of VAPP cases occurred in persons with immunologic abnormalities (27 in vaccine recipients and 7 in contacts of vaccine recipients). None of the vaccine recipients were known to be immunologically abnormal prior to vaccination.

The risk of VAPP is not equal for all OPV doses in the vaccination series. The risk of VAPP is 7 to 21 times higher for the first dose than for any other dose in the OPV series. From 1980 through 1994, 303 million doses of OPV were distributed and 125 cases of VAPP were reported, for an overall risk of VAPP of one case per 2.4 million doses. Forty-nine paralytic cases were reported among immunologically normal recipients of OPV during this period. The overall risk to these recipients was one VAPP case per 6.2 million OPV doses. However, 40 (82%) of these 49 cases occurred following receipt of the first dose, making the risk of VAPP one case per 1.4 million first doses. The risk for all other doses was one per 27.2 million doses. The reason for this difference by dose is not known with certainty, but it is probably because the vaccine virus is able to replicate longer in a completely non immune infant. This prolonged replication increases the chance of the emergence of a revertant virus that may cause paralysis. The situation is similar for contacts. A non-immune child may shed virus longer, increasing the chance of exposure of a contact.

The last case of VAPP acquired in the United States was reported in 1999. As noted above a U.S. resident with VAPP was reported in 2005, but the vaccine virus infection was acquired in Costa Rica.

Contraindications and Precautions to Vaccination

Severe allergic reaction to a vaccine component, or following a prior dose of vaccine, is a contraindication to further doses of that vaccine. Since IPV contains trace amounts of streptomycin, neomycin, and polymyxin B, there is a possibility of allergic reactions in persons sensitive to these antibiotics. Persons with allergies that are not anaphylactic, such as skin contact sensitivity, may be vaccinated.

Moderate or severe acute illness is a precaution for IPV.

Breastfeeding does not interfere with successful immunization against poliomyelitis with IPV. IPV may be administered to a child with diarrhea. Minor upper respiratory illnesses with or without fever, mild to moderate local reactions to a prior dose of vaccine, current antimicrobial therapy, and the convalescent phase of an acute illness are not contraindications for vaccination with IPV.

Contraindications to combination vaccines that contain IPV are the same as the contraindications to the individual components (e.g., DTaP, hepatitis B).

Vaccine Storage and Handling

IPV may be shipped without refrigeration provided it is delivered within 4 days. It should be maintained at 35°–46°F (2°–8°C). The vaccine should be clear and colorless. Any vaccine showing particulate matter, turbidity, or change in color should be discarded.

Outbreak Investigation and Control Collect preliminary clinical and epidemiologic information (including vaccine history and contact with OPV vaccines) on any suspected case of paralytic polio. Notify the National Immunization Programme, after appropriate local and state health authorities have been notified. Intensify field investigation to verify information and collect appropriate specimens for viral isolation and serology.

A single case of paralytic poliomyelitis demands immediate attention. If the evidence indicates vaccine-associated disease, no outbreak control programme is needed. If, however, evidence indicates wild virus (for example, two cases in a community),all unvaccinated persons in the epidemic area who are 6 weeks of age and older and whose vaccine histories are uncertain should be vaccinated.

Polio Eradication

Following the widespread use of poliovirus vaccine in themid-1950s, the incidence of poliomyelitis declined rapidly in many industrialized countries. In the United States, the number of cases of paralytic poliomyelitis reported annually declined from more than 20,000 cases in 1952 to fewer than100 cases in the mid-

1960s. The last documented indigenous transmission of wild poliovirus in the United States was in 1979.

In 1985, the member countries of the Pan American Health Organization adopted the goal of eliminating poliomyelitis from the Western Hemisphere by 1990. The strategy to achieve this goal included increasing vaccination coverage; enhancing surveillance for suspected cases (i.e., surveillance for acute flaccid paralysis); and using supplemental immunization strategies such as national immunization days, house-to-house vaccination, and containment activities. Since 1991, when the last wild-virus–associated indigenous case was reported from Peru, no additional cases of poliomyelitis have been confirmed despite intensive surveillance. In September 1994, an international commission certified the Western Hemisphere to be free of indigenous wild poliovirus. The commission based its judgment on detailed reports from national certification commissions that had been convened in every country in the region.

In 1988, the World Health Assembly (the governing body of the World Health Organization) adopted the goal of global eradication of poliovirus by the year 2000. Although this goal was not achieved, substantial progress has been made. One type of poliovirus appears to have already been eradicated. The last isolation of type 2 virus was in India in October 1999.

The polio eradication initiative is supported by a coalition of international organizations that includes WHO, the United Nations Children's Fund (UNICEF), and other bilateral and multilateral organizations. Rotary International has contributed more than $500 million to support the eradication initiative.

Postpolio Syndrome

After an interval of 30–40 years, 25%–40% of persons who contracted paralytic poliomyelitis in childhood experience new muscle pain and exacerbation of existing weakness, or develop new weakness or paralysis. This disease entity is referred to as postpolio syndrome. Factors that increase the risk of postpolio syndrome include increasing length of time since acute poliovirus infection, presence of permanent residual impairment after recovery from the acute illness, and female sex. The pathogenesis of postpolio syndrome is thought to involve the failure of oversized motor units created during the recovery process of paralytic poliomyelitis. Postpolio syndrome is not an infectious process, and persons experiencing the syndrome do not shed poliovirus.

6 Learning Disabilities and other Disorders

Unlike other disabilities, such as paralysis or blindness, a learning disability (LD) is a hidden handicap. A learning disability doesn't disfigure or leave visible signs that would invite others to be understanding or offer support. A woman once blurted to Wallace, "You seem so intelligent—you don't *look* handicapped!"

LD is a disorder that affects people's ability to either interpret what they see and hear or to link information from different parts of the brain. These limitations can show up in many ways—as specific difficulties with spoken and written language, coordination, self-control, or attention. Such difficulties extend to schoolwork and can impede learning to read or write, or to do math.

Learning disabilities can be lifelong conditions that, in some cases, affect many parts of a person's life: school or work, daily routines, family life, and sometimes even friendships and play. In some people, many overlapping learning disabilities may be apparent. Other people may have a single, isolated learning problem that has little impact on other areas of their lives.

Types of Learning Disabilities

"Learning disability" is not a diagnosis in the same sense as "chickenpox" or "mumps." Chickenpox and mumps imply a single, known cause with a predictable set of symptoms. Rather,

LD is a broad term that covers a pool of possible causes, symptoms, treatments, and outcomes. Partly because learning disabilities can show up in so many forms, it is difficult to diagnose or to pinpoint the causes. And no one knows of a pill or remedy that will cure them.

Not all learning problems are necessarily learning disabilities. Many children are simply slower in developing certain skills. Because children show natural differences in their rate of development, sometimes what seems to be a learning disability may simply be a delay in maturation. To be diagnosed as a learning disability, specific criteria must be met.

The criteria and characteristics for diagnosing learning disabilities appear in a reference book called the DSM (short for the *Diagnostic and Statistical Manual of Mental Disorders*). The DSM diagnosis is commonly used when applying for health insurance coverage of diagnostic and treatment services.

Learning disabilities can be divided into three broad categories:

- Developmental speech and language disorders
- Academic skills disorders
- "Other," a catch-all that includes certain coordination disorders and learning handicaps not covered by the other terms

Each of these categories includes a number of more specific disorders.

Developmental Speech and Language Disorders

Speech and language problems are often the earliest indicators of a learning disability. People with developmental speech and language disorders have difficulty producing speech sounds, using spoken language to communicate, or understanding what other people say. Depending on the problem, the specific diagnosis may be:

- Developmental articulation disorder

- Developmental expressive language disorder
- Developmental receptive language disorder

Developmental Articulation Disorder—Children with this disorder may have trouble controlling their rate of speech. Or they may lag behind playmates in learning to make speech sounds. For example, Wallace at age 6 still said "wabbit" instead of "rabbit" and "thwim" for "swim." Developmental articulation disorders are common. They appear in at least 10 percent of children younger than age 8. Fortunately, articulation disorders can often be outgrown or successfully treated with speech therapy.

Developmental Expressive Language Disorder—Some children with language impairments have problems expressing themselves in speech. Their disorder is called, therefore, a developmental expressive language disorder. Susan, who often calls objects by the wrong names, has an expressive language disorder. Of course, an expressive language disorder can take other forms. A 4-year-old who speaks only in two-word phrases and a 6-year-old who can't answer simple questions also have an expressive language disability.

Developmental Receptive Language Disorder—Some people have trouble understanding certain aspects of speech. It's as if their brains are set to a different frequency and the reception is poor. There's the toddler who doesn't respond to his name, a preschooler who hands you a bell when you asked for a ball, or the worker who consistently can't follow simple directions. Their hearing is fine, but they can't make sense of certain sounds, words, or sentences they hear. They may even seem inattentive. These people have a receptive language disorder. Because using and understanding speech are strongly related, many people with receptive language disorders also have an expressive language disability.

Of course, in preschoolers, some misuse of sounds, words, or grammar is a normal part of learning to speak. It's only when these problems persist that there is any cause for concern.

Academic Skills Disorders

Students with academic skills disorders are often years behind their classmates in developing reading, writing, or arithmetic skills. The diagnoses in this category include:

- Developmental reading disorder
- Developmental writing disorder
- Developmental arithmetic disorder

Developmental Reading Disorder—This type of disorder, also known as dyslexia, is quite widespread. In fact, reading disabilities affect 2 to 8 percent of elementary school children.

When you think of what is involved in the "three R's"—reading, 'riting, and 'rithmetic—it's astounding that most of us do learn them. Consider that to read, you must simultaneously:

- Focus attention on the printed marks and control eye movements across the page
- Recognize the sounds associated with letters
- Understand words and grammar
- Build ideas and images
- Compare new ideas to what you already know
- Store ideas in memory

Such mental juggling requires a rich, intact network of nerve cells that connect the brain's centers of vision, language, and memory.

A person can have problems in any of the tasks involved in reading. However, scientists found that a significant number of people with dyslexia share an inability to distinguish or separate the sounds in spoken words. Dennis, for example, can't identify the word "bat" by sounding out the individual letters, b-a-t. Other children with dyslexia may have trouble with rhyming games, such as rhyming "cat" with "bat." Yet scientists have found these skills fundamental to learning to read. Fortunately, remedial reading specialists have developed techniques that can help many children with dyslexia acquire these skills.

However, there is more to reading than recognizing words. If the brain is unable to form images or relate new ideas to those stored in memory, the reader can't understand or remember the new concepts. So other types of reading disabilities can appear in the upper grades when the focus of reading shifts from word identification to comprehension.

Developmental Writing Disorder—Writing, too, involves several brain areas and functions. The brain networks for vocabulary, grammar, hand movement, and memory must all be in good working order. So a developmental writing disorder may result from problems in any of these areas. For example, Dennis, who was unable to distinguish the sequence of sounds in a word, had problems with spelling. A child with a writing disability, particularly an expressive language disorder, might be unable to compose complete, grammatical sentences.

Developmental Arithmetic Disorder—If you doubt that arithmetic is a complex process, think of the steps you take to solve this simple problem: 25 divided by 3 equals?

Arithmetic involves recognizing numbers and symbols, memorizing facts such as the multiplication table, aligning numbers, and understanding abstract concepts like place value and fractions. Any of these may be difficult for children with developmental arithmetic disorders. Problems with numbers or basic concepts are likely to show up early. Disabilities that appear in the later grades are more often tied to problems in reasoning.

Many aspects of speaking, listening, reading, writing, and arithmetic overlap and build on the same brain capabilities. So it's not surprising that people can be diagnosed as having more than one area of learning disability. For example, the ability to understand language underlies learning speak. Therefore, any disorder that hinders the ability to understand language will also interfere with the development of speech, which in turn hinders learning to read and write. A single gap in the brain's operation can disrupt many types of activity.

Learning Disabilities Related to Differences in the Brain

In comparing people with and without learning disabilities, scientists have observed certain differences in the structure and functioning of the brain. For example, new research indicates that there may be variations in the brain structure called the planum temporale, a language-related area found in both sides of the brain. In people with dyslexia, the two structures were found to be equal in size. In people who are not dyslexic, however, the left planum temporale was noticeably larger. Some scientists believe reading problems may be related to such differences.

With more research, scientists hope to learn precisely how differences in the structures and processes of the brain contribute to learning disabilities, and how these differences might be treated or prevented.

How Learning Disabilities Identified?

When a baby is born, the parents eagerly wait for the baby's first step, first word, a myriad of other "firsts." During routine checkups, the pediatrician, too, watches for more subtle signs of development. The parents and doctor are watching for the child to achieve developmental milestones. The developmental milestones chart (omitted here; see page 18 of brochure) lists a few of these markers and the ages and grades that they typically appear.

Parents are usually the first to notice obvious delays in their child reaching early milestones. The pediatrician may observe more subtle signs of minor neurological damage, such as a lack of coordination. But the classroom teacher, in fact, may be the first to notice the child's persistent difficulties in reading, writing, or arithmetic. As school tasks become more complex, a child with a learning disability may have problems mentally juggling more information.

The learning problems of children who are quiet and polite in school may go unnoticed. Children with above average intelligence, who manage to maintain passing grades despite their disability, are even less likely to be identified. Children with hyperactivity, on the other hand, will be identified quickly by their impulsive behaviour and excessive movement. Hyperactivity usually begins before age 4 but may not be recognized until the child enters school.

What should parents, doctors, and teachers do if critical developmental milestones haven't appeared by the usual age? Sometimes it's best to allow a little more time, simply for the brain to mature a bit. But if a milestone is already long delayed, if there's a history of learning disabilities in the family, or if there are several delayed skills, the child should be professionally evaluated as soon as possible. An educator or a doctor who treats children can suggest where to go for help.

How are Learning Disabilities Diagnosed?

By law, learning disability is defined as a significant gap between a person's intelligence and the skills the person has achieved at each age. This means that a severely retarded 10-year-old who speaks like a 6-year-old probably doesn't have a language or speech disability. He has mastered language up to the limits of his intelligence. On the other hand, a fifth grader with an IQ of 100 who can't write a simple sentence probably does have LD.

Learning disorders may be *informally flagged* by observing significant delays in the child's skill development. A 2-year delay in the primary grades is usually considered significant. For older students, such a delay is not as debilitating, so learning disabilities aren't usually suspected unless there is more than a 2-year delay. *Actual diagnosis* of learning disabilities, however, is made using standardized tests that compare the child's level of ability to what is considered normal development for a person of that age and intelligence.

For example, as late as fifth grade, any student couldn't add two numbers, even though she rarely missed school and was good in other subjects. Her mother took her to a clinician, who observed students behaviour and administered standardized math and intelligence tests. The test results showed that Susan's math skills were several years behind, given her mental capacity for learning. Once other possible causes like lack of motivation and vision problems were ruled out, his math problem was formally diagnosed as a specific learning disability.

Test outcomes depend not only on the child's actual abilities, but on the reliability of the test and the child's ability to pay attention and understand the questions. Children like Ram, with poor attention or hyperactivity, may score several points below their true level of ability. Testing a child in an isolated room can sometimes help the child concentrate and score higher.

Each type of LD is diagnosed in slightly different ways. To diagnose speech and language disorders, a speech therapist tests the child's pronunciation, vocabulary, and grammar and compares them to the developmental abilities seen in most children that age. A psychologist tests the child's intelligence. A physician checks for any ear infections, and an audiologist may be consulted to rule out auditory problems. If the problem involves articulation, a doctor examines the child's vocal cords and throat.

In the case of academic skills disorders, academic development in reading, writing, and math is evaluated using standardized tests. In addition, vision and hearing are tested to be sure the student can see words clearly and can hear adequately. The specialist also checks if the child has missed much school. It's important to rule out these other possible factors. After all, treatment for a learning disability is very different from the remedy for poor vision or missing school.

"Other" Learning Disabilities

The DSM also lists additional categories, such as "motor skills disorders" and "specific developmental disorders not otherwise specified." These diagnoses include delays in acquiring language, academic, and motor skills that can affect the ability to learn, but do not meet the criteria for a specific learning disability. Also included are coordination disorders that can lead to poor penmanship, as well as certain spelling and memory disorders.

Attention Disorders

Nearly 4 million school-age children have learning disabilities. Of these, at least 20 percent have a type of disorder that leaves them unable to focus their attention.

Some children and adults who have attention disorders appear to daydream excessively. And once you get their attention, they're often easily distracted. Geeta, for example, tends to mentally drift off into a world of her own. Children like Susan may have a number of learning difficulties. If, like Susan, they are quiet and don't cause problems, their problems may go unnoticed. They may be passed along from grade to grade, without getting the special assistance they need.

In a large proportion of affected children—mostly boys—the attention deficit is accompanied by hyperactivity. Dennis is an example of a person with attention deficit hyperactivity disorder—ADHD. They act impulsively, running into traffic or toppling desks. Like young Ram, who jumped on the sofa to exhaustion, hyperactive children can't sit still. They blurt out answers and interrupt. In games, they can't wait their turn. These children's problems are usually hard to miss. Because of their constant motion and explosive energy, hyperactive children often get into trouble with parents, teachers, and peers.

By adolescence, physical hyperactivity usually subsides into fidgeting and restlessness. But the problems with attention and concentration often continue into adulthood. At work, adults with ADHD often have trouble organizing tasks or completing their work. They don't seem to listen to or follow directions. Their work may be messy and appear careless.

Attention disorders, with or without hyperactivity, are not considered learning disabilities in themselves. However, because attention problems can seriously interfere with school performance, they often accompany academic skills disorders.

Errors in Fetal Brain Development

Throughout pregnancy, the fetal brain develops from a few all-purpose cells into a complex organ made of billions of specialized, interconnected nerve cells called neurons. During this amazing evolution, things can go wrong that may alter how the neurons form or interconnect.

In the early stages of pregnancy, the brain stem forms. It controls basic life functions such as breathing and digestion. Later, a deep ridge divides the cerebrum—the thinking part of the brain—into two halves, a right and left hemisphere. Finally, the areas involved with processing sight, sound, and other senses develop, as well as the areas associated with attention, thinking, and emotion.

As new cells form, they move into place to create various brain structures. Nerve cells rapidly grow to form networks with other parts of the brain. These networks are what allow information to be shared among various regions of the brain.

Throughout pregnancy, this brain development is vulnerable to disruptions. If the disruption occurs early, the fetus may die, or the infant may be born with widespread disabilities and possibly mental retardation. If the disruption occurs later, when the cells are becoming specialized and moving into place, it may leave errors in the cell makeup, location, or connections. Some scientists believe that these errors may later show up as learning disorders.

Other Factors that Affect Brain Development

Through experiments with animals, scientists at NIMH and other research facilities are tracking clues to determine what disrupts brain development. By studying the normal processes of brain development, scientists can better understand what can go wrong. Some of these studies are examining how genes, substance abuse, pregnancy problems, and toxins may affect the developing brain.

Genetic Factors—The fact that learning disabilities tend to run in families indicates that there may be a genetic link. For example, children who lack some of the skills needed for reading, such as hearing the separate sounds of words, are likely to have a parent with a related problem. However, a parent's learning disability may take a slightly different form in the child. A parent who has a writing disorder may have a child with an expressive language disorder. For this reason, it seems unlikely that specific learning disorders are inherited directly. Possibly, what is inherited is a subtle brain dysfunction that can in turn lead to a learning disability.

There may be an alternative explanation for why LD might seem to run in families. Some learning difficulties may actually stem from the family environment. For example, parents who have expressive language disorders might talk less to their children, or the language they use may be distorted. In such cases, the child lacks a good model for acquiring language and therefore, may seem to be learning disabled.

Tobacco, Alcohol, and Other Drug Use—Many drugs taken by the mother pass directly to the fetus. Research shows that a mother's use of cigarettes, alcohol, or other drugs during pregnancy may have damaging effects on the unborn child. Therefore, to prevent potential harm to developing babies, the U.S. Public Health Service supports efforts to make people aware of the possible dangers of smoking, drinking, and using drugs.

Scientists have found that mothers who smoke during pregnancy may be more likely to bear smaller babies. This is a concern because small newborns, usually those weighing less than 5 pounds, tend to be at risk for a variety of problems, including learning disorders.

Alcohol also may be dangerous to the fetus' developing brain. It appears that alcohol may distort the developing neurons. Heavy alcohol use during pregnancy has been linked to fetal alcohol syndrome, a condition that can lead to low birth weigh, intellectual impairment, hyperactivity, and certain physical defects. Any alcohol use during pregnancy, however, may influence the child's development and lead to problems with learning, attention, memory, or problem solving. Because scientists have not yet identified "safe" levels, alcohol should be used cautiously by women who are pregnant or who may soon become pregnant.

Drugs such as cocaine—especially in its smokable form known as crack—seem to affect the normal development of brain receptors. These brain cell parts help to transmit incoming signals from our skin, eyes, and ears, and help regulate our physical response to the environment. Because children with certain learning disabilities have difficulty understanding speech sounds or letters, some researchers believe that learning disabilities, as well as ADHD, may be related to faulty receptors. Current research points to drug abuse as a possible cause of receptor damage.

Problems During Pregnancy or Delivery—Other possible causes of learning disabilities involve complications during pregnancy. In some cases, the mother's immune system reacts to the fetus and attacks it as if it were an infection. This type of disruption seems to cause newly formed brain cells to settle in the wrong part of the brain. Or during delivery, the umbilical cord may become twisted and temporarily cut off oxygen to the fetus. This, too, can impair brain functions and lead to LD.

Toxins in the Child's Environment—New brain cells and neural networks continue to be produced for a year or so after the child is born. These cells are vulnerable to certain disruptions, also.

Researchers are looking into environmental toxins that may lead to learning disabilities, possibly by disrupting childhood brain development or brain processes. Cadmium and lead, both prevalent in the environment, are becoming a leading focus of neurological research. Cadmium, used in making some steel products, can get into the soil, then into the foods we eat. Lead was once common in paint and gasoline, and is still present in some water pipes. A study of animals sponsored by the National Institutes of Health showed a connection between exposure to lead and learning difficulties. In the study, rats exposed to lead experienced changes in their brainwaves, slowing their ability to learn. The learning problems lasted for weeks, long after the rats were no longer exposed to lead.

In addition, there is growing evidence that learning problems may develop in children with cancer who had been treated with chemotherapy or radiation at an early age. This seems particularly true of children with brain tumors who received radiation to the skull.

Education Options

Although obtaining a diagnosis is important, even more important is creating a plan for getting the right help. Because LD can affect the child and family in so many ways, help may be needed on a variety of fronts: educational, medical, emotional, and practical.

In most ways, children with learning disabilities are no different from children without these disabilities. At school, they eat together and share sports, games, and after-school activities. But since children with learning disabilities do have specific learning needs, most public schools provide special programmes.

Schools typically provide special education programmes either in a separate all-day classroom or as a special education class that the student attends for several hours each week. Some parents hire trained tutors to work with their child after school. If the problems are severe, some parents choose to place their child in a special school for the learning disabled.

If parents choose to get help outside the public schools, they should select a learning specialist carefully. The specialist should be able to explain things in terms that the parents can understand. Whenever possible, the specialist should have professional certification and experience with the learner's specific age group and type of disability. Some of the support groups listed at the end of this booklet can provide references to qualified special education programmes.

Planning a special education programme begins with systematically identifying what the student can and cannot do. The specialist looks for patterns in the child's gaps. For example, if the child fails to hear the separate sounds in words, are there other sound discrimination problems? If there's a problem with handwriting, are there other motor delays? Are there any consistent problems with memory?

Special education teachers also identify the types of tasks the child can do and the senses that function well. By using the senses that are intact and bypassing the disabilities, many children can develop needed skills. These strengths offer alternative ways the child *can* learn.

Medication

For nearly six decades, many children with attention disorders have benefited from being treated with medication. Three drugs, Ritalin (methylphenidate), Dexedrine (dextroamphetamine), and Cylert (pemoline), have been used successfully. Although these drugs are stimulants in the same category as "speed" and "diet pills," they seldom make children "high" or more jittery. Rather, they temporarily improve children's attention and ability to focus. They also help children control their impulsiveness and other hyperactive behaviours.

The effects of medication are most dramatic in children with ADHD. Shortly after taking the medication, they become more able to focus their attention. They become more ready to learn. Studies by NIMH scientists and other researchers have shown that at least 90 percent of hyperactive children can be helped by either Ritalin or Dexedrine. If one medication does not help a hyperactive child to calm down and pay attention in school, the other medication might.

The drugs are effective for 3 to 4 hours and move out of the body within 12 hours. The child's doctor or a psychiatrist works closely with the family and child to carefully adjust the dosage and medication schedule for the best effect. Typically, the child takes the medication so that the drug is active during peak school hours, such as when reading and math are taught.

In the past few years, researchers have tested these drugs on adults who have attention disorders. Just as in children, the results show that low doses of these medications can help reduce distractibility and impulsivity in adults. Use of these medications has made it possible for many severely disordered adults to organize their lives, hold jobs, and care for themselves.

In trying to do everything possible to help their children, many parents have been quick to try new treatments. Most of these treatments sound scientific and reasonable, but a few are pure quackery. Many are developed by reputable doctors or specialists—but when tested scientifically, cannot be proven to help. Following are types of therapy that have *not* proven effective in treating the majority of children with learning disabilities or attention disorders:

- Megavitamins
- Colored lenses
- Special diets
- Sugar-free diets
- Body stimulation or manipulation

Although scientists hope that brain research will lead to new medical interventions and drugs, at present there are no medicines for speech, language, or academic disabilities.

Role of Families

The effects of learning disabilities can ripple outward from the disabled child or adult to family, friends, and peers at school or work. Children with LD often absorb what others thoughtlessly say about them. They may define themselves in light of their disabilities, as "behind," "slow," or "different."

Sometimes they don't know how they're different, but they know how awful they feel. Their tension or shame can lead them to act out in various ways—from withdrawal to belligerence. Like Wallace, they may get into fights. They may stop trying to learn and achieve and eventually drop out of school. Or, like Susan, they may become isolated and depressed.

Children with learning disabilities and attention disorders may have trouble making friends with peers. For children with ADHD, this may be due to their impulsive, hostile, or withdrawn behaviour. Some children with delays may be more comfortable with younger children who play at their level. Social problems may also be a product of their disability. Some people with LD seem unable to interpret tone of voice or facial expressions. Misunderstanding the situation, they act inappropriately, turning people away.

Without professional help, the situation can spiral out of control. The more that children or teenagers fail, the more they may act out their frustration and damage their self-esteem. The more they act out, the more trouble and punishment it brings, further lowering their self-esteem. Wallace, who lashed out when teased about his poor pronunciation and was repeatedly suspended from school, shows how harmful this cycle can be.

Having a child with a learning disability may also be an emotional burden for the family. Parents often sweep through a range of emotions: denial, guilt, blame, frustration, anger, and despair. Brothers and sisters may be annoyed or embarrassed by their sibling, or jealous of all the attention the child with LD gets.

Counseling can be very helpful to people with LD and their families. Counseling can help affected children, teenagers, and adults develop greater self-control and a more positive attitude toward their own abilities. Talking with a counselor or psychologist also allows family members to air their feelings as well as get support and reassurance.

Many parents find that joining a support group also makes a difference. Support groups can be a source of information, practical suggestions, and mutual understanding. Self-help books written by educators and mental health professionals can also be helpful. A number of references and support groups are listed at the end of this booklet.

Behaviour modification also seems to help many children with hyperactivity and LD. In behaviour modification, children receive immediate, tangible rewards when they act appropriately. Receiving an immediate reward can help children learn to control their own actions, both at home and in class. A school or private counselor can explain behaviour modification and help parents and teachers set up appropriate rewards for the child.

Parents and teachers can help by structuring tasks and environments for the child in ways that allow the child to succeed. They can find ways to help children build on their strengths and work around their disabilities. This may mean deliberately making eye contact before speaking to a child with an attention disorder. For a teenager with a language problem, it may mean providing pictures and diagrams for performing a task. For students like Ram with handwriting or spelling problems, a solution may be to provide a word processor and software that checks spelling. A counselor or school psychologist can help identify practical solutions that make it easier for the child and family to cope day by day.

Every child needs to grow up feeling competent and loved. When children have learning disabilities, parents may need to work harder at developing their children's self-esteem and relationship-building skills. But self-esteem and good relationships are as worth developing as any academic skill.

Attention Deficit Hyper-activity Disorder (ADHD) is a condition that becomes apparent in some children in the preschool and early school years. It is hard for these children to control their behavior and/or pay attention. It is estimated that between 3 and 5 percent of children have attention deficit hyperactivity disorder

(ADHD), or approximately 2 million children in the United States. This means that in a classroom of 25 to 30 children, it is likely that at least one will have ADHD.

ADHD was first described by Dr. Heinrich Hoffman in 1845. A physician who wrote books on medicine and psychiatry, Dr. Hoffman was also a poet who became interested in writing for children when he couldn't find suitable materials to read to his 3-year-old son. The result was a book of poems, complete with illustrations, about children and their characteristics. The Story of Fidgety Philip" was an accurate description of a little boy who had attention deficit hyperactivity disorder. Yet it was not until 1902 that Sir George F. Still published a series of lectures to the Royal College of Physicians in England in which he described a group of impulsive children with significant behavioral problems, caused by a genetic dysfunction and not by poor child rearing—children who today would be easily recognized as having ADHD.' Since then, several thousand scientific papers on the disorder have been published, providing information on its nature, course, causes, impairments, and treatments.

A child with ADHD faces a difficult but not insurmountable task ahead. In order to achieve his or her full potential, he or she should receive help, guidance, and understanding from parents, guidance counselors, and the public education system. This brochure offers information on ADHD and its management, including research on medications and behavioral interventions, as well as helpful resources on educational options.

Because ADHD often continues into adulthood, this brochure contains a section on the diagnosis and treatment of ADHD in adults.

Symptoms

The principle characteristics of ADHD are inattention, hyperactivity, and impulsivity. These symptoms appear early in a child's life. Because many normal children may have these symptoms, but at a low level, or the symptoms may be caused by another disorder, it is important that the child receive a thorough examination and appropriate diagnosis by a well qualified professional.

Symptoms of ADHD will appear over the course of many months, often with the symptoms of impulsiveness and hyperactivity preceding those of inattention that may not emerge for a year or more. Different symptoms may appear in different settings, depending on the demands the situation may pose for the child's self-control. A child who "can't sit still" or is otherwise disruptive will be noticeable in school, but the inattentive daydreamer may be overlooked. The impulsive child who acts before thinking maybe considered just a "discipline problem," while the child who is passive or sluggish may be viewed as merely unmotivated. Yet both may have different types of ADHD. All children are sometimes restless, sometimes act without thinking, sometimes daydream the time away. When the child's hyperactivity, distractibility, poor concentration, or impulsivity begin to affect performance in school, social relationships with other children, or behavior at home, ADHD may be suspected. But because the symptoms vary so much across settings, ADHD is not easy to diagnose. This is especially true when inattentiveness is the primary symptom.

According to the most recent version of the *Diagnostic and Statistical Manual (Mental Disorder* (DSM-IV-TR), there are three patterns of behavior that indicate ADHD. People with ADHD may show several signs of being consistently inattentive. They may have a pattern of being hyperactive and impulsive far more than others of their age. Or they may show all three types of behavior. This means that there are three subtypes of ADHD recognized by professionals. These are the predominantly hyperactive-impulsive type (that does not show significant inattention); the predominantly inattentive type (that does not show significant hyperactive-impulsive behavior) sometimes called ADD—an outdated term for this entire disorder; and the combined type (that displays both inattentive and hyperactive-impulsive symptoms).

Hyperactivity-impulsivity

Hyperactive children always seem to be "on the go" or constantly in motion. They dash around touching or playing with whatever is in sight, or talk incessantly. Sitting still at dinner or during a school lesson or story can be a difficult task. They squirm and fidget in their seats or roam around the room. Or they may wiggle their feet, touch everything, or noisily tap their pencil. Hyperactive teenagers or adults may feel internally restless. They often report needing to stay busy and may try to do several things at once.

Impulsive children seem unable to curb their immediate reactions or think before they act. They will often blurt out inappropriate comments, display their emotions without restraint, and act without regard for the later consequences of their conduct. Their impulsivity may make it hard for them to wait for things they want or to take their turn in games. They may grab a toy from another child or hit when they're upset. Even as teenagers or adults, they may impulsively choose to do things that have an immediate but small payoff rather than engage in activities that may take more effort yet provide much greater but delayed rewards.

Some signs of hyperactivity-impulsivity are:

- Feeling restless, often fidgeting with hands or feet, or squirming while seated
- Running, climbing, or leaving a seat in situations where sitting or quiet behavior is expected
- Blurting out answers before hearing the whole question
- Having difficulty waiting in line or taking turns.

In attention

Children who are inattentive have a hard time keeping their minds on any one thing and may get bored with a task after only a few minutes. If they are doing something they really enjoy, they have no trouble paying attention. But focusing deliberate, conscious attention to organizing and completing a task or learning something new is difficult.

Homework is particularly hard for these children. They will forget to write down an assignment, or leave it at school. They will forget to bring a book home, or bring the wrong one. The homework, if finally finished, is full of errors and erasures. Homework is often accompanied by frustration for both parent and child.

The DSM-IV-TR gives these signs of inattention:

- Often becoming easily distracted by irrelevant sights and sounds
- Often failing to pay attention to details and making careless mistakes
- Rarely following instructions carefully and completely losing or forgetting things like toys, or pencils, books, and tools needed for a task
- Often skipping from one uncompleted activity to another.

Children diagnosed with the Predominantly Inattentive Type of ADHD are seldom impulsive or hyperactive, yet have significant problems paying attention. They appear to be daydreaming, "spacey," easily confused, slow moving and lethargic. They may have difficulty processing information as quickly and accurately as other children. When the teacher gives oral or even written instructions, this child has a hard time understanding what he or she is supposed to do and makes frequent mistakes. Yet the child may sit quietly, unobtrusively, and even appear to be working but not fully attending to or understanding the task and the instructions.

These children don't show significant problems with impulsivity and over activity in the classroom, on the school ground, oral home. They may get along better with other children than the more impulsive and hyperactive types of ADHD, and they may not have the same sorts of social problems so common with the combined type of ADHD. So often their problems with inattention are overlooked. But they need help just as much as do the other types of ADHD who cause more obvious problems in the classroom.

Diagnosis

Some parents see signs of inattention, hyperactivity, and impulsivity in their toddler long before the child enters school. The child may lose interest in playing a game, watching a TV show, or may run around completely out of control. But because children mature at different rates and are very different in personality, temperament, and energy levels, it's useful to get an expert's opinion of whether the behavior is appropriate for the child's age. Parents can ask their child's pediatrician, or a child psychologist or psychiatrist, to assess whether their toddler has an attention deficit hyperactivity disorder or is, more likely at this age, just immature or unusually exuberant.

ADHD may be suspected by a parent or caretaker or may go unnoticed until the child runs into problems at school. Given that ADHD tends to affect functioning most strongly in school, sometimes the teacher is the first to recognize that a child is hyperactive or inattentive and may point it out to the parents and/or consult with the school psychologist. Because teachers work with many children, they come to know how "average" children behave in learning situations that require attention and self-control. However, teachers sometimes fail to notice the needs of children who may be more inattentive and passive yet who are quiet and cooperative, such as those with the predominantly inattentive form of ADHD.

What Causes ADHD?

One of the first questions a parent will have is "Why? What went wrong?" "Did I do something to cause this?" There is little compelling evidence at this time that ADHD can arise purely from social factors or child-rearing methods. Most substantiated causes appear to fall in the realm of neurobiology and genetics. This is not to say that environmental factors may not influence the severity of the disorder, and especially the degree of impairment and suffering the child may experience, but that such factors do not seem to give rise to the condition by themselves.

The parents' focus should be on looking forward and finding the best possible way to help their child. Scientists are studying causes in an effort to identify better ways to treat, and perhaps someday, to prevent ADHD. They are finding more and more evidence that ADHD does not stem from home environment, but from biological causes. Knowing this can remove a huge burden of guilt from parents who might blame themselves for their child's behavior.

Over the last few decades, scientists have come up with possible theories about what causes ADHD. Some of these theories have led to dead ends, some to exciting new avenues of investigation.

Environmental Agents: Studies have shown a possible correlation between the use of cigarettes and alcohol during pregnancy and risk for ADHD in the offspring of that pregnancy. As a precaution, it is best during pregnancy to refrain from both cigarette and alcohol use.

Another environmental agent that may be associated with a higher risk of ADHD is high levels of lead in the bodies of young preschool children. Since lead is no longer allowed in paint and is usually found only in older buildings, exposure to toxic levels is not as prevalent as it once was. Children who live in old buildings in which lead still exists in the plumbing or in lead paint that has been painted over may be at risk.

Brain Injury: One early theory was that attention disorders were caused by brain injury. Some children who have suffered accidents leading to brain injury may show some signs of behavior similar to that of ADHD, but only a small percentage of children with ADHD have been found to have suffered a traumatic brain injury.

Food Additives and Sugar: It has been suggested that attention disorders are caused by refined sugar or food additives, or that symptoms of ADHD are exacerbated by sugar or food additives.

In 1982, the National Institutes of Health held a scientific consensus conference to discuss this issue. It was found that diet restrictions helped about 5 per cent of children with ADHD, mostly young children who had food allergies. A more recent study on the effect of sugar on children, using sugar one day and a sugar substitute on alternate days, without parents, staff, or children knowing which substance was being used, showed no significant effects of the sugar on behavior or learning.

In another study, children whose mothers felt they were sugar-sensitive were given aspartame as a substitute for sugar. Half the mothers were told their children were given sugar, half that their children were given aspartame. The mothers who thought their children had received sugar rated them as more hyperactive than the other children and were more critical of their behavior.

Genetics: Attention disorders often run in families, so there are likely to be genetic influences. Studies indicate that 25 percent of the close relatives in the families of ADHD children also have ADHD, whereas the rate is about 5 percent in the general population. Many studies of twins now show that a strong genetic influence exists in the disorder.

Researchers continue to study the genetic contribution to ADHD and to identify the genes that cause a person to be susceptible to ADHD. Since its inception in 1999, the Attention—Deficit Hyperactivity Disorder Molecular Genetics Network has served as a way for researchers to share findings regarding possible genetic influences on ADHD.

Recent Studies on Causes of ADHD: Some knowledge of the structure of the brain is helpful in understanding the research scientists are doing in searching for a physical basis for attention deficit hyperactivity disorder. One part of the brain that scientists have focused on in their search is the *frontal lobes* of the *cerebrum.* The frontal lobes allow us to solve problems, plan ahead, understand the behavior of others, and restrain our impulses. The two frontal lobes, the right and the left, communicate with each other through the *corpus callosum,* (nerve fibers that connect the right and left frontal lobes).

The *basal ganglia* are the interconnected gray masses deep in the cerebral hemisphere that serve as the connection between the cerebrum and the *cerebellum* and, with the cerebellum are responsible for motor coordination. The cerebellum is divided into three parts. The middle part is called the *vermis.*

All of these parts of the brain have been studied through the use of various methods for seeing into or imaging the brain. These methods include functional magnetic resonance imaging (FMRI) positron emission tomography (PET), and single photon emission computed tomography (SPECT). The main or central psychological deficits in those with ADHD have been linked through these studies. By 2002 the researchers in the NIMH Child Psychiatry Branch had studied 152 boys and girls with ADHD, matched with 139 age and gender-matched controls without ADHD. The children were scanned at least twice, some as many as four times over a decade. As a group, the ADHD children showed 3 to 4 per cent smaller brain volumes in all regions—the frontal lobes, temporal gray matter, caudate nucleus, and cerebellum.

This study also showed that the ADHD children who were on medication had a white matter volume that did not differ from that of controls. Those never-medicated patients had an abnormally small volume of white matter. The white matter consists of fibers that establish long-distance connections between brain regions. It normally thickens as a child grows older and the brain matures.

Although this long-term study used MRI to scan the children's brains, the researchers stressed that MRI remains a research tool and cannot be used to diagnose ADHD in any given child. This is true for other neurological methods of evaluating the brain, such as the PET and the SPECT.

Disorders that Sometimes Accompany ADHD

Oppositional defiant disorder: As many as one third to one-half of all children with ADHD—mostly boys—have another condition, known as Oppositional defiant disorder (ODD). These children are often defiant, stubborn, non-compliant, have outbursts of temper, or become belligerent. They argue with adults and refuse to obey.

Conduct disorder: About 20 to 40 percent of ADHD children may eventually develop conduct disorder (CD), a more serious pattern of antisocial behavior. These children frequently lie or steal, fight with or bully others, and are at a real risk of getting into trouble at school or with the police. They violate the basic rights of other people, are aggressive toward people and/or animals, destroy property, break into people's homes, commit thefts, carry or use weapons, or engage in vandalism. These children or teens are at greater risk for substance use experimentation, and later dependence and abuse. They need immediate help.

Anxiety and Depression: Some children with ADHD often have co-occurring anxiety or depression. If the anxiety or depression is recognized and treated, the child will be better able to handle the problems that accompany ADHD. Vice versa, effective treatment of ADHD can have a positive impact on anxiety as the child is better able to master academic tasks.

Bipolar Disorder: There are no accurate statistics on how many children with ADHD also have bipolar disorder. Differentiating between ADHD and bipolar disorder in childhood can be difficult. In its classic form, bipolar disorder is characterized by mood cycling between periods of intense highs and lows. But in children, bipolar often seems to be a rather chronic mood dysregulation with a mixture of elation, depression, and irritability. Furthermore, there are some symptoms that can be present both in ADHD and bipolar disorder, such as a high level of energy and a reduced need for sleep. Of the symptoms differentiating children with ADHD from those with bipolar disorder, elated mood and grandiosity of the bipolar child are distinguishing characteristics.

The Treatment of ADHD

Every family wants to determine what treatment will be most effective for their child. This question needs to be answered by each family in consultation with their health care professional. To help families make this important decision, the National Institute of Mental Health (NIMH) has funded many studies of treatments for ADHD and has conducted the most intensive study ever undertaken for evaluating the treatment of this disorder. This study is known as the Multimodal Treatment Study of Children with Attention Deficit Hyperactivity Disorder (MTA).'[2] The N1MH is now conducting a clinical trial for younger children ages 3 to 5.5 years (Treatment of ADHD in Preschool-Age Children).

The Multimodal Treatment Study of Children with Attention Deficit Hyperactivity Disorder

The MTA study included 579 (95-98 at each of 6 treatment sites) elementary school boys and girls with ADHD, randomly assigning them to one of four treatment programs; (1) medication management alone; (2) behavioral treatment alone; (3) a combination of both; or (4) routine community care.

In each of the study sites, three groups were treated for the first 14 months in a specified protocol and the fourth group was referred for community treatment of the parents' choosing. All of the children were reassessed regularly throughout the study period. An essential part of the program was the cooperation of the schools, including principals and teachers. Both teachers and parents rated the children on hyperactivity, impulsivity, and inattention, and symptoms of anxiety and depression, as well as social skills.

The children in two groups (medication management alone and the combination treatment) were seen monthly for one-half hour at each medication visit. During the treatment visits, the prescribing physician spoke with the parent, met with the child, and sought to determine any concerns that the family might have regarding the medication or the child's ADHD-related difficulties. The physicians, in addition, sought input from the teachers on a monthly basis. The physicians in the medication-only group did not provide behavioral therapy but did advise the parents when necessary concerning any problems the child might have.

In the behavior treatment-only group, families met up to 35 times with a behavior therapist, mostly in group sessions. These therapists also made repeated visits to schools to consult with children's teachers and to supervise a special aide assigned to each child in the group. In addition, children attended a special 8-week summer treatment program where they worked on academic, social, and sports skills, and where intensive behavioral therapy was delivered to assist children in improving their behavior.

Children in the combined therapy group received both treatments, that is, all the same assistance that the medication-only received, as well as all of the behavior therapy treatments.

In routine community care, the children saw the community-treatment doctor of their parents' choice one to two times per year for short periods of time. Also, the community-treatment doctor did not have any interaction with the teachers.

The results of the study indicated that long-term combination treatments and the medication-management alone were superior to intensive behavioral treatment and routine community treatment. And in some areas—anxiety, academic performance, oppositionality, parent-child relations, and social skills—the combined treatment was usually superior. Another advantage of combined treatment was that children could be successfully treated with lower doses of medicine, compared with the medication-only group.

Adjustment Disorders

States of subjective distress and emotional disturbance, usually interfering with social functioning and performance, and arising in the period of adaptation to a significant life change or to the consequences of a stressful life event (including the presence or possibility of serious physical illness). The stressor may have affected the integrity of an individual's social network (through bereavement or separation experiences) or the wider system of social supports and values (migration or refugee status). The stressor may involve only the individual or also his or her group or community.

Individual predisposition or vulnerability plays a greater role in the risk of occurrence and the shaping of the manifestations of adjustment disorders than it does in the other conditions in F43, but is nevertheless assumed that the condition would not have arisen without the stressor. The manifestations vary, and include depressed mood, anxiety, worry (or a mixture of these), a feeling of inability to cope, plan ahead, or continue in the present situation, and some degree of disability in the performance of daily routine. The individual may feel liable to dramatic behaviour or outbursts of violence, but these rarely occur. However, conduct disorders (e.g. aggressive or dissocial behaviour) may be an associated feature, particularly in adolescents. None of the symptoms is of sufficient severity or prominence in its own right to justify a more specific diagnosis. In children, regressive phenomena such as return to bed-wetting, babyish speech, or thumb-sucking are frequently part of the symptom pattern.

Diagnostic Guidelines

Diagnosis depends on a careful evaluation of the relationship between:

(*a*) form, content, and severity of symptoms;

(*b*) previous history and personality; and

(*c*) stressful event, situation, or life crisis.

The presence of this third factor should be clearly established and there should be strong, though perhaps presumptive, evidence that the disorder would not have arisen without it. If the stressor is relatively minor, or if a temporal connection (less than 3 months) cannot be demonstrated, the disorder should be classified elsewhere, according to its presenting features includes:

- culture shock
- grief reaction
- hospitalism in children

It Excludes:

- separation anxiety disorder of childhood

Dyslexia

Although there is no universally recognised definition of dyslexia, the one presented by the World Federation of Neurology has won broad respect: "A disorder manifested by difficulty in learning to read despite conventional instruction, adequate intelligence and socio-cultural opportunity. It is dependent upon fundamental cognitive disabilities which are frequently of constitutional origin."

The Single most important hallmark of dyslexia is underachievement in writing and reading skills. There are a number of characteristics of dyslexia which appear singly but more often in combination:

Characteristics of Dyslexia

- Problems with reading, accuracy, speed, and comprehension
- Repeated spelling errors
- Reversal of orientation of letters, or sequences of letters in words, when read or written: e.g. b-d; was-saw; quite-quiet
- Delayed spoken language
- Errors in letter naming
- Difficulty in learning and remembering printed words
- Cramped or illegible handwriting
- Difficulty in finding the "right" word when speaking
- Slow rate of writing
- Lack of awareness of sounds in words—sound order, rhymes

- Similar problems among relatives
- Uncertainty as to right-or left-handedness
- Confusion about directions in space or time (right and left, up and down, yesterday and tomorrow, days and months)
- Difficulties in mathematics

Fortunately, very few persons exhibit all these signs of the disorder, but they have enough in common to distinguish them as a group with unique educational needs. The problems is not one of intelligence but of a specific difficulty in mastering language.

The dyslexic as a school child recognizes his problem all too well:... "I can think okay. What's wrong with me is just my words. I forget them, and I can't manage them."

"I forget them." He cannot learn and remember whole words by sight so he has trouble with reading in the regular classroom. And he can't. remember letters, so he gets them twisted: "b" for "d", "p" for "q" and so on. Often he cannot call up the words he wants to say: "Oh, you know, that thing you used to write with... "Yesterday—I mean tomorrow—sometime or other."

1.	cat	cat
2.	rUN	run
3.	[illegible]	arm
4.	traN	train
5.	Shot	shout
6.	cVit	correct
7.	SrCl	circle
8.	heViN	heaven
9.	eckt	educate
10.	Mt	material
11.	rcN	ruin
12.	falk	fashion

The spelling performance of a dyslexic child.

"And I can't manage them." The words come out incorrectly:

...or in the wrong order.."please up hurry!" Managing letters in spelling is even harder. He writes "left" for "felt" and "oil" may flipflop into "710". What we call "nuclear" may be "unclear" to him.

He may have trouble with math, which is another language; its numbers, like letters, take a lot of remembering and managing.

He may be clumsy, or he may have beautiful coordination except for handling a pencil. His handwriting may be irregular, slow, cramped and hard to read.

The dyslexic often finds organization—managing his life—difficult. His homework instructions, his sense of direction or time, the sequence of things to do often may get mixed up. It is often discovered that other members of his family, through the generations, have found language hard to master in several ways: reading, writing and especially spelling.

The dyslexics, their parents and teachers should understand that dyslexia is not a "disease" but a product of a special kind of mind. Very often it is a unique and gifted mind if it can be freed to work. The dyslexic is not an impaired person! There have been many famous dyslexics: Einstein, Edison, Leonardo D Vinci, Hans Christian Andersen,

George Patton, Woodrow Wilson, Nelson Rockefeller, to name only a few.

There are well-known people today in medicine, psychology, banking, college teaching, architecture, engineering and sports who are dyslexics. And finally, there are literally thousands of ordinary people who have identified their problem and concentrated on their strengths. These people have mastered the language and become successful men and women, even though they are dyslexics.

Dyslexia is far more widespread than most people imagine. Studies show that as many as 15% of U.S. school children may be dyslexic. This statistic is being supported by preliminary research conducted in Indian Schools. This is more than the combined total of those suffering from epilepsy, cerebral palsy, and mental retardation. Chances are, someone close to you is dyslexic. You may not know it, and neither may he or she.

Part of the burden on many dyslexic youngesters is that they don't always know why they are different. They experience confusion and an inability to learn in the same manner as others. Their difficulties are not always shown in ways that are easily recognizable. All they know is that they are different, that they fail when their friends succeed, and that however hard they try, they cannot live up to the expectations of parents and teachers.

Dyslexia respects no geographical boundaries. It affects children of all races, girls as well as boys. A disproportionate number of dyslexic children wind up as juvenile offenders or as enemies of themselves or society. Dyslexia is more than an "invisible handicap." The implications of the problems are far-reaching and affect both the dyslexic and the society in general.

Our problem is ignorance. We fail to understand the dyslexics problem. We think of them as lazy or stupid. We tell them to try harder and scold them when they fail. Our ignorance becomes a part of their problem. Dyslexia breeds frustration, anxiety and resentment. Without appropriate help, the dyslexic will suffer. Effects of dyslexia can include severe learning and emotional problems, illiteracy and delinquency. With appropriate help. The dyslexic has an excellent chance of coping with his problem. He can go on to bring his intelligence and special talents to the service of society.

Follow up studies of dyslexics who have received appropriate teaching have been greatly exciting and encouraging. Many of the children have mastered their disability, often at great effort, but are now no longer considered "poor risks" for academic and occupational pursuits.

This is just a beginning. All children should receive an education appropriate to their needs. In the case of dyslexia, the concept that they require alternative teaching strategies is only beginning to be acknowledged by many. Educators recognize evident problems of children with retardation, or with physical handicapts. A "hidden disability^ is harder to accept.

Dyslexia is serious and widespread, a national problem on a vast scale. People with dyslexia can be helped but the fact is, that at present, very few of them are receiving the necessary support that they need. The majority are forced to struggle with education, to live with frustration and resentment, and to deny to society the potential of their special gifts and talents.

Dyscalculia

Many students have difficulty learning mathematics for a variety of reasons. Not all of these students have dyscalculia. However, there are some basic areas of mathematical activity in everyday life that may indicate a dyscalculic tendency if persistently difficult and frustrating for a person. Such symptoms manifest as: mathematics anxiety and dyscalculia.

The term *dyscalculia* is derived from new-Latin stems, there being two words or word stems being distinguishable in it The word stem *dys* indicates that a state of dysfunction is involved, the word *calculus*, which comes originally from Greek, denoting in direct translation a stone used for making calculations. The resulting word, *dyscalculia*, means difficulties in performing mathematical calculations of certain types.

In very simple terms, analogous to dyslexia—which is dysfunction in the reception, comprehension, or production of linguistic information, dyscalculia can be defined as the dysfunction in the reception, comprehension, or production of quantitative and spatial information.

What distinguishes dyscalculia from other types of difficulties with math is the fact that particular aspects of mathematical calculations are involved. If a person has difficulties in performing the four basic types of arithmetic operations, for example, this creates problems for the person in regard to higher mathematics as well. The basic difficulties may involve not being able to gain access quickly enough to principles pertaining to arithmetic operations. This can affect not only simple but also more complex mathematical operations, which then require longer to perform. One should note, however, that many persons with dyscalculia can master difficult mathematical tasks but require a considerable time in carrying out the operations. This shows the importance of giving pupils with dyscalculia tasks that are of the right level. If the level is too low, this can be insulting to them and be poorly motivating. It can contribute to the child's giving up, something which my experience suggests to occur rather frequently.

Dyscalculia is a collection of symptoms of learning disability involving the most basic aspect of arithmetical skills. On the surface, these relate to basic concepts such as: telling the time, calculating prices and handling change, and measuring and estimating things such as temperature and speed.

Dyscalculia is an individual's difficulty in conceptualizing numbers, number relationships, outcomes of numerical operations and estimation—what to expect as an outcome of an operation. Dyscalculia manifests in a person as having difficulty:

- Mastering arithmetic facts by the traditional methods of teaching, particularly the methods involving counting.
- Dealing with exchange of money-handling a bank account, giving and receiving change, and tipping.
- Learning abstract concepts of time and direction / schedules, telling and keeping track of time, and the sequence of past and future events.
- Acquiring spatial orientation/space organisation / direction, easily disoriented (including left/right orientation), trouble reading maps, and grappling with mechanical processes.
- Learning musical concepts, following directions in sports that demand sequencing or rules, and keeping track of scores and players during games such as cards and board games.

- Following sequential directions—sequencing (including reading numbers out of sequence, substitutions, reversals, omissions and doing operations backwards), organizing detailed information, remembering specific facts and formulas for completing their mathematical calculations.

Dyscalculia can be quantitative, which is a difficulty in counting and calculating; or qualitative, which is a difficulty in the conceptualizing of mathematics processes and spatial sense; or mixed, which is the inability to integrate quantity and space.

One can speak of at least four types of difficulties in mathematics:

- Acalculia
- Dyscalculia
- Difficulties with mathematics generally
- Pseudo-dyscalculia

The differences between them in terms of the causal factors involved and the difficulties the child experiences mean that the forms of intervention called for differ considerably. Being given mathematical exercises of the wrong sort could make the situation for a child with dyscalculia worse, for example, and giving a child with acalculia conventional mathematical training at all should be avoided, since he/she would scarcely be able to master it. Accurate differential diagnosis is thus important, just as it is in medicine.

Dyscalculia is of a number of different types, each involving a specific type of problem in solving mathematical tasks. It corresponds in mathematics performance to dyslexia in the area of reading. The majority of children and adults with dyscalculia have it in a pure form in which both the ability to read and the ability to understand what is read are unaffected, although about 20–30% with dyscalculia have a mixed form of it characterized by having difficulties both with reading and with math Their often requiring a long time to carry out even simple arithmetic tasks. They count on their fingers until far into the upper grades. Difficulties of this sort are termed automatization difficulties.

Children and adults with dyscalculia tend nevertheless to be of normal intelligence, but often present an uneven picture in their results on intelligence tests. Their problems reflect, not emotional problems but difficulties in connection with certain specific types of thought processes.

Warning Sings

Since math disabilities are varied, the signs that a person may have a difficulty in this area can be just as varied. However, having difficulty learning math skills does not necessarily mean a person has a learning disability. All students learn at different paces, and particularly among young people, it takes time and practice for formal math procedures to make practical sense.

If a person has trouble in any of the areas below, additional help may be beneficial.

Below is a list of signs of dysfunction that teachers frequently notice in pupils who have difficulties with mathematics:

Direct signs

- Symbols, often numeric ones, are written either backwards or in a rotated position.
- Digits that are similar in appearance, such as 6 and 9 or 3 and 8, are confused with each other.
- Failure to take proper note of the distance between digits, so that the numbers 8 and 12 when appearing in succession, for example, are read as 812.
- Difficulties in recognizing and making use of the symbols for the four basic types of arithmetic operations.
- Problems in understanding maps.
- Problems in taking note of objects or symbols when these appear, not singly, but together with other objects or symbols.
- Problems in copying numbers, digits or geometric drawings or figures one is shown, or in reproducing them from memory.

- Problems in understanding matters of weight, direction, space or time.
- Failure to write down or to read off the correct value of a number that consists of two or more digits.
- Problems in understanding the meaning of the symbols for the four basic types of arithmetic operations, such as failure to recall what use of a minus-sign involves.
- Problems in shifting from one type of arithmetic operation to another.
- Problems in understanding differences in size between different numbers, such as in realizing or remembering that 93 is 4 more than 89.
- Problems in grasping the position of a number relative to other numbers, such as in being able to say what number immediately precedes or immediately follows 19.
- Having a 'bad memory' for numeric facts.
- Having difficulties in carrying out computations in one's head
- Problems in associating words with visual symbols or vice versa, or in reciting the names of things.
- Inability to discover a satisfactory way of solving a particular problem.
- Problems in shifting from a concrete to an abstract level (in children 10-11 yrs. old or older).
- Problems in remembering what steps to follow in carrying out particular arithmetic or mathematical calculations.
- Difficulties in understanding, and in answering either orally or in writing, problems presented to one in either verbal or visual terms.
- Problems in carrying out practical, everyday tasks.
- Problems in dealing with geometric figures.
- Problems in judging what can be regarded as reasonable.
- Problems in planning generally or in following a correct strategy in solving a mathematical problem.

- Difficulties in maintaining the overall picture of a given problem, getting lost in details.
- Problems in dealing with various mathematical units.
- Good at speaking, reading, and writing, but slow to develop counting and math problem-solving skills.
- Good memory for printed words, but difficulty reading numbers, or recalling numbers in sequence.
- Good with general math concepts, but frustrated when specific computation and organization skills need to be used.
- Trouble with the concept of time-chronically late, difficulty remembering schedules, trouble with approximating how long something will take.
- Poor sense of direction, easily disoriented and easily confused by changes in routine.
- Poor long term memory of concepts—can do math functions one day, but is unable to repeat them the next day.
- Poor mental math ability—trouble estimating grocery costs or counting days until vacation.
- Difficulty playing strategy games like chess, bridge or role-playing video games.
- Difficulty keeping score when playing board and card games.

Indirect signs

- Difficulties in connection with abstract concepts such as those of time and movement.
- Difficulties with such concepts as present and future; difficulties in changing the time perspective.
- Difficulties in planning tasks or activities.
- Difficulties in assessing tasks or activities that have been carried out.
- Weaknesses in spatial orientation or in the ability to solve spatial problems, as shown by having a limited sense of

direction or having difficulties in adjusting to new surroundings.

- Limitations in working memory or in short-term memory.
- Fluctuations in attentiveness and difficulties in concentrating.
- Weaknesses in long-term memory as shown by the individual's having problems in recalling information that has been learned, such as that of a numeric character."
- Limited memory for names or faces.
- Lack of confidence.
- Dislike of mathematics or lack of interest in carrying out mathematical computations.
- Difficulties in managing money.
- Difficulties in reading the time off the hands of a clock or a watch.
- Difficulties in processing information presented rapidly and also in distinguishing what is important.
- Problems in the coordination of fine movements and the tendency in writing for letters to be reversed, rotated, unexpectedly large or poorly formed.
- Difficulties in parlour games that involve mathematical computations of some sort or the question of whose turn is next.
- Difficulties in learning about geography.
- Problems of the sort the child has being found in the family among close relatives.

A typical picture is that of a competent child that rather unexpectedly shows signs of serious difficulties of one or more of the sorts just described.

It is rather frequent that children with dyscalculia have had, or have, difficulties in learning to read a clock, its taking a long time for them to learn it.

For anyone who has learned to read a clock, doing so usually appears simple. Yet reading a clock calls for many different functions. The first to be done is to note the position of the hands. Thereafter one needs to figure out in one's head what time it is. It cannot be read off the clock that it is twenty to two in the afternoon or that it is five after nine in the morning.

Reading the time off a clock with hands also requires that one have good visual perception, a good working memory and an adequate linguistic understanding of time concepts.

For many children with dyscalculia, reading the time off a clock with hands can be considerably more difficult than reading it off a digital clock, since the latter involves simply reading off the digits from left to right. Reading off 01.40 is easy enough. Certain difficulties remain, nevertheless, since there is no indication on the clock that this means twenty to two. That is a transformation one needs to do oneself.

Difficulties in reading clocks are not the only problems other than those of math itself with which children with dyscalculia are faced while growing up. Many of them are also poor in time perception. This can be reflected in their having difficulties in estimating the time which an hour or a day represents. This in turn can have a negative effect on their ability to plan and thus on how they get things done generally. Weaknesses in time perception can in part be a matter of having difficulties in grasping the sequence involved in a particular course of events

How to Recognize Dyscalculia?

A typical picture is that of a competent child that rather unexpectedly shows signs of serious difficulties of one or more of the sorts just described.

It is rather frequent that children with dyscalculia have had, or have, difficulties in learning to read a clock, its taking a long time for them to learn it.

For anyone who has learned to read a clock, doing so usually appears simple. Yet reading a clock calls for many different functions. The first to be done is to note the position of the hands. Thereafter one needs to figure out in one's head what time it is. It cannot be read off the clock that it is *twenty to two* in the afternoon or that it is *five after nine* in the morning.

Reading the time off a clock with hands also requires that one have good visual perception, a good working memory and an adequate linguistic understanding of time concepts.

For many children with dyscalculia, reading the time off a clock with hands can be considerably more difficult than reading it off a digital clock, since the latter involves simply reading off the digits from left to right. Reading off *01.40* is easy enough. Certain difficulties remain, nevertheless, since there is no indication on the clock that this means *twenty to two.* That is a transformation one needs to do oneself.

Difficulties in reading clocks are not the only problems other than those of math itself with which children with dyscalculia are faced while growing up. Many of them are also poor in time perception. This can be reflected in their having difficulties in estimating the time which an hour or a day represents. This in turn can have a negative effect on their ability to plan and thus on how they get things done generally. Weaknesses in time perception can in part be a matter of having difficulties in grasping the sequence involved in a particular course of events

We do not have any inborn, innate feeling for time. Rather, this is developed and maintained through constant practice. The latter allows us to gradually learn how much we will succeed in doing in the course of an hour, for example. Learning about such time-related matters is never complete, however, as our basic knowledge of how to cycle, swim or wash dishes is. The continual practice we get enables our *time-planning ability* to develop and be maintained.

Difficulties in time perception lead to serious problems when a child needs to plan his/her activities, such as studying or doing homework. Such problems are particularly marked when school-related tasks are to be done not for the following day but by some time say two weeks ahead. One should nevertheless emphasize that many pupils overestimate the time they have available for various tasks without this necessarily meaning that they suffer from dyscalculia. Children with dyscalculia are not only prone to problems of time perception, but also have difficulties in imagining in what order various tasks should be carried out.

Everyday problems for the child with dyscalculia manifest themselves, however, not only in the planning of homework and the like, but also in planning generally, even in such concrete situations as the child's planning how to clean and cleaning his/her own room. Many children with dyscalculia have a need of a clear structure in their everyday life, although few of them, unfortunately, actively seek help in this respect.

Dyscalculia Symptoms

- Normal or accelerated language acquisition: verbal, reading, writing 'Poetic ability'. Good visual memory for the printed word. Good in the areas of science (until a level requiring higher math skills is reached), geometry (figures with logic not formulas), and creative arts.
- Difficulty with the abstract concepts of time and #direction. Inability to recall schedules, and sequences of past or future events. Unable to keep track of time. May be chronically late.
- Mistaken recollection of names. Poor name/face retrieval. Substitute names beginning with same letter.
- Inconsistent results in addition, subtraction, multiplication and division. Poor mental math ability. Poor with money and credit. Cannot do financial planning or budgeting. Checkbooks not balanced. Short term, not long term financial thinking. Fails to see big financial picture. May have fear of money and cash transactions. May be unable to mentally figure change due back, the amounts to pay for tips, taxes, etc.

- When writing, reading and recalling numbers, these common mistakes are made: number additions, substitutions, transpositions, omissions, and reversals.
- Inability to grasp and remember math concepts, rules, formulas, sequence (order of operations), and basic addition, subtraction, multiplication and division facts. Poor long term memory (retention & retrieval) of concept mastery— may be able to perform math operations one day, but draw a blank the next! May be able to do book work but fails all tests and quizzes.
- May be unable to comprehend or "picture" mechanical processes. Lack "big picture/ whole picture" thinking. Poor ability to "visualize or picture" the location of the numbers on the face of a clock, the geographical locations of states, countries, oceans, streets, etc.
- Poor memory for the "layout" of things. Gets lost or disoriented easily. May have a poor sense of direction, loose things often, and seem absent minded. (Remember the absent minded professor?)
- May have poor athletic coordination, difficulty keeping up with rapidly changing physical directions like in aerobic, dance, and exercise classes. Difficulty remembering dance step sequences, rules for playing sports.
- May have difficulty grasping concepts of formal music education. Difficulty sight—reading music, learning fingering to play an instrument, etc.
- Difficulty keeping score during games, or difficulty remembering how to keep score in games, like bowling, etc. Often looses track of whose turn it is during games, like cards and board games. Limited strategic planning ability for games, like chess.

How does Dyscalculia Develop?

Schools have supported children who experience difficulties with mathematics, but dyscalculia has only recently been identified as a distinct condition for children and adults. It means that there are many adults and children who have never had their difficulties with mathematics formally identified. Furthermore, while there is currently a great deal of interest, little is known about the causes of dyscalculia. It is a complex phenomenon and may have several underlying causes.

Our work at Cambridge College in America with children and adults with learning problems in mathematics suggests that there seem to be several factors that may be implicated as the causes of mathematics learning problems:

- Cognitive factors.
- Inadequate and poor teaching-mismatch between the mathematics learning personality of a student and teaching style.
- Lack of prerequisite skills for mathematics learning.
- Delay in the development of mathematics language—vocabulary, syntax, and translation ability—from mathematics to English and English to mathematics.
- Inadequate mastery at levels of knowing: movement from intuitive to concrete, concrete to representational, representational to abstract, abstract to applications, and from applications to communication.

In all cases, it seems, the prerequisite skills for mathematics learning are affected. These prerequisite skills include: following sequential directions, spatial orientation/space organization, pattern recognition, visualization, estimation, inductive and deductive thinking. These prerequisite skills act as "anchors" for mathematics ideas. The degree to which these prerequisite skills are not developed or affected varies from learner to learner.

Incidence of Dyscalculia?

Since people are just becoming aware of this condition, it is hard to quantify exactly how many people have dyscalculia. Although many people experience difficulty or disability in mathematics, recent studies show that approximately 4% of students show classical symptoms of dyscalculia. They may have normal abilities in other areas and appropriate or higher cognitive development. Each class may have one or two such students.

A link between dyslexia and dyscalculia hasn't been proved. The International Dyslexia Association has suggested that 60% of dyslexics have some difficulty with numbers or number relationships. Of the 40% of dyslexics who don't have mathematics difficulties, about 11% excelled in mathematics. The remaining 29% have the same mathematical abilities as those who don't have learning difficulties.

Since some of the same prerequisite skills are involved in both language acquisition and mathematics—at least in the early learning levels—the coincidence of dyslexia and dyscalculia is not uncommon. Our observations show that about 40% of dyslexics also exhibit some symptoms of dyscalculia. However, the group of dyscalculic children/adults, like the group of dyslexics, is not a homogeneous one. Most people with dyscalculia don't necessarily suffer from any other learning difficulty. Indeed, they may well excel in non-mathematical areas.

Is Dyscalculia Widely Understood?

All mathematics teachers have encountered children with mathematics learning difficulties and mathematics anxiety. Most of these teachers have some awareness of the nature of learning disabilities/problems in mathematics. However, few teachers are aware of the causes of these problems—learning disabilities, mathematics anxiety, and dyscalculia. In fact, very few of them are able to recognize and deal with the problems of dyscalculics.

American Academies of Neurology and Paediatrics have identified dyscalculia as one of the neurological conditions with a cluster of syndromes associated with it. Similarly, in 2001, as part of the national Numeracy Strategy, the government published guidance for teachers to help them support dyscalculic pupils. Dyscalculia is likely to be a more familiar condition to people who specialize in learning difficulties such as special needs coordinators and educational psychologists. In the U.S., many school psychologists, neurologists and neuro-psychologists have begun to diagnose this as a condition.

How is Dyscalculia is Identified?

When a teacher or trained professional evaluates a student for learning disabilities in math, the student is interviewed about a full range of math-related skills and behaviors. Pencil and paper math tests are often used, but an evaluation needs to accomplish more. It is meant to reveal how a person understands and uses numbers and math concepts to solve advanced-level, as well as everyday, problems. The evaluation compares a person's expected and actual levels of skill and understanding while noting the person's specific strengths and weaknesses. Below are some of the areas that may be address:

- Ability with basic math skills like counting, adding, subtracting, multiplying and dividing.
- Ability to predict appropriate procedures based on understanding patterns—knowing when to add, subtract, multiply, divide or do more advanced computations.
- Ability to organize objects in a logical way.
- Ability to measure-telling time, using money.
- Ability to estimate number quantities.
- Ability to self-check work and find alternate ways to solve problems.

What are the Effects of Dyscalculia?

Since disabilities involving math can be so different, the effects they have on a person's development can be just as different. For instance, a person who has trouble processing language will face different challenges in math than a person who has difficulty with visual-spatial relationships. Another person with trouble remembering facts and keeping a sequence of steps in order will have yet a different set of math-related challenges to overcome.

Early Childhood

Building a solid foundation in math involves many different skills. Young children with learning disabilities can have difficulty learning the meaning of numbers (number sense), trouble with tasks like sorting objects by shape, size or color; recognizing groups and patterns; and comparing and contrasting using concepts like smaller/bigger or taller/shorter. Learning to count, recognizing numbers and matching numbers with amounts can also be difficult for these children.

School-Age Children

As math learning continues, school-age children with language processing disabilities may have difficulty solving basic math problems using addition, subtraction, multiplication and division. They struggle to remember and retain basic math facts (i.e. times tables), and have trouble figuring out how to apply their knowledge and skills to solve math problems.

Difficulties may also arise because of weakness in visual-spatial skills, where a person may understand the needed math facts, but have difficulty putting them down on paper in an organized way. Visual-spatial difficulties can also make understanding what is written on a board or in a textbook challenging.

Teenagers and Adults

If basic math facts are not mastered, many teenagers and adults with dyscalculia may have difficulty moving on to more advanced math applications. Language processing disabilities can make it hard for a person to get a grasp of the vocabulary of math. Without the proper vocabulary and a clear understanding of what the words represent, it is difficult to build on math knowledge.

Success in more advanced math procedures requires that a person be able to follow multi-step procedures. For individuals with learning disabilities, it may be hard to visualize patterns, different parts of a math problem or identify critical information needed to solve equations and more complex problems.

Strategies to Deal with Dyscalculia

Dyscalculia is a special need, and requires diagnosis, support and special methods of teaching. The support should give the learners an understanding of their condition, and equip them with coping and learning strategies that they can use in the classroom and in their day-to-day encounters with quantity and space. Since this is a heterogeneous group no general or single intervention can be recommended.

Dyscalculic learners lack an intuitive grasp of numbers and have problems learning number facts and procedures by the usual methods of teaching. Even when these learners produce a correct answer or use a correct method, they may do so mechanically and without confidence; they are anxious about it.

One objective of remedial instruction should be to improve learners' self-esteem by giving them real-life exposure to mathematics as a part of everyday life: ingredients needed in baking a cake, checking the change after purchasing something, or making estimations.

The milestone concepts for learning mathematics are: understanding number, place value, fractions, integers, spatial sense and variability. Because a person's mathematics difficulties generally originate from some dysfunction in one of these milestone concepts, one should begin instruction in these areas systematically.

Individuals with dyscalculia need help in organizing and processing information related to quantity and space. Since mathematics is a form of language, one should spend time on its vocabulary, syntax and translation—from mathematics to English and from English to mathematics.

These individuals can benefit from tutoring that can accomplish three objectives. First, to help them make-up the missing arithmetic concepts. Second, to help them connect these to their current mathematical needs. And, third, to help them develop the prerequisite skills for mathematics learning.

Effective teaching combines direct instruction (teacher-directed tasks, discussion, and concrete models) with strategy instruction (teaching ways to learn, such as memorization techniques for arithmetic facts, study skills and metacognition-learners identify strategies that help them to learn). Such teaching include:

- Sequencing and task-analysis (breaking down the task into parts and then synthesizing the parts into a whole, providing step-by-step prompts).
- Repetition and practice (automatizing arithmetic facts, daily testing, sequenced review).
- Socratic questioning and responses (structured questioning where teacher asks process or content questions to scaffold learning).
- Control of task difficulty (the teacher provides necessary assistance or tasks sequenced from easy to difficult).
- Use of technology.
- Teacher-modeled problem solving.
- Strategy cues (reminders to use strategies).

Helping a student identify his/her strengths and weaknesses is the first step to getting help. Following identification, parents, teachers and other educators can work together to establish strategies that will help the student learn math more effectively. Help outside the classroom lets a student and tutor focus specifically on the difficulties that student is having, taking pressure off moving to new topics too quickly. Repeated reinforcement and specific practice of straightforward ideas can make understanding easier. Other strategies for inside and outside the classroom include Every remedial/instructional session should have the following components:

- Developing the prerequisite and support skills.

- Learning arithmetic facts orally.
- Visualizing problems and information.
- Verbalizing and recording procedures and estimation.
- Helping the child form problems relating to the given concept.
- Counting forward beginning with a given number e.g. begin with 53 and count forward by two's, by three's, etc.
- Counting backwards beginning with a given number, e.g., begin with 97 and count backward, by 1's, 2's, 5's, and 10's.
- Showing patterns of number facts, e.g., $4 + 4 = 8$, then $4 + 5 = 9$; $8 + 10 = 18$, then $18 + 10 = 28$, $78 + 10 = 88$, etc.
- Use graph paper for students who have difficulty organizing ideas on paper.
- Practice estimating as a way to begin solving math problems.
- Introduce new skills beginning with concrete examples and later moving to more abstract applications.
- For language difficulties, explain ideas and problems clearly and encourage students to ask questions as they work.
- Provide a place to work with few distractions and have pencils, erasers and other tools on hand as needed.

Help students become aware of their strengths and weaknesses. Understanding how a person learns best is a big step in achieving academic success and confidence.

The three components of a mathematical idea: linguistic, conceptual and procedural should be carefully included in all mathematical instruction. Therefore, before the student performs any arithmetic operations he should be asked about the language, procedure, and the conceptual model of the problem first. When the student has completed the problem, they should be asked whether they know any other problems that are similar to the one just completed.

Dipression

Large-scale research studies have reported that up to 3 percent of children and up to 8 percent of adolescents in the U.S. suffer from depression, a serious mental disorder that adversely affects mood, energy, interest, sleep, appetite, and overall functioning. In contrast to normal emotional experiences of sadness or passing mood states, the symptoms of depression are extreme and persistent and can interfere significantly with the ability to function at home or at school. There is evidence that depression emerging early in life often recurs and continues into adulthood, and that early onset depression may predict more severe illness in adult life. Diagnosing and treating children and adolescents with depression is critical in preventing impairment in academic, social, emotional, and behavioural functioning and to allow children to live up to their full potential.

Depression in children and adolescents is associated with an increased risk of suicidal behaviours. Since 1964, the suicide rate among adolescents and young adults has doubled. In 1996, the most recent year for which statistics are available, suicide was the 3rd leading cause of death in 15 to 24 year olds and the 4th leading cause among 10 to 14 year olds.

Antidepressant medications are prescribed to treat children and adolescents with depression. Recent studies indicate that certain selective serotonin reuptake inhibitors (SSRIs) are safe and efficacious treatments for depression in young people. However, care must be used in prescribing and monitoring all medication. Special forms of psychotherapy, such as cognitive-behavioural therapy, have proved effective for adolescents with depression, and current studies are evaluating the effectiveness of individual, family, and group therapies for young people. A current multi-site study of adolescents who are depressed is evaluating the comparative effectiveness of medication, psychosocial, or combined treatments.

Anxiety

Anxiety disorders are the most common mental health problems that occur in children and adolescents. According to one large-scale study of 9 to 17 year olds, entitled Methods for the Epidemiology of Child and Adolescent Mental Disorders (MECA), as many as 13 percent of young people had an anxiety disorder in a year.

Generalized Anxiety Disorder: symptoms include exaggerated worry and tension over everyday events.

Obsessive Compulsive Disorder (*OCD*): characterized by intrusive, unwanted, repetitive thoughts and rituals performed out of a feeling of urgent need; at least one-third of adult cases begins in childhood.

Panic Disorder: characterized by feelings of extreme fear and dread that strike unexpectedly and repeatedly for no apparent reason, often accompanied by intense physical symptoms, such as chest pain, pounding heart, shortness of breath, dizziness, or abdominal distress.

Post Traumatic Stress Disorder (*PTSD*): a condition that can occur after exposure to a terrifying event, most often characterized by the repeated re-experience of the ordeal in the form of frightening, intrusive memories, and brings on hypervigilance and deadening of normal emotions.

Phobias: *social phobia*, extreme fear of embarrassment or being scrutinized; *specific phobia*, excessive fear of an object or situation, such as dogs, heights, loud sounds, flying, costumed characters, enclosed spaces, etc.

Other disorders: *separation anxiety*, excessive anxiety concerning separation from the home or from those to whom the person is most attached; and *selective mutism*, persistent failure to speak in specific social situations.

Various forms of psychotherapy, including cognitive-behavioural therapy and family therapy, as well as certain medications, particularly selective serotonin reuptake inhibitors (SSRIs), are used to treat anxiety disorders in children and adolescents. Research on the safety and efficacy of these treatments is ongoing.

Eating Disorders

Eating disorders are most common among adolescent and young women. In addition to causing various physical health problems, eating disorders are associated with illnesses such as depression, substance abuse, and anxiety disorders. Among adolescent and young adult women in the U.S., it is estimated that between 0.5 and 1.0 percent suffer from anorexia nervosa, 1 to 3 percent have bulimia nervosa, and 0.7 to 4 percent experience binge-eating disorder. There are limited data concerning the prevalence in males.

Similar to other mental disorders, such as obsessive-compulsive disorder and depression, patients with eating disorders have little control over their symptoms, and suffer from often serious and sometimes life-threatening illnesses that require medical and psychiatric attention. Because of their complexity, eating disorders call for a comprehensive treatment plan involving medical care and monitoring, psychotherapy, nutritional counseling, and medication management. Studies are investigating the causes of eating disorders and effectiveness of treatments.

Manic Depressive Illness

Manic-depressive illness causes extreme shifts in mood, energy, and functioning. Overly energized, disruptive, and reckless periods alternate with periods of sadness, withdrawal, hopelessness, and other depressive symptoms. Unlike normal mood states of happiness and sadness, symptoms of manic-depressive illness can interfere with school performance, family relationships, peer interactions, and other everyday activities. Although manic-depressive illness typically emerges in late adolescence or early adulthood, there is increasing evidence that the disorder also can begin in childhood. According to one study, one percent of adolescents ages 14-18 were found to have met criteria for manic-depressive illness or cyclothymia, a milder form of the illness, in their lifetime.

Evidence suggests that manic-depressive illness beginning in childhood or early adolescence may be a different, possibly more severe form of the disorder than older adolescent and adult-onset manic-depressive illness. When the illness begins before or soon after puberty, it is often characterized by a continuous, rapid-cycling, and mixed symptom state that may co-occur with ADHD or other behavioural disorders, or may have features of these disorders as initial symptoms. In contrast, later onset manic-depressive illness appears to begin suddenly, often with a manic episode, and to have a more episodic pattern with relatively stable periods between episodes.

Various treatments known to be effective in adults with manic-depressive illness also may help relieve the symptoms in young people. The essential treatment for this disorder is the use of appropriate doses of mood stabilizing medications. The most typical is lithium, known to be very effective in adults for controlling mania and preventing recurrences of manic and depressive episodes. Research on the effectiveness of this and other medications in children and adolescents with manic-depressive illness is ongoing. In addition, studies are investigating various forms of psychotherapy to complement medication treatment for this illness in young people.

Autism and Other Pervasive Developmental Disorders

Autism and other pervasive developmental disorders are brain disorders that occurs in as many as 2 in 1,000 Americans. They typically affect the ability to communicate, form relationships with others, and respond appropriately to the outside world. The signs of autism usually develop by 3 years of age. The symptoms and deficits associated with autism may vary among people with the disorder. While some individuals with autism function at a relatively high level, with speech and intelligence intact, others are developmentally delayed, mute, or have serious language difficulty.

Research has made it possible to identify earlier those children who show signs of developing autism and thus initiate early intervention. Both psychosocial and pharmacological interventions can improve the behavioural and cognitive functioning of children with autism. Studies to evaluate medications such as risperidone and valproate are investigating their effects on cognition, behaviour, and development, as well as their safety and efficacy. Emerging evidence is suggesting that certain genetic factors may confer susceptibility to the disorder and studies are underway to better understand this process. The prospect of acquiring basic biologic knowledge about autism holds hope for the development of future therapies.

Schizophrenia

Schizophrenia is a chronic, severe, and disabling brain disorder that affects about 1 percent of the population during their lifetime. Symptoms include hallucinations, delusions, disordered thinking, and social withdrawal. Schizophrenia appears to be extremely rare in children; more typically, the illness emerges in late adolescence or early adulthood. However, research studies are revealing that various cognitive and social impairments may be evident early in children who later develop schizophrenia. These and other findings may lead to the development of preventive interventions for children.

Only in this decade have researchers begun to make significant headway in understanding the origins of schizophrenia. In the emerging picture, genetic factors, which confer susceptibility to schizophrenia, appear to combine with other factors early in life to interfere with normal brain development. These developmental disturbances eventually appear as symptoms of schizophrenia many years later, typically during adolescence or young adulthood. A number of new, effective medications for schizophrenia have been introduced during the past decade.

Tourette's Syndrome

Tourette's Syndrome (TS) is characterized by repeated, involuntary movements and uncontrollable vocal sounds, known as tics. Although the basic cause of TS is unknown, current research suggests there is a genetic abnormality affecting certain neurotransmitters in the brain, and that varying environmental factors, possibly including infections, modifies the clinical expression of the disorder. Symptoms of TS are seen in association with some other neurological disorders, particularly OCD. Researchers are investigating the neurological similarities between OCD and TS to determine whether a genetic relationship exists.

In most cases, Tourette's Syndrome is not disabling, symptoms don't impair patients, development proceeds normally, and there is no need for treatment. However, some effective medications are available in the rare instances when symptoms interfere with functioning. Children with TS can generally function well at home and in the regular classroom. If they have an accompanying learning disability or other disorder, such as ADHD or OCD, they may require tutoring, special classes, psychotherapy, or medication.

7 Identification and Assessment

Identification and assessment has become an arena of battle. Teachers in classrooms are coping with more and more children with special needs and are overwhelmed because they perceive lack of adequate support. Different parts of the curriculum battle for resources, particularly at secondary level to keep up with demands of government led initiatives. Staff battle staff for scarce resources as administrators assign special education resources to teach subjects. Teachers battle principals, principals battle school district personnel, school district personnel battle department and other professionals and departments battle other departments for resources. At every turn an argument has to be made to justify the resources required and not necessarily those with the best evidence wins, but those who cause more fuss, or plea with a stronger emotional message, or who are in position of power to make the decision.

Identification

Some children identify themselves by being conspicuous in the school environment by either:

- not being able to do the work required; or
- will not do the work required.

What teachers' do and the framework in which they do it, are significant when considering why certain children are identified as having a special need. This is sometimes referred to as the label of convenience since the situation is deemed bad enough for someone else to do something about. There is a need for some standard related to such notions as the level of stress generated by the child who varies from the norm of the ideal students. What is the current norm? What is regular? Is ideal becoming the norm as in the Department saying "Ideally all students will graduate from high school having gone through a rigorous curriculum of mathematics, language, and science with an excellent level of achievement?"

Identification is a complex interaction of social effects and the people involved. The criteria used by teachers may relate to individual perspectives not objective characteristics of the child. Identification in the system usually means the child cannot cope in the classroom. The work or the demands within the classroom are beyond the child's capabilities. This does not only mean children with learning difficulties but also those who place teachers under stress for other reasons. Students who are low achievers, non-readers or have learning difficulties are disabled in the classroom when the work they are asked to do does not match their needs.

Early identification of difficulties is important to begin ruling out the obvious impairments of vision, hearing, orthopedic, health, neurological, developmental, or other medical impairments that my affect learning. Locating students who are at risk academically, socially, cognitively, physically, or due to delay in language development is prerequisite to early intervention and/or more in depth assessment.

Some children will come to school with special educational needs already identified and with a history of interventions. In many instances, however, the special need is first realized when the child comes to school. Many of these needs fall within a learning difficulty without known cause. That is, it is not visible to the naked eye. In order to prevent labels from driving the student's programme or placement, it is necessary to develop a profile of needed supports that would individually define the child's educational programme. In this case, the programme is not equivalent to placement. It is supportive of inclusion with peers as a primary means of reducing functional disability and the kinds of support required to advance the success of that inclusion. It is the combined responsibility of school personnel, other professionals, and parents to gather the information and document any concerns.

Many learning needs evolve from factors which are environmental in nature. These factors include what teachers do, how they make decisions about learning, their attitudes, and their classroom management approaches. These ideas challenge us to examine the role that our education system plays in the creation and remediation of certain learning needs.

The context for identification and assessment involves three key components. These are curriculum, environment, and the context at hand. Relevant environmental factors and the impact that teaching strategies have on student learning are extremely important. Identification and assessment provides a backdrop for making necessary adjustments to the instruction, the environment, and the learning context. These are the variables which individual teachers can control. When these variables are not controlled, an outcome is increased referral for assessment services.

Only those learning needs that arise from multiple sources including factors related to disabilities, disorders, and special abilities should fall within the realm of special. How teachers respond to learning needs, the decisions they make, and the attitudes they hold. all impact on what is a special need. Differentiation must become a normal part of lesson planning, with naturally supported learning and with students needing to support each other's learning more. In other words, differentiated instruction not differentiated curriculum.

Teachers often face a professional dilemma. They fear compromising on academics because of need to face the difficulties that students present. The reform movement for raising standards has no clear idea of what this means in the practical terms for schools. It is usually talked about through structures like new curriculum and requirements for graduation. It seldom gets talked about in reference to how children learn and are motivated to learn, because this is often dismissed as irrelevant in the drive for standards. In schools the questions asked are more related to medical, emotional, physiological, psychological, and social than to how the child is being taught, what approaches and materials are used, what is the classroom organization like, and what attitudes and emphases prevail in the classroom.

Many children may exhibit a variety of needs relative to learning and the learning environment. However, some students exhibit significant difficulties that require a level of response beyond the differentiation in classrooms. The behavioural dimension of schooling impacts directly on the pedagogical dimension. What a student brings to the learning environments is probably more important to that student than the learning environment itself. Often, it is easier to change the learning environment than to have the students' needs conform to a particular environment. The behavioural functioning of students with disabilities and special abilities impacts on the learning function. As such, the whole school community must share responsibility and respond accordingly.

In conclusion, identification is an attempt to define a problem. It involve such things as observations, interventions, contacts with parents, counselors and others. This usually takes place in the context of the curriculum and instructional environment. When the problem cannot be solved in this context, it is usually referred for a more comprehensive assessment for further clarification and obtain more specific information for educational programming.

Identifying Exceptional Students

How can a teacher determine if a child is gifted? When establishing an identification procedure, teachers and administrators must be sensitive to factors which may inhibit student identification:

- language,
- culture,
- gender,
- physical ability,
- learning or sensory disabilities, and
- personality style.

Some students jump out as highly exceptional and capable learners. They catch our attention with exceptional responses to classroom activities. Others may provide a mixed picture, demonstrating strengths in some areas, but average or below average functioning in others. The question is not whether to enhance the programme for these students, but how to enhance the programme.

Some students have exceptional potential that is masked by individual characteristics or underachievement. Exceptional potential can be missed when the learning environment does not offer the student an opportunity to demonstrate or develop a talent. Establishing a systematic process of identification will ensure that most, if not all, gifted students are identified.

Identification of strengths and talents should be ongoing and should involve using multiple criteria. Several of the following sources of information should be used as part of the identification process:

- Formal test results including indicators of cognitive ability, achievement, aptitude and creativity.
- Teacher observations including anecdotal records, checklists and inventories.
- Records of student achievement including assignments,

portfolios, grades and outstanding talents and accomplishments.

In addition, the following may contribute to a deeper understanding of individual student strengths:

- Nominations by educators, parents, peers and self.
- Interviews of parents and students.

Early Identification for Children with Special Needs

You may be the first to notice that a child in your child care setting has special needs. Perhaps no one has realized that a problem exists or perhaps parents deny that their child has a problem. The family physician may have told the parents that the child will outgrow it. Yet parents need to know if you think their child has special needs. However, it is ultimately the parent's decision to seek help.

Following 10 steps can lead to securing help for the child, the family and child care providers—everyone on the team.

Step 1. Observation

Observe the child at different times of the day. Document your observations without interpretation. Provide clear evidence of the child's difficulties and always include the child's strengths. Be concrete.

For example: In morning circle, child imitated hand and body gestures to songs. When story was read, got up from circle three times; teacher had to bring child back to the group.

Step 2. Strengths and Needs

Develop a list of the child's strengths and needs.

For example: Strengths—enjoys the programme; likes water play; plays with cars. Needs—unable to verbally communicate, grabs toys from other children.

Step 3. Consultation

Share observations of the child with a supervisor. Decide on the best overall approach to help the child and family.

For example: Assign one person to spend more time with the child to build a positive relationship. That person should play a key role in communicating with the family.

Step 4. Building Rapport

Develop relationship with the child's parents. Ask about the child at home: favourite toys, communication skills, response to routines. This valuable information can help you better understand the child. Often the parent has the same concerns about their child and is waiting for someone to validate and assist them in accessing help.

Step 5. Meeting with the Family

Arrange a meeting with the child's family. Be specific: "I'd like to set up a time to talk with you about helping Johnny with his speech." During the meeting, share specific examples of your observations, noting both the child's strengths and needs. Never diagnose or label the child. Put your feedback in the context of the child's ability to manage in a group setting. Come prepared with information about specialized services available to help the child and family.

Step 6. Patience

Allow the parent time to consider their options and make an informed decision. If the parent agrees to involve additional services to help their child, have the parent sign a consent form so you can make a referral to the appropriate service. If a parent chooses not to pursue the issue further, continue maintaining communication with the parent. Gaining a parent's trust takes time. Parents' concerns can emerge gradually. Invite parents into the programme to observe and discuss their child's progress.

Step 7. Support Plan

Make a plan to support the child in your programme using the expertise of your team. Set one or two specific goals that both teachers and parents can work on. Make goals achievable. Make a date for the team to review the child's progress. Set the child and team up for success. Teach the child skills that he needs.

For example: To facilitate play skills, turn taking and appropriate language, have one teacher sit with the child with special needs and another child from the group.

Step 8. Resources

Involve outside resources to provide support. Your provincial licensing consultant can help identify available services. A resource consultant can visit your programme, assess the child with special needs and assist in developing an individual support plan. An effective consultant facilitates the partnership between the centre, the family and any outside resources needed.

Step 9. Training

Educate staff about the child's special needs through training by appropriate professionals. Circulate articles and/or videos to help staff better understand the child's particular needs.

Step 10. Policies

Ensure that your centre has an inclusion policy that covers ways to access support for the team. This policy should be included and reviewed with parents upon the child's enrollment. Make all community resource information available to all parents.

Suicide and the Exceptional Child

From last couple of years, suicide rates have increased dramatically among young people in the India as well as in U.S. and Canada and other counturies also. Suicide is the third leading cause of death of young people between the ages of 15 and 24 in the U.S.

(National Center for Health Statistics, 1989), and the second leading cause in Canada (Health and Welfare Canada, 1987). Although official suicide rates are much lower for children under 15, suicidal behaviour has been reported even in very young children. It is generally accepted that many suicides are unreported or misreported as accidents or death due to undetermined causes (particularly for young children). It has been estimated that the actual number of suicides may be two to three times greater than official statistics indicate (American Psychiatric Association, 1985).

The presence of a psychiatric disorder—particularly a mood disorder such as depression or bipolar illness, a conduct disorder, or a psychosis—contributes to the likelihood of suicide. Depression often exists in conjunction with other mental disorders or with other long-lasting social or behavioural problems. However, not all students with depression or other psychiatric disorders are suicidal.

Very little information is available regarding the prevalence of depression or suicide in students who receive special education services, although relationships between cognitive deficits and depression and between diminished problem-solving abilities and suicidal behaviour have been noted. Medical problems have also been associated with depression and suicide. Estimates of the prevalence of depression or symptoms of depression among children and youth with learning or behaviour problems tend to be higher than those for the general population (e.g., Forness, 1988). Children with symptoms of depression, particularly gifted children or children who do not also exhibit symptoms of another disorder, may be overlooked in the school referral process for special education services.

Factors Place Students at Risk of Suicide

Researchers have attempted to identify situations, experiences, or characteristics that contribute to the likelihood that a child will complete a suicide. When a child has more than one of these factors, the risk of suicide is increased. In addition to mental illness and behaviour disorders, suicide has been associated with demographic factors, such as being between the ages of 15 and 24, being white or male, or having a history of attempted suicide. Psychosocial conditions, such as parental loss, family disruption, exposure to suicide, unwanted pregnancy, and particularly, having a relative who has committed suicide are additional factors. Certain biological conditions have also been associated with suicide; these include perinatal factors, decreases in levels of serotonin, and decreases in the secretion of growth hormone, among others.

How Can a Student Who is Potentially Suicidal be Recognized?

Suicidal ideas, threats, and attempts often precede a suicide. The most commonly cited warnings of potential suicide include:

(*a*) extreme changes in behaviour,

(*b*) a previous suicide attempt,

(*c*) a suicidal threat or statement, and

(*d*) signs of depression.

Young children who have depression may have physical complaints, be agitated, or hear imaginary voices. Adolescents may have school difficulties, may withdraw from social activities, have negative or antisocial behaviour, or may use alcohol or other drugs. They may display increased emotionality, and their moods may be restless, grouchy, aggressive, or sulky. They may not pay attention to their personal appearance. They may refuse to cooperate in family ventures or want to leave home. They may feel that they are not understood or that they are not approved of, or they may be very sensitive to rejection in love relationships.

Role of Educators

The primary role of all school personnel is to detect the signs of depression and potential suicide, to make immediate referrals to the contact person within the school, to notify parents, to secure assistance from school and community resources, and to assist as members of the support team in follow-up activity after a suicide threat or attempt. Special educators should be aware that many exceptional students, particularly those with emotional or behavioural disorders, may be depressed or potentially suicidal, and also that many depressed or suicidal youngsters are not referred for special education services. Discussions with students should stress the individuals and agencies that are available to help students and the steps they can take in seeking help for themselves, their friends, and their families in case of emergencies.

When a classroom teacher notices changes in a student that may be an indicator of suicidal behaviour, immediate action is crucial. Teachers and other school personnel who detect signs of depression or potential suicide in a student must immediately notify the school contact person, who will in turn notify the parents and other appropriate individuals in the school or community. The student should be kept under close supervision and must not be left alone. It is important to let the student know that adults in the school are concerned about his or her welfare. Students who are depressed or suicidal may misinterpret uncertainty or failure to respond as a lack of caring.

One course of action for students who show signs of depression or potential suicide is referral for special education assessment. A special education teacher can provide a safe, structured, and positive classroom environment and an appropriate, effective educational programme. Classroom behaviour management systems that emphasize support, encouragement, gains, and rewards rather than punishment should be implemented.

School's Responsibilities Regarding Assessment

School assessments should be regarded as additional to, rather than a substitute for, an assessment by a mental health professional. Authorities have often suggested that evaluation for suicide potential should be included in the diagnostic procedure for any child referred for any reason to a physician or psychiatrist. The assessment process provides a means of consulting with parents and other school professionals and an opportunity to assess the risk factors present in the student's life. Alleviation of the risk factors should be goals on the student's IEP. The involvement of the family as part of the school programme for depressed and potentially suicidal youngsters is extremely important.

School psychologists are important members of the IEP team for depressed or suicidal children. Assessment instruments suitable for use by school psychologists who have received specific training are available. Many clinicians feel that a battery of screening and assessment instruments, including a variety of assessment techniques such as interviews, checklists, questionnaires, and inventories is required for an accurate assessment of depression and suicidal risk. The role of the school psychologist may also include crisis intervention and treatment within the school. If these responsibilities are part of the school psychologist's role, they should be included in the job description, and the psychologist should carry liability insurance.

Components of an Effective School Programme

Many school suicide prevention programmes have not been evaluated for efficacy and safety. Researchers have questioned the effectiveness of curricular programmes, and some research suggests that such programmes may actually increase the risk for students who have attempted suicide. They recommended instead that schools concentrate on providing individual assistance to students who are most at risk. Schools should exercise caution in developing a plan for suicide prevention, but a written and approved plan must be developed.

Each school plan should be developed by the district's own committee and should be a team effort by all individuals, groups, and agencies that may be affected by its implementation. A comprehensive programme will include procedures related to all three levels of prevention—for the aftermath of a suicide crisis (tertiary prevention), for dealing with suicide attempts, threats, and ideation, (secondary prevention), and for the enhancement of mental health (primary prevention). The full continuum of special education services—ranging from counseling, special materials, and specialized instruction within the regular school programme to short-and long-term residential placements—is an essential component of the intervention plan. It is advisable to seek legal counsel regarding the plan to address issues of liability. A comprehensive plan would include the following:

- Crisis teams at the school and district levels as well as a community crisis team or network of professionals.
- A contact person, such as the school counselor, who is designated to maintain communication among teachers, students, parents, and community treatment providers.
- Case management.
- Procedures for documenting referrals, notifying parents and working with depressed or suicidal students.
- Policies and procedures that clearly delineate the appropriate steps to follow in the event of suicidal behaviour and the responsibilities of the various school personnel in carrying out the plan.
- Training for teachers and other school personnel.
- Provision of positive information to students about the symptoms of depression and suicidal behaviour, resources available in the school and community, and procedures for referring themselves or others to these services.

Assessment

In its initial phases, assessment is not complex. It usually begins with an awareness or discovery that the student has difficulty in coping with every day matters compared with his or her peers. Assessment is best regarded as a process of involving observations of a student over a period of time and not a short exercise. If the difficulty is pronounced a formal assessment should be carried out. At this stage it gets a little more complex. The assessment may be educationally, psychologically, medically, or socially based and may be across multiple environments in functional terms. Parents and other professionals play key roles in this aspect of assessment and requires clarity of purpose, coordination, collaboration and translating results of assessment into functional terms for the provision of educational and related services.

The purpose of assessment is to determine the most effective instructional interventions for the student and any related support services that are needed. The functional assessment approach whereby a comparison is made with a standard and a discrepancy noted is most useful. The standard serves as the desired behaviour and reflects the level of functioning required for the student to be successful in specific tasks. The two decisions that have to be faced in this context are "what do we call it" and "what are going to do about it." That is, it involves dealing with the issues of assigning a label, assignment to grade level, placement in special programme and what to teach, how to teach and what/how to support through related services. This requires a functional analysis that is based in all areas including those related to the curriculum, environment, and present context. It involves creating a data base through direct observations and records of ongoing performance.

Assessment in special education is designed to find specific answers to specific questions in order to determine the type and level of special educational need. The following is an illustration of these questions:

- Does the student require different or modified curriculum in order to meet the assessed need?
- Does the student require specialized teaching and specialized material supports to access his/her curriculum?
- Does the student require therapeutic support such as speech and language, physical therapy, occupational therapy, and behavioural therapy, in order to function in the school and classroom environment?

- Does student require support with everyday personal care items such as operating equipment, eating, toileting, and mobility?
- Are parents involved as "equal partners" who provide observations and indicate their level of support?
- Are other agencies involved as "equal partners" in determining the level of related services required and in the provision of these services?

Functional assessments based on these, and other pertinent, questions will be helpful in determining the nature of the special need and the level at which that need presents itself. This provides a critical picture for those who are responsible for meeting those needs. It is by no means evident, however, what counts as a special educational need. At what point is a child deemed to have a difficulty in learning or in difficulty learning that is significantly greater than the majority of other children? Should school failure be the basis of a special educational need? At what point do significant difficulties become complex or profound or specific enough to require special education? This is the role of comprehensive assessment.

Comprehensive and functional assessment is the bridge between identification and intervention. It is a continuous, multilevel process in which the student, family, educators, and professionals from other agencies act in unison. Children with special needs cannot wait months for batteries of psycho-educational tests before interventions are attempted. The form of information generated must be useful and usable for programme planning. If strengths and needs are not identified it does not matter how dependable the assessment tool is.

Observation

Observing the student and his or her environment is an important part of any assessment process. Observations in the classroom and in other settings where the student operates can provide valuable information about his or her academic, motor, communication, or social skills; behaviours that contribute to or detract from learning; and overall attitude or demeanor.

Observing the student's environment(s) and his or her behaviour within those environments can identify the factors that are influencing the student. For the information from observations to be useful, the team must first define the purpose for the observation and specify:

1. Who will make the observation;
2. Who or what will be observed;
3. Where the observation will take place (observing a range of situations where the student operates is recommended);
4. When the observation will take place (a number of observations at different times is also important); and
5. How the observations will be recorded.

Observations are a key part of some of the assessment methods that will be discussed later in this section, including curriculum-based assessment, ecological assessment, and task analysis. There are many ways in which to record what is observed; the box below entitled "Common Observational Techniques" lists and briefly describes the more common observational methods.

Common Observational Techniques

Anecdotal Records

The observer describes incidents or behaviours observed in a particular setting in concrete, narrative terms (as opposed to drawing inferences about feelings or motives). This type of record allows insight into cause and effect by detailing what occurred before a behaviour took place, the behaviour itself, and consequences or events that occurred after the behaviour.

Event Recording

The observer is interested in recording specific behavioural events (such as how many times the student hits or gets out of his or her seat). A tally sheet listing the behaviours to be observed and counted is useful; when the observer sees the behaviour of interest, he or she can simply make a tick mark on the sheet.

Duration Recording

This method usually requires a watch or clock, so that a precise measurement of how much time a student spends doing something of concern to the teacher or assessment team (e.g., talking to others, tapping, rocking) can be recorded.

Time-Sampling Recording

With this technique observers count the number of times a behaviour occurs during a specific time interval. Rather than observe for long periods of time and tally all incidences of the behaviour causing concern, the observer divides the observation period into equal time units and observes and tallies behaviour only during short periods of time. Based upon the time sampling, predictions can then be made about the student's total behaviour.

Checklists and Rating Scales

A checklist usually requires the observer to note whether a particular characteristic is present or absent, while a rating scale typically asks the observer to note the degree to which a characteristic is present or how often a behaviour occurs. There are many commercially available checklists and rating scales, but they may be developed locally as well.

While observations can yield useful information about the student and his or her environments, there are a number of errors that can occur during observations and distort or invalidate the information collected. One source of error may come from the observer—he or she must record accurately, systematically, and without bias. If his or her general impression of the student influences how he or she rates that student in regards to specific characteristics, the data will be misleading and inaccurate. This can be especially true if the student comes from a background that is different from the majority culture. In such cases, it is important that the observer have an understanding of, and a lack of bias regarding, the student's cultural or language group. Often, multiple observers are used to increase the reliability of the observational information collected. All observers should be fully trained in how to collect information using the specific method chosen (e.g., time-sampling using a checklist) and how to remain unobtrusive while observing and recording, so as not to influence the student's behaviour. It is also important to observe more than once, in a number of situations or locations, and at various times, and to integrate these data with information gathered through other assessment procedures. Decisions should not be made based upon a narrow range of observational samples.

Interviews

Interviewing the student in question, his or her parents, teachers, and other adults or peers can provide a great deal of useful information about the student. Ultimately, "an interview should be a conversation with a purpose" with questions designed to collect information that "relates to the observed or suspected disability of the child". Preparing for the interview may involve a careful review of the student's school records or work samples, for these may help the assessment team identify patterns or areas of specific concern that can help determine who should be interviewed and some of the questions to be asked. Parents, for example, may be able to provide detailed information about the child's academic or medical background. It is especially important that they contribute their unique, "insider" perspective on their child's functioning, interests, motivation, difficulties, and behaviour in the home or community. They may have valuable information to share about possible solutions to the problems being noted. Teachers can provide insight into the types of situations or tasks that the child finds demanding or easy, what factors appear to contribute to the child's difficulties, and what has produced positive results (e.g., specific activities, types of rewards). The student, too, may have much to say to illuminate the problem. "All persons interviewed should be asked if they know of information important to the solution of the academic or behaviour problem that was not covered during the interview".

Organizing interview results is essential. Interviewer might summarize the "perceptions of each person interviewed in a way that conveys similarities and differences in viewpoints", including:

1. Perceptions of the primary problem and its cause,
2. What attempts have been made to solve or address the problem,
3. Any recent changes in the problem's severity, and
4. Student strengths and weaknesses.

Testing

Most assessments include tests, although this has become increasingly controversial. Many educators question the usefulness of the information gained from tests, for reasons that will be discussed in a moment. However controversial testing may be, this News Digest will nonetheless present a basic overview of the issues, because testing so often forms a part of the assessment process. Parents, teachers, and other professionals may find this basic information helpful (*a*) for understanding some of the controversy surrounding testing and, thus, what principles schools need to consider when using standardized tests, and (*b*) for identifying what resources of information about tests are available and what alternatives to testing exist.

Standardized tests are very much a part of the education scene, as we all know. Most of us have taken many such tests in our lifetime. Tests may be informal—meaning a measure developed locally—or they may be commercially developed, formal measures, commonly called standardized tests. Unlike informal tests, standardized tests have detailed procedures for administration, timing, and scoring. There is a wide variety of tests available to assess the different skill areas.

Some tests are known as criterion-referenced tests. This means that they are scored according to a standard, or criterion, that the teacher, school, or test publisher decides represents an acceptable level of mastery. An example of a criterion-referenced test might be a teacher-made spelling test where there are 20 words to be spelled and where the teacher has defined an "acceptable level of mastery" as 16 correct (or 80%). These tests, sometimes called content-referenced tests, are concerned with the mastery of specific, defined skills; the student's performance on the test indicates whether or not he or she has mastered those skills.

Other tests are known as norm-referenced tests. Scores on these tests are not interpreted according to an absolute standard or criterion (i.e., 8 out of 10 correct) but, rather, according to how the student's performance compares with that of a particular group of individuals. In order for this comparison to be meaningful, a valid comparison group—called a norm group—must be defined. A norm group is a large number of children who are representative of all the children in that age group. Such a group can be obtained by selecting a group of children that have the characteristics of children across the United States—that is, a certain percentage must be from each gender, from various ethnic backgrounds (e.g., Caucasian, African American, American Indian, Asian, Hispanic), from each geographic area (e.g., Southeast, Midwest), and from each socioeconomic class. By having all types of children take the test, the test publisher can provide information about how various types of children perform on the test. (This information—what type of students comprised the norm group and how each type performed on the test—is generally given in the manuals that accompany the test.) The school will compare the scores of the child being evaluated to the scores obtained by the norm group. This helps evaluators determine whether the child is performing at a level typical for, below, or above that expected for children of a given ethnicity, socioeconomic status, age, or grade.

Not all tests use large, representative norm groups. This means that such tests were normed using a group of individuals who were not representative of the population in general. For example, on one such test, the norm group may have included few or no African American, Hispanic, or Asian students. Because it is not known how such students typically perform on the test, there is nothing to which an individual student's scores can be compared, which has serious implications for interpretation of results.

Thus, before making assumptions about a child's abilities based upon test results, it is important to know something about the group to which the child is being compared—particularly whether or not the student is being compared to children who are similar in ethnicity, socioeconomic status, and so on. The more unlike the child the norm group is, the less valuable the results of testing will generally be. This is one of the areas in which standardized testing has fallen under considerable criticism. Often, test administrators do not use the norm group information appropriately, or there may not be children in the norm group who are similar to the child being tested. Furthermore, many tests were originally developed some time ago, and the norm groups reported in the test manual are not similar at all to the children being tested today.

Behaviour and Emotional and Social Development

Behaviour–how a student conducts himself or herself in school—is often a key factor in educational performance. Certainly, behaviour that is off-target academically or socially—inattention, being out of seat, talking too much, hitting or biting, skipping school—can detract from learning. When a student's behaviour appears to be interfering with school performance and relationships with others, or when that behaviour is maladaptive, bizarre, or dangerous, it becomes important to assess the student's behaviour (when the behaviour occurs, how often, and for what reasons) as well as his or her emotional and social development.

Negative or inappropriate behaviours may occur for different reasons. One child may be disruptive in class because of attention deficit disorder. A second child may exhibit similar behaviours due to a mental illness, while another's inappropriate behaviour may be linked to environmental factors such as his or her parents' recent divorce. Still another child may be disruptive only in one or two classes, for reasons associated with the way instruction is organized (e.g., a predominance of small group, large group, or self-paced activities) or something in that environment which the student finds disturbing. Thus, identifying why a child is exhibiting certain behaviours is an important part of the assessment process. The reasons why, if they can be determined, will influence whether or not the child is determined eligible for special education services and, if so, will certainly affect the nature of decisions made regarding educational and other interventions.

Assessing Problem Behaviour

For children exhibiting signs of emotional, social, or behavioural problems, the assessment team will generally conduct a behavioural assessment. The goal of behavioural assessment is to gain an increased understanding of how environmental factors may be influencing the child's behaviour. This includes identifying (a) what expectations and rules are established by significant others in the settings where the problem behaviour occurs, and (b) what "specific variables in a particular situation… may be maintaining problem behaviours" (Berdine & Meyer, 1987, p. 151). This knowledge will then be used directly in designing intervention strategies. "Behavioural assessment depends on keen observation and precise measurement" (Swanson & Watson, 1989, p. 246). Assessment is tied to observing a specific situation (e.g., how the child responds during lunch or reading) at a particular point in time. It is important that a behavioural assessment involve multiple measures and take place in various settings (e.g., the classroom, school playground, chorus, home) and at different times during the day (e.g., morning, afternoon, and night). The ability to observe and record behaviour, select the most appropriate places to observe the child, and find efficient and clear means of interpreting results are all critical in behavioural assessment.

Collectively, the observations should provide information which:

1. Pinpoints and quantifies the nature of the behaviour problem (including what variables in the environment are contributing to or maintaining the behaviour);
2. Allows eligibility and placement decisions to be made;
3. Illuminates what type of instruction or intervention is needed; and
4. Provides baseline information against which progress can be measured once intervention begins.

Interviews are also a useful means of gathering information about a child's behaviour. Parents and significant others may be able to offer insight into the nature and history of the child's difficulties. The child may also be an excellent source of information. Of primary interest here is determining the child's "awareness of the problem behaviours and their controlling variables, degree of motivation to change, and skill at behavioural self-control"

Assessing Adaptive Behaviour

Other aspects of behaviour may be important to assess as well. Adaptive behaviour is a frequent focus of assessment, and is a required area of assessment when a classification of mental retardation is being considered for a student. Adaptive behaviour refers to "the effectiveness or degree with which individuals meet the standards of personal independence and social responsibility expected for age and cultural groups". When assessing a person's adaptive behaviour, examiners may investigate his or her strengths and weaknesses in a variety of different skill areas, such as: communication, self-care, home living, social skills, community use, self-direction, health and safety, functional academics, leisure, and work. According to the American Association on Mental Retardation (1992), these are the skills with which individuals most often require assistance or some specialized support.

The IDEA specifies "deficits in adaptive behaviour" as one of the two characteristics necessary for a student to be classified as having mental retardation (the other characteristic being "significantly subaverage general intellectual functioning". Measuring a student's adaptive behaviour, however, should not be limited to only those students suspected of having mental retardation; this type of assessment has much to offer the decision-making associated with students with other disabilities as well, particularly in regards to IEP development and instructional and transition planning.

Many commercially-developed adaptive behaviour instruments exist to help educators evaluate a student's adaptive skills. Using these instruments typically does not require the student to be involved directly; rather, examiners record information collected from a third person who is familiar with the student (e.g., parent, teacher, direct service provider) and who can report what types of adaptive skills the student has mastered and which he or she has not. Unfortunately, there is some concern that many of the available adaptive behaviour scales do not meet the technical requirements of good instrumentation and that there may be bias inherent in assessing the behaviour of children who are culturally or linguistically different from the majority culture. Therefore, care must be taken with the selection of the adaptive behaviour scale to be used. It is also a good idea to use other methods to collect information about the student's skills, such as direct observation and interviewing the student. For minority students, it is imperative to develop an understanding of what types of behaviour are considered adaptive (and, thus, appropriate) in the minority culture, before making judgments about the particular functioning of a student.

Assessing Emotional and Social Development

No child lives in a vacuum. His or her relative freedom from internal and external stressors, ability to interact with others comfortably, and ability to respond consistently and positively in the learning environment all are important for the child to benefit maximally from school experiences. In assessing a child's emotional and social adjustment, questions need to be answered related to the child's intrapersonal and interpersonal experience. Assessment of the child's intrapersonal world involves knowledge about how the child views him or herself, how the child responds emotionally, how much conflict or anxiety he or she is currently experiencing, the degree to which the individual believes that personal behaviours can actually make a difference in his or her own life, his or her tolerance for frustration, and general activity level. Interpersonal characteristics are related to how the individual views the world and other people. Such characteristics are developed in response to the child's experiences within the environment. If the child sees the world as a hostile place and views people as untrustworthy, negative interactive patterns and behaviours may emerge.

The development of the child's intrapersonal experience and interpersonal behaviours is, at least in part, related to the way basic physiological and psychological needs (e.g., to be fed, feel safe, belong, be productive, unique, empowered) are being met. If a child is abused, ignored, or neglected, there are often negative behavioural, cognitive, and emotional outcomes. Problem behaviours such as tantrums, aggression toward others, or withdrawal may result from the child's emotional and social turmoil. However, as was mentioned above, it is important to remember that negative behaviours may arise from vastly different reasons than experiences of abuse or neglect (e.g., biochemical or physiological factors).

There are many instruments available to assess a child's emotional and social functioning. Several ways in which personality variables may be measured. The use of Rating Scales was discussed above under "Behavioural Assessment" and is applicable here as well. A second approach, using projective techniques, asks students to respond to vague or ambiguous stimuli such as inkblots or pictures, draw pictures, or express themselves through the use of puppets or dolls. The responses are then interpreted by a person trained in such procedures. A third approach is to administer personality inventories or questionnaires that vary in their focus. Some may measure self-concept or learning style, while others are intended to indicate the possible presence of mental illness. These latter instruments are generally lengthy and present the individual taking them with a substantial reading load, both in terms of how much there is to read and in terms of how complex and abstract many of the ideas are. Thus, many such inventories are not suitable for individuals with low literacy. Many of these measures suffer from technical inadequacies and yield esoteric results that are difficult to translate into treatment goals" (p. 144). For this reason, while information gathered through these instruments may help the assessment team understand the student more fully, information collected through approaches such as direct observation and interviews may be more useful and reliable.

Identification and Assessment of the Disabilities

Timely identification of impairments, a secondary prevention, can reduce the impact of the impairment on the functional level of the individual and also in checking the impairments from becoming a disabling condition. Initially they need to be identified as soon as possible at home by the parents and outside (in the anganwadi centres/schools/sub-health centres/through camps), and then they need to be assessed by a team of specialists in order to plan necessary interventions.

Identification

At Home Parents can observe and identify the children with disabilities by using the following checklist for early identification of disabilities:

I. Hearing Impairment

Screening new born

1. Is there any one in the family with deafness since childhood.

2. Did the mother take an abortificient drug or any drug or any other medicine in large doses during the first three months of pregnancy?
3. Is the birth weight below 1500 gms.?
4. Did the child have a delayed cry after birth?
5. Did the child have significant jaundice (yellowness of eyes) during the first 10 days after birth?
6. Does the child have a cleft in the lip or palate, or a malformed pinna?

Screening children in the age group of 6 months to 2 years

1. Does a child turn towards the source of sound which is located either at the back or towards one side of the body?
2. Does he/she has discharge from the ear?

Screening children above 2 years age

1. Does he/she turn when called from behind?
2. Uses gestures excessively.
3. The child does not speak or has a defective speech.
4. The child does not understand the spoken language.
5. The child has an ear discharge.

II. Visual Impairment

1. The child does not follow an object moving before his eyes by one month's age.
2. The child does not reach for toys and things held in front of him by three months age.
3. One eye moves differently from the other; including squint.
4. Eyes are either red or have a yellow discharge, or the tears flow continuously.
5. The child has a tendency to bring pictures or books very close to the eyes.

III. Mental Retardation

1. Does the child respond to name/voice by fourth month?
2. Does the child smiles at others by sixth month?
3. Does the child hold the head steadily by sixth month?
4. Does the child sit without support by twelfth month?
5. Can the child stand without support by eighteenth month?
6. Can the child walk well by twentieth month?

8 Strategies for Teaching Students with Disabilities

Most people know, or are taught, at an early age, how to process information and develop an organized plan or strategy when confronted with a problem, whether that problem is social, academic, or job related. Others find such cognitive processes quite difficult. Learning disabilities have only recently been recognized as disabilities. This neurological disorder causes difficulty in organizing information received, remembering them, and expressing information and therefore affects a person's basic function such as reading, writing, comprehension, and reasoning. However, these students with learning disabilities can be taught effective learning strategies that will help them approach tasks more effectively. (From: Learning Strategies for Problem Learners, by Thomas Lombardi).

General Information

Bring to the student's attention *science role models with disabilities* with a similar disability to that of the student. Point out that this individual got ahead by a combination of effort and by asking for help when needed.

There are many types of learning disabilities as one person vary from another. Some of the situations commonly found are dyslexia (inability to read), dyscalcula (inability in math reasoning), dysgraphia (difficulty with syntax), visual, and audio difficulties. Generally, a person with learning disabilities experience difficulties in study skills, writing skills, oral skills, reading skills, math skills, and social skills.

In studying, students experience inability to organize time therefore unable to finish assignments on time, and they have trouble taking notes and following instructions. They often have difficulty spelling correctly and have frequent grammatical errors which results in poor sentence stucture and poor penmanship. If the lecturer speaks too fast, they will have difficulty understanding the lecture and recalling the words. They are usually slow readers and sometimes hae incorrect comprehension and poor retention. Confusion with math symbols are common, as well as difficulty with concepts of time and money. Realizing their inabilities result in low self-esteem which greatly affects their social skills. They might have impulsive behaviour and disorientated in time.

Dealing with students with learning disabilities takes patience. The following are some suggestions and guidelines for a teacher with students with learning disabilities.

- Don't assume that the person is not listening just because you are getting no verbal or visual feedback.
- Don't assume that you have to explain everything to students with learning disabilities. They do not necessarily have a problem with general comprehension.
- Consult with the special education specialist to obtain help in understanding the specific nature of the learning disability for each student.
- Never assess a student's capabilities based solely on their IQ or other standardized test scores.
- Give student with learning disabilities priority in registration for classes.
- Allow course substitution for nonessential course requirements in their major studies.

- A student may have documented intelligence with test scores in the average to superior range with adequate sensory and motor systems and still have a learning disability. Learning disabilities often go undiagnosed, hence teacher observation can be a major source of identification.
- Bring to the student's attention *science role models with disabilities* with a similar disability to that of the student. Point out that this individual got ahead by a combination of effort and by asking for help when needed.

Teacher Presentation

- Always ask questions in a clarifying manner, then have the students with learning disabilities describe his or her understanding of the questions.
- Use an overhead projector with an outline of the lesson or unit of the day.
- Reduce course load for student with learning disabilities.
- Provide clear photocopies of your notes and overhead transparencies, if the student benefits from such strategies.
- Provide students with chapter outlines or study guides that cue them to key points in their readings.
- Provide a detailed course syllabus before class begins. Ask questions in a way that helps the student gain confidence.
- Keep oral instructions logical and concise. Reinforce them with a brief cue words. Repeat or re-word complicated directions.
- Frequently verbalize what is being written on the chalkboard.
- Eliminate classroom distractions such as, excessive noise, flickering lights, etc.
- Outline class presentations on the chalkboard or on an overhead transparency. Outline material to be covered during each class period unit. (At the end of class, summarize the important segments of each presentation.)

- Establish the clarity of understanding that the student has about class assignments.
- Give assignments both in written and oral form.
- Have more complex lessons recorded and available to the students with learning disabilities.
- Have practice exercises available for lessons, in case the student has problems.
- Have students with learning disabilities underline key words or directions on activity sheets (then review the sheets with them).
- Have complex homework assignments due in two or three days rather than on the next day.
- Pace instruction carefully to ensure clarity.
- Present new and or technical vocabulary on the chalkboard or overhead.
- Provide and teach memory associations (mnemonic strategies).
- Support one modality of presentation by following it with instruction and then use another modality.
- Talk distinctly and at a rate that the student with a learning disability can be follow.
- Technical content should be presented in small incremental steps.
- Use plenty of examples, oral or otherwise, in order to make topics more applied.
- Use straight forward instructions with step-by-step unambiguous terms. (Preferably, presented one at a time).
- Write legibly, use large type; do not clutter the blackboard with non-current/non-relevant information.
- Use props to make narrative situations more vivid and clear.
- Assist the student, if necessary, in borrowing classmates' notes.
- Consider cross-age or peer tutoring if the student appears unable to keep up with the class pace or with complex subject

matter. The more capable reader can help in summarizing the essential points of the reading or in establishing the main idea of the reading.

Laboratory

- Clearly label equipment, tools, and materials. Color code them for enhanced visual recognition.
- Consider alternate activities/exercises that can be utilized with less difficulty for the student, but has the same or similar learning objectives.
- Provide clear photocopies of your notes and overhead transparencies.
- For students with learning disabilities, make available cue cards or labels designating the steps of a procedure to expedite the mastering.
- Use an overhead projector with an outline of the lesson or unit of the day.
- Allow extended time for responses and the preparation and delivery of reports.
- In dealing with abstract concepts, use visual tools such as charts and graphs. Also, paraphrase and present them in specific terms, and sequence and illustrate them with concrete examples, personal experiences, or hands-on exercises.
- To minimize student anxiety, provide an individual orientation to the laboratory and equipment and give extra practice with tasks and equipment.
- Find areas of strength in the student's lab experiences and emphasize those as much as possible.
- Allow the students with learning disabilities the use of computers and spell checking programmes on assignments.

Reading

- Announce readings as well as assignments well in advance.
- Find materials paralleling the textbook, but written at a lower

reading level. (Also, include activities that make the reading assignment more relevant.)

- Introduce simulations to make abstract content more concrete.
- Make lists of required readings available early and arrange to obtain texts on tape from Recording for the Blind or a Reading/Typing Service.
- Offer to read written material aloud, when necessary.
- Read aloud material that is written on the chalkboard and on the overhead transparencies.
- Review relevant material, preview the material to be presented, present the new material then summarize the material just presented.
- Suggest that the students use both visual and auditory senses when reading the text.
- Rely less on textbooks. Reading for students with learning disabilities may be slow and deliberate, and comprehension may be impaired for the student, particularly when dealing with large quantities of material. Comprehension and speed usually dramatically increase with the addition of auditory input.
- Spend more time on building background for the reading selections and creating a mental scheme for the organization of the text.
- Encourage students to practice using technical words in exchanges among peers.
- Choose books with a reduced number of difficult words, direct non convoluted syntax, and passages that deliver clear meaning. Also, select readings that are organized by subheads because this aids in the flow of ideas.
- When writing materials for reading by students with learning disabilities, some of the strategies referred to in the *reading section of the hearing impaired presentation* will be appropriate.
- Allow the student to use a *tape recorder*.

Group Interaction and Discussion

- Always ask questions in a clarifying manner, then have the students with learning disabilities describe his or her understanding of the questions.
- Assist the student, if necessary, in borrowing classmates discussion notes.
- Encourage questions during or after class to ensure that materials are understood by students with learning disabilities.
- Give individual conferences to guide students with learning disabilities to monitor progress and understanding of the assignment and of the course content.
- Give plenty of reinforcement when it is evident that the student with a learning disability is trying things that are made difficult by the disability.
- Have frequent question-and-answer sessions for students with learning disabilities.

Field Experiences

- Allow the students with learning disabilities the use of computers and spell checking programmes on field notes and reports.
- Consider alternate activities/exercises that can be utilized with less difficulty for the student, but has the same or similar learning objectives.

Research

- Review and discuss with the student the steps involved in a research activity. Think about which step(s) may be difficult for the student's specific functional limitations and jointly devise accommodations for that student.
- Use appropriate laboratory and field strategies.

Testing

- Avoid overly complicated language in exam questions and clearly separate items when spacing them on the exam sheet.

(Refer to writing for students with hearing impairments in the *reading section.*)

- Consider other forms of testing (oral, hands-on demonstration, open-book etc.). Some students with learning disabilities find that large print helps their processing ability.
- Consider the use of illustrations by the students with learning disabilities as an acceptable form of response to questions in lieu of written responses.
- Eliminate distractions while students are taking exams.
- For students with perceptual problems, for whom transferring answers is especially difficult, avoid answer sheets, especially computer forms. Allow them to write answers (check or circle) on the test (or try to have them dictate their responses on a tape recorder.)
- For students who have reading difficulties, have a proctor read the test to the student.
- For students with writing difficulties, have someone scibe the answers for them or use a tape recorder to take down the answers.
- Gradually increase expectations as the students with learning disabilities gains confidence.
- Grant time extensions on exams and written assignments when there are significant demands on reading and writing skills.
- If distractions are excessive, permit the students with learning disabilities to take examinations in a separate quiet room with a proctor.
- Provide study questions for exams that demonstrate the format along with the content of the exam.
- Review with the student how to proofread assignments and tests.
- Do not test material just presented or outcomes just produced, since for the students with learning disabilities, additional time is generally required to assimilate new knowledge and concepts.

- Permit the students with learning disabilities the use of a dictionary, thesaurus, or a calculator during tests.
- Provide computer with spell check/grammar/cut & paste features

Strategies for Children having Visual Impairment

There are two main functional categories of visual impairments: Low Vision and Blind. Low vision students usually are print users, but may require special equipment and materials. The definition of legal blindness covers a broad spectrum of visual impairments. The extent of visual disability depends upon the physical sensory impairment of the student's eyes, the age of the student at the onset of vision impairment, and the way in which that impairment occurred. Vision also may fluctuate or may b e influenced by factors such as inappropriate lighting, light glare, or fatigue. Hence, there is no "typical" vision impaired student. The major challenge facing visually impaired students in the science educational environment is the overwhelming mass of visual material to which they are continually exposed, viz., textbooks, class outlines, class schedules, chalkboards writing, etc. In addition, the increase in the use of films, videotapes, computers, laser disks, and television adds to the volume of visual material to which they have only limited access. To assist in overcoming a students' visual limitation requires unique and individual strategies based on that student's particular visual impairment and his/her skill of communication (e.g., Braille, speed listening, etc.).

General Courtesy for Childrens

- Speak to the class upon entering and leaving the room or site.
- Call the student with a vision impairment by name if you want his/her attention.
- Seat the student away from glaring lights (e.g. by the window) and preferably infront of the class.
- Use descriptive words such as straight, forward, left, etc. in

relation to the student's body orientation. Be specific in directions and avoid the use of vague terms with unusable information, such as "over there", "here", "this", etc.

- Describe, in detail, pertinent visual occurrences of the learning activities.
- Describe and tactually familiarize the student to the classroom, laboratory, equipment, supplies, materials, field sites, etc.
- Give verbal notice of room changes, special meetings, or assignments.
- Offer to read written information for a person with a visual impairment, when appropriate.
- Order the appropriate text books for the students in their preferred medium.
- Identify yourself by name, don't assume that the student who is visually impaired will recognize you by your voice even though you have met before.
- If you are asked to guide a student with a visual impairment, identify yourself, offer your services and, if accepted, offer your arm to the student's hand. Tell them if they have to step up or step down, let them know if the door is to their left or right, and warn them of possible hazards.
- Orally, let the student know if you need to move or leave or need to end a conversation.
- If a student with a visual impairment is in class, routinely check the instructional environment to be sure it is adequate and ready for use.
- When communicating with a student who has a vision impairment, always identify yourself and others who are present.
- Do not pet or touch a guide dog. Guide dogs are working animals. It can be hazardous for the visually impaired person if the dog is distracted.

- Be understanding of the slight noise made by a *portable translator.*
- Also use an auditory or tactile signal where a visual signal is normally used.
- It is not necessary to speak loudly to people with visual impairments.
- Always notify changes of class schedule in advance.

General Strategies

The degree of impairment and the student's background and training (like the degree of proficiency in Braille) will affect the usefulness of the various strategies and suggestions. The student with a vision impairment will most likely need assistance in all aspects of science programmes. The various strategies given below will work for most vision impaired students—some may not. Accessible description will be necessary for pictures, graphics, displays, or field sites, etc.; the student's identification queries; and differentiation of items where touch will not discriminate; and in orientation and mobility aspects in unfamiliar situations.

- Bring to the student's attention *science role models with disabilities* with a similar disability to that of the student. Point out that this individual achieved by a combination of effort and by asking for help when needed.
- A wide selection of *magnifying devices* are available that can be used by visually impaired students to assist in reading or working with objects that need to be observed.
- A *screen reader, low vision projection screen,* or an item like *outSPOKEN* or a similar system can be used to read a computer screens.
- A screen magnifier may be used to enlarge print on a computer screen.

General Information Access for Persons with Vision Loss

1. Visual material needs to be accompanied by a verbal description. If you are demonstrating how to use a piece of equipment, be sure to describe the equipment and what you are doing to operate it. Read overheads aloud and describe the content of slides (see note below about large print). In a conference presentation setting, you will probably want to provide all descriptions yourself. If you are showing a videotape, describe the action. If you distribute videotapes as handouts, any action or an explanatory text that is crucial to understanding the text of the presentation should be narrated.
2. If there are multiple speakers (such as a panel), have each speaker introduce himself or herself to the audience so that the speakers' voices are keyed for the audience as to their identity.
3. Be certain that your presentation can be clearly heard by everyone in the room and repeat all questions from the audience, prior to answering.
4. Handouts should be available in large print, audiotape, computer disk, and/or Braille formats. If this is not possible prior to your presentation, note the various individuals' preferred formats and then make your materials available to them within a short time after your presentation.
5. Large Print *-People who have some functional vision may be able to see print if it is large enough. Prepare print information on white paper with sharp, black ink. Standard print is generally 10-12 point type. Large print is 16-18 point and up, generally an enlargement setting of 160-175 per cent on a copy machine. In the case of documents that already exist in print form, use a copy machine to enlarge each page onto 11 x 17 paper. Try darker settings on the copy machine to increase contrast without producing streaks. Many computer programmes offer a variety of font types and sizes.

6. (On most newer versions of browsers, you can select Text Zoom from View Menu of the browser for larger view).

Teacher Presentation

- By verbally spelling out a new or technical word, you will be helping the student with a vision impairment, as well as for other students.
- An *enlarged activity script, directions, or readings* of a detailed lesson can be used for a low vision person and for use in describing *tactile 3D models* .
- Use an *overhead projector* to show step-by-step instructions. Mask all the instructions except the one(s) that you want to present.
- Use an *opaque projector* whenever possible to enlarge a text or manual.
- All colored objects used for identification related to a lesson, experiment, or other directions should be labeled with a *Braille label maker* or otherwise tacitly coded for most students with vision impairments.
- Describe, in detail, visual occurrences, visual media, and directions including all pertinent aspects that involve sight.
- Use a sighted narrator or *descriptive video* (preferably the latter) to describe aspects of videos or laser disks.
- Describe, in detail, all pertinent visual occurrences or chalkboard writing.
- Where needed, have lesson or direction materials Brailled, use an *enlarged activity script*, or recorded ahead of time, for class handouts.
- Have *tactile 3D models, raised line drawings*, or *thermoforms* available to supplement drawings or graphics in a tactile format when needed.
- Whenever possible, use actual objects for three dimensional representations.

- Modify instructions for auditory/tactile presentation.
- Use *raised line drawings* for temporary tactile presentations.
- Use an *overhead projector*, chalkboard, graphs, or slides as you would normally, but provide more detailed oral descriptions, possibly supplemented with *thermoforms* where appropriate.
- Allow student to use a *tape recorder* for recording classroom presentations or the text.
- Make all handouts and assignments available in an appropriate form: e.g., regular print, large print, Braille, or on a cassette, depending on the students optimal mode of communication.
- Use a *monocular* or a *private eye* (electronic miniature television) or similar devices for long range observations of chalk board or demonstration table presentations.

Laboratory

1. Describe and tactually/spatially familiarize the student with the lab and all equipment to be used.
2. Consider alternate activities/exercises that can be utilized with less difficulty for the student, but has the same or similar learning objectives.
3. Use an *enlarged activity script, directions, or readings* for a low vision student (or taped script for a student who is blind) for use with *tactile 3D models.*
4. Make all handouts and assignments available in the appropriate form for the student: e.g., regular print, large print, Braille, or tape depending on the students optimal mode of communication.
5. Assistance may be needed for converting certain laboratory materials from a visual to a tactile format.

6. Have the student with a vision impairment do a trial run on the equipment before the activity.
7. Allow more time for the laboratory activities.
8. Always try to keep materials, supplies, and equipment in the same places.
9. Use a *microprojector* or similar device to help the visually impaired student to examine images from a microscope.
10. Place the student and/or *tape recorder* an appropriate distance from the activity to permit hearing and/or the recording of results or observations.
11. Use an *overhead projector* or *opaque projector* to show step-by-step instructions. Mask all the instructions except the one(s) that you want followed for students with vision impairments.
12. Use *Descriptive Video* for videos or laser disks. If Descriptive Video is not available, use a sighted narrator to describe movies, videos, laser disks, or slides.
13. Provide means for the acquisition and/or recording of data in an appropriate mode for the student.
14. Use tag shapes for showing relationships (such as distance comparisons) buttons, or other markers on a "layout" board.
15. A *Braille label maker* will be useful for identifying materials and containers in the laboratory for the vision impaired student with a vision impairment who reads Braille.
16. Make equipment available that the student with a vision impairment can access in interpreting and understanding the results of laboratory exercises (e.g. *audible readout voltmeters, calculators, talking thermometers, magnifiers*, etc.
17. Use a hot plate for heating instead of Bunsen burner.
18. Label material, supplies, and equipment with regular print, large print, and/or Braille, as appropriate for the vision impaired student.

19. Pair the student with a vision impairment with a sighted student. Then have the non-impaired student describe the activities and outcomes as they are observed.
20. A *low vision projection screen* can be use to magnify images up to 720X.
21. Use a *portable communication board* to provides auditory scanning of laboratory materials such as: pictographic symbols, letters, and/or words.
22. When using a computer, the student with a visual disability can use a *voice input device* or a *remote voice system* to verbally enter commands.
23. Prior to the enrollment of a student with a visual impairment in class, obtain laboratory equipment that have available ability to produce adaptive outputs such as: a large screen, print materials, or various *audio output devices.*
24. Various *Braille devices* can be used to assists vision impaired students when reading.
25. For "reading" the outputs of balances and other instruments, one can use a Braille N' Speak device *(Blazie Engineering)*
26. Have a lab assistant help you if necessary to make sure that students with visual impairments are being assisted.

Group Interaction and Discussion

- Describe and tactually/spatially familiarize the student to the classroom.
- Place the student and/or recorder an appropriate distance from the activity to permit recording of material.
- Use a tape recorder.
- If the student is partially sighted, be sure he/she is seated where lighting is appropriate.
- Use a note taker who takes notes in the appropriate mode.

Text Reading Systems

- Paid or volunteer readers or writers can assist a student with a visual impairment with texts, materials, and library readings.

- Offer to read, or arrange to have read, written information for a person with a visual impairment, when appropriate.
- Arrange, ahead of time, for audio book acquisition of the text or other reading materials through the *Talking Book Service, Recordings for the Blind and Dyslexic, text reading systems*, or *audio output devices.*
- Various *Braille devices* can be used to assists vision impaired students when reading.

Field Experiences

- Make all handouts, safety information, and assignments available in an appropriate form (e.g., regular print, large print, tactile Braille, or cassette).
- Consider alternate activities/exercises that can be utilized with less difficulty for the student, but has the same or similar learning objectives.
- Use a sighted guide.
- Do detailed description and narration of objects seen in science centers, museums, and/or field activities.
- The use of a *laser cane* or *mowat sensor* can be useful in assisting the student in unfamiliar surroundings.
- An *enlarged activity script, directions, or readings* for descriptions of a field/activity for a low vision person to use with field observations.
- Suggest that the student use a *standard tape recorder.*

Research

- Review and discuss with the student the steps involved in a research activity. Think about which step(s) may be difficult for the specific functional limitations of the student and jointly devise accommodations for that student.
- Use appropriate lab and field strategies according to the nature of the research.
- Various *Braille Devices* can be used to assists vision impaired students when reading.

- Suggest that the student use a *tape recorder* with a sighted person on the various activities.
- Research on *Mowatt sensor*

Testing

- Make arrangements for tactile examinations, if touch is not normally permitted (say, in a museum) then contact the curator for tactile access to a museum display items or say, in a zoo for access to a plant/animal species and/or collection).
- Place the student being tested close to the activity if tactile examination is necessary.
- Present examinations in a form that will be unbiased to visually impaired students. Ask the student for the approach he/she finds to be most accessible.
- One possible accessible method is to record test questions on tape and have the students record their answers on tape in an area which has minimal disturbance for other students.
- Use an *enlarged activity script, directions, or readings* to go along with the testing material.
- Allow more time.
- Allow *calculators* to be used during the test.
- Make use of larger print (e.g. 14 pt; 20 pt sized or as needed).
- Make use of visual magnification (magnifier or magnifying machine), audiocassette, Braille/Braille graphs/Braille device for written responses, large block answer sheet.

Strategies for Childrens Hearing Impairment

Over time, the average hearing impaired student shows an ever increasing gap in vocabulary growth, complex sentence comprehension and construction, and in concept formation as compared to students with normal hearing. Hearing impaired students often learn to "feign" comprehension with the end result being that the student does have optimal learning opportunities. Therefore, facilitative strategies for hearing impaired students are primarily concerned with various aspects of communication. Other problems arise because deafness is an invisible disability. It is easy for teachers to "forget about it" and treat the student as not having a disability. It has also been shown that hearing impaired students with good English skills also have good science concept formation.

Deaf: "A hearing impairment which is so severe that a child is impaired in processing linguistic information through hearing, with or without amplification, which adversely affects educational performance."

Hard of Hearing: "A hearing impairment, whether permanent of fluctuating, which adversely affects a child's educational performance but which is not included under the definition of 'deaf'."

Deaf-Blind: "Simultaneous hearing and visual impairments, the combination of which causes such severe communication and other developmental and educational problems that a child cannot be accommodated in special education programmes solely for deaf children or blind children."

General Courtesy

These strategies will work on some of the students—some strategies will not. The degree of impairment and the background training of the student will affect the usefulness of the various strategies).

- Since facial expressions, gestures, and other body language will help convey your message:
- Get the attention of a student with a hearing impairment before speaking and communicating and always face the student.
- If not facing a student with a hearing impairment, gently

touch a student on the shoulder or on the arm to indicate that you want to talk to him/her.

- Do not be alarmed if the student does not understand and you cannot understand him/her. Generally, you will become accustomed to each other in time.
- When communicating, always face the student with a hearing impairment.
- Facial expressions, gestures, and other body language will help convey your message.
- For reinforcement repeat new vocabulary in different contexts.
- Sequence topics so that new material is related to that previously learned.
- The use of visual aids is most helpful since vision is the student's primary means of receiving information.
- Use written announcements (assignments, due dates, exam dates, changes in the class schedule, special event dates, etc.).
- If ambiguities or difficulties arise in the home concerning assignments or lessons, have the parents make a note of these difficulties. Follow-up in written detail.
- Provide an outline in advance of the lesson/activity to give to the student in advance, also list your expectations.
- Write all homework assignments, class instructions, and procedural changes on the chalkboard.
- Use captioned films, videos, and laser disks.
- Use interpreter where needed (see general strategies).
- Avoid seating the student in heavy traffic areas.
- Do not touch or pet a hearing dog. These animals are working animals and it may be hazardous for the hearing impaired student if the dog is distracted.
- Avoid vibrations and excessive noise.
- Make chalkboard notes legible.
- Do not talk while writing on chalkboard.

- Eliminate background noises. Sounds taken for granted and normally ignored by hearing individuals, are amplified by a hearing aid and interfere with the communication of the person who is hard of hearing.
- Establish, with the student, a procedure in case of an emergency. For example, agree that for a fire drill (or fire) the teacher will write on board "Fire drill FIRE—go out backdoor." (Also, if you have a signing student, learn the signs for emergency, fire, go, etc.)
- Get the attention of a person with a hearing impairment before speaking.
- If necessary, use written notes to communicate.
- Supplement audible alarm systems with simple visual alarms such as flashing lights.
- When teaching a student with a hearing impairment, ask where he/she would like to sit, in order to communicate in an optimal manner.

General Strategies

- Bring to the student's attention *science role models with disabilities* with a similar disability to that of the student. Point out that this individual got ahead by a combination of effort and by asking for help when needed.
- Obtain feedback from your hearing impaired students at every opportunity as an indicator of the student's level of understanding.
- If the student lip-reads:
    - Have students sit closer to the lecturer.
    - Look directly at the student.
    - Speak slowly, naturally, and clearly.
    - Slowing down slightly may help.
    - Do not exaggerate your lip movements or shout.
    - If you have a mustache, keep it well trimmed.
- If the student uses an interpreter:

- Speak directly to the student rather than to the interpreter.
- Signing may be distracting at first, but you and the other students will soon become accustomed to the interpreter's presence.
- Give the student and the interpreter outlines of the lecture or written material, in advance, so that they can become familiar with new technical vocabulary.
- Interpreters should not give their opinion of a student's progress as this can violate the student's rights.
- Provide scripts of video and laser media when possible for both the interpreter and the student with a hearing disability (with or without captioning).
- The interpreter is not to answer lesson related questions from the student with a hearing impairment. The student should direct all lesson related questions to the instructor.
- The interpreter should stand closer to the section of the chalkboard that is being used by the instructor, thereby allowing the student to simultaneously see both the signs and the writing on the board.

• When writing materials for hearing impaired students:

  - Break up long sentences.
  - Reduce difficult vocabulary load.
  - Reduce concept density.
  - When using a pronoun be sure that the antecedent is very clear.
  - Do not omit words such as: "that" where such words will clarify a sentence connection.
  - Stay with simple coordinating conjunctions (e.g., but, so, for, and) and avoid less common transitional words (e.g., however, as a consequence, nevertheless, although).
  - Keep cause-and-effect expressions in a very simple in form.
  - Keep conditional expressions which influence the meaning of a statement to a minimum (such as; if, when, assuming that, suppose, provided that, etc.).

- If there is no other way to avoid using a difficult word, include a brief explanation in parentheses, however keep parenthetical explanations to a minimum.
- If an important basic or technical word is to be taught:
- Make meaning and application absolutely clear.
- Use context as a memory aid.
- For a new term, repeat the word numerous times in a variety of contexts.

- Certain language forms are generally to be AVOIDED:
  - Passive voice verbs.
  - Negative forms of verbs and other expressions of negation.
  - Too many modifying forms, such as prepositional phrases, relative clauses. (If a relative clause must be used, the relative pronoun [who, which, that, where, etc.] should be next to the word to which it refers).
  - Stylistic embellishments, such as rhetorical inversions.
  - Colloquial and idiomatic expressions.
  - Cut wordiness while retaining simple English.
  - Avoid the use of idioms.

Teacher Presentation

- Avoid standing in front of windows or light sources that may silhouette the instructor and hinder visual cues.
- Begin explanations with concrete examples, working from the concrete to the abstract.
- Present only one source of visual information at a time.
- Erase the chalkboard except for the items being discussed to reduce "visual pollution."
- Engage the attention of the student with a hearing impairment before communicating with the class.
- If possible, face the light source and keep your hands away from your face when speaking.
- Use an *FM audio trainer* for hard-of-hearing students.

- If a lip reader, refer to General Strategies.
- Use *captioned films/videos/laser disks,* whenever possible.
- If the student with a hearing impairment does not understand, try repeating. If the student still does not understand, rephrase a thought or use a different word order.
- Repeat the questions other students in the class asked so that students with hearing impairments know what you are refering to.
- Maximize the use of visual media.
- It is crucial that students with hearing impairments have good note takers. It is impossible to simultaneously lip-read and take notes, or to watch/read an interpreter and take notes.
- *Carbonless* note taking paper can be used. The paid or volunteer note taker needs to take legible notes and then give the student with a hearing impairment the original (or a copy).
- Obtain feedback from your student at every opportunity as an indicator of the student's level of understanding.
- For reinforcement repeat new vocabulary in different contexts.
- Sequence topics so that new material is related to that previously learned.
- The use of visual aids is most helpful since vision is the student's primary means of receiving information.
- Use written announcements (assignments, due dates, exam dates, changes in the class schedule, special event dates, etc.).
- If ambiguities or difficulties arise in the home concerning assignments or lessons, have the parents make a note of these difficulties. Follow-up in written detail.
- Provide an outline in advance of the lesson/activity to give to the student in advance, also list your expectations.
- Write all homework assignments, class instructions, and procedural changes on the chalkboard.
- Use captioned films, videos, and laser disks.

- Use interpreter where needed (see general strategies).
- Avoid seating the student in heavy traffic areas.
- Reduce excessive noise as much as possible to facilitate communication.

Laboratory

1. Refer to the section on interpreters and lip reading above in the General Strategies.
2. Consider alternate activities/exercises that can be utilized with less difficulty for the student, but has the same or similar learning objectives.
3. Avoid seating the student in heavy traffic areas.
4. As you demonstrate a procedure or technique, deliberately alternate between speaking (use FM audio trainer for hard-of-hearing) and manipulating the materials. This allows the student who is hearing impaired to look at one thing at a time.
5. If the student does not understand, try repeating; if the student still does not understand, rephrase a thought or use a different word order.
6. Keep visual pollution on chalkboard to a minimum. Leave on the chalkboard only what you are discussing.
7. Write new vocabulary words on the chalk board before a lesson or laboratory.
8. Make chalkboard notes legible.
9. Do not talk while writing on chalkboard.
10. Maximize the use of visual media and demonstrations.
11. Repeat new vocabulary in different contexts for reinforcement.
12. Assign students with hearing impairments to a laboratory station that allows an unobstructed view of the chalkboard and the instructor and/or interpreter.

13. Begin explanations with concrete examples, working from the concrete to the abstract.
14. Insure that the student with a hearing impairment receives information about any changes in experimental procedure by writing on the board or paper.
15. Label equipment and materials to aid in the learning of new vocabulary items.
16. Provide concise, step-by-step directions prior to the laboratory activity and preview it with the student, if possible.
17. Provide indicator lights for the on/off status of equipment.
18. When a partner is needed, the teacher should assist in finding an understanding lab partner for a student with a hearing impairment.
19. Use *captioned film/video/laser disk* material.
20. Obtain feedback from your hearing impaired students at every opportunity as an indicator of the student's level of understanding.
21. Use signaling devices to alert the student to a significant sound in the lab.
22. Use an *overhead projector* to show step-by-step instructions.
23. Mask all the instructions except the one that you want followed next.
24. Write all homework assignments and laboratory procedural changes on the chalkboard.
25. Present only one source of visual information at a time.
26. Use written announcements (assignments, due dates, exam dates, changes in the class schedule, special event dates, etc.).
27. In advance, provide an outline of the activity and give to the student your expectations.
28. If non-captioned videos or movies are shown, a dim light is needed so that the student who uses an interpreter can see the interpreter's signing.

Reading

- Provide or adapt reading materials at appropriate reading levels and provide resource material at these same reading levels (see writing section in the general strategies).
- Use highly visual materials (e.g., many figures, pictures, diagrams) in reading assignments.
- Use reading materials that follow the writing guidelines given above in the General Strategies section.

Writing Styles for Hearing Impaired Individuals

When writing materials for hearing impaired students:

- Break up long sentences.
- Reduce difficult vocabulary load.
- Reduce concept density.
- When using a pronoun be sure that the antecedent is very clear.
- Do not omit words such as: "that" where such words will clarify a sentence connection.
- Stay with simple coordinating conjunctions (e.g., but, so, for, and) and avoid less common transitional words (e.g., however, as a consequence, nevertheless, although).
- Keep cause-and-effect expressions in a very simple in form.
- Keep conditional expressions which influence the meaning of a statement to a minimum (such as; if, when, assuming that, suppose, provided that, etc.).
- If there is no other way to avoid using a difficult word, include a brief explanation in parentheses, however keep parenthetical explanations to a minimum.
- If an important basic or technical word is to be taught:
- Make meaning and application absolutely clear.
- Use context as a memory aid.

- For a new term, repeat the word numerous times in a variety of contexts.

Certain Language Forms are generally to be Avoided:

- Passive voice verbs.
- Negative forms of verbs and other expressions of negation.
- Too many modifying forms, such as prepositional phrases, relative clauses. (If a relative clause must be used, the relative pronoun [who, which, that, where, etc.] should be next to the word to which it refers).
- Stylistic embellishments, such as rhetorical inversions.
- Colloquial and idiomatic expressions.
- Cut wordiness while retaining simple English.
- Avoid the use of idioms.

Group Interaction and Discussion

- Be quite clear as to which topic is being discussed.
- Expect and encourage the student to participate in class by answering questions, giving reports, and volunteering for other verbal activities.
- Clearly identify who is speaking or asking a question (pointing is OK).
- In group or team settings, develop procedures so the student who is hearing impaired can express his/her communication needs to others.
- In group situations or discussions which include a student who is speech reading (lip reading) it is very helpful to have students sit in a horseshoe or circle for better inclusion of students with hearing impairments.
- Repetitions or summaries of the most relevant classroom questions, responses, and discussions are helpful to the student with a hearing impairment.
- Show special awareness. Call the person who has a hearing

impairment by name to initiate communication, (or a nod or a hand gesture is acceptable).

- You may need to get the student's attention by tapping him/her gently on the shoulder, arm, or waving your hand or using a similar visual signal.
- A circle is the best seating arrangement for a hearing impaired student. Seat the student with his/her "better" ear towards the class.

Field Experiences

- Adapt as many activities as possible to a visual mode.
- Consider alternate activities/exercises that can be utilized with less difficulty for the student, but has the same or similar learning objectives.
- Whenever possible, allow for direct access to and manipulation of materials.
- Use flash cards for clarity in field exercises.
- Use an Interpreter.

Research

- Review and discuss with the student the steps involved in a research activity. Think about which step(s) may be difficult for the specific functional limitations of the student and jointly devise accommodations for that student.
- Use appropriate lab and field strategies.

Testing

- Refer to the writing section of the general strategies prior to writing test questions.
- After tests or quizzes, give answers by using the overhead projector or give answers in writing.
- Avoid overly complicated language in exam questions and clearly separate items when spacing them on the exam sheet. (See last part of Reading section above on writing for students with hearing impairments.)

- Avoid the use of abbreviations or idioms, except for standard ones.
- Due to difficulty with vocabulary, students may require extra time.
- Interpreters may be asked to interpret a test. Because of the complex language involved, an interpreter can often rephrase a question so that a student is able to better understand the intent of the question.
- Interpreters should not be used as proctors for tests.
- Supplement oral or signed explanations with written material.
- Use short sentences because they are easier and quicker to comprehend than longer sentences.
- Keep the test reading materials at appropriate reading levels.
- Provide small group setting with preferetial seating, auditory amplification, and screens to block out distraction, allowing students to hear more clearly.

Guidelines For Making Teachers Presentations and Materials Accessible to Persons with Hearing Loss

It is a good idea to assume that there will always be people in your audience who have difficulties seeing your material or hearing your presentation. When you make your presentation accessible to persons with hearing or vision loss, everyone in your audience will benefit.

Strategies to Create Information Access for Persons with Hearing Loss

Environment

- Provide the audience with a clear and direct view of your mouth and face.
- Speak from a well-lighted area of the room.
- Reduce background noise by turning off slide projectors or other types of apparatus when not in use.

- Speak clearly and naturally and at your normal pace, unless you are asked to slow down.
- For those with mustaches, trim so the lips show clearly

Interpreters

- Sign language interpreters are certified professionals who use American Sign Language or Signed English to interpret spoken English for people who are deaf or hard of hearing.
- If a sign language interpreter is used, introduce yourself to the interpreter and go over technical and specialized vocabulary before beginning presentations.
- Interpreters at conference presentations should stand on one side of the platform at the front of the room, even with extra lighting if needed, in order to be clearly seen from anywhere in the audience.
- When replying to a query from a hearing impaired individual using an interpreter, speak to the hearing impaired person, NOT to the interpreter.

Captioning

- Captioning is the on screen text display of spoken words or sounds that are part of a video or film presentation. Captioners are usually trained as stenographers and use special software to add captions to a previously produced video.
- Video or film production services can also include captions as part of your original production.
- If showing a videotape, have it captioned. (Open captions are preferred for this purpose as closed captions can be seen only with the use of a decoder.) If there is a script or transcription already available, this will make the captioner's job easier.
- If captioning is not feasible, arrange for an interpreter to sign the audio portion of the tape. If possible, make the tape available to the interpreter a day, or so, before your presentation.

Auditory Materials

- Audiotapes, videotapes, and other auditory materials can be translated into print format to make them accessible to people who are deaf or hard-of-hearing. When transcribing video, be sure to mention any sounds and actions that may occur independent of the spoken text, and indicate settings or changes of scene as well."
- If available, use Assistive Learning Devices. These devices consist of a transmitter that sends electronically enhanced sound to receivers worn by individuals who are hard-of-hearing.
- If available, use A Computer-Aided Realtime Translation (CART), which, usually originally trained as a court or stenographer, uses a stenotype machine with a phonetic keyboard and special software. A computer translates the phonetic symbols into English captions almost instantaneously. Presenters should provide conference organizers with a copy of their presentation or outline and a list of any unusual or technical words that will be used. The CART reporters will add these words to their computer to make translation faster and more accurate. For conference workshops, captions should be output to a large screen located to one side of the presentation area. Lights in this section of the room should be kept low so that the words on the screen can be easily read.

Bibliography

Achenbach, T.M., (1991). *Teacher's report form of the child behavior checklist.* Burlington, VT: University of Vermont.

Aggarwal, Pratap and Ashraf, Mohd Siddiqi: *A Study of Special Privileges of Scheduled Castes in Haryana*, New Delhi, 1976.

Alberto, P. and Troutman, A. (1990). *Applied Behavior Analysis for Teachers.* Columbus: Merrill Publishing Company.

Arthritis Foundation, (2004). *Raising a Child with Arthritis: A Parent's Guide.* Atlanta, GA.

Arthritis Foundation, (2004). *Safe or Sorry: What Parents Need to Know About Kids and Sports Injuries*, Atlanta, GA.

Attention Deficit Disorder in Adults. *Harvard Mental Health Letter*, 2002:19; 5:3-6.

Barkley, R.A., *Taking Charge of ADHD.* New York: The Guilford Press, 2001, p.21.

Biederman, J., Faraone, S.V., Keenan, K., Knee, D., Tsuang, M.F., Family-genetic and psychosocial risk factors in DSM-III attention deficit disorder. *Journal of the American Academy of Child and Adolescent Psychiatry*, 1990: 29(4); 526-533.

Bryant, D.P., & Bryant, B.R. (1998). Using Assistive Technology Adaptations to Include Students With Learning disabilities in Cooperative learning Activities. *Journal of Learning Disabilities*, 31 (1),. 41-54.

Caine, T., (1998). Getting the most out of Technology in the Classroom. *The Exceptional Parent NOV.*

Castellanos, F.X., Lee, P.P., Sharp, W., Jeffries, N.O., Greenstein, D.K., Clasen, L.S., Blumenthal, J.D., James, R.S., Ebens, C.I., Walter, J.M., Zijdenbos, A., Evans, A.C., Giedd, J.N., Rapoport, J.L.,

Developmental trajectories of brain volume abnormalities in children and adolescents with attentiondeficit/hyperactivity disorder. *Journal of the American Medical Association*, 2002, 288:14; 1740-1748.

Central Institute of Research and Training in Public Cooperation, *School Dropout Among Harijan Children: Causes & Cure*, March 1975.

Chalmers, L., (1991, September).Classroom modifications for the mainstreamed student with mild handicaps. *Intervention in School and Clinic*, 27(1), 40-42, 51.

Chaudhuri, Manas, Kamal, "Trends of Stagnation among the Students of different sectors of Population", *Bulletin of the Cultural Research Institute*, Vol. XIII, No. I + II, 1978.

Chauhan, B.R., 'Special Problems Regarding the Education among the Scheduled Castes' in M.S. Gore, I.P. Desai, and Suma Chitnis Papers in *Sociology of Education in India*, NCERT, New Delhi, 1967, p. 246.

Chitnis, S., *Literacy and Educational Enrolment of Scheduled Castes in Maharashtra*, Unit for Research in Sociology of Education, Bombay, 1974.

Chitnis, Suma, 'Education For Equality: Case of Scheduled Castes in *Economic and Political Weekly*, Annual Number,1972, pp. 167581.

Consensus Development Panel. Defined Diets and Childhood Hyperactivity National Institutes of Health Consensus Development Conference, *Summary*, Volume 4, Numbers, 1982.

DSM-IV-TR workgroup. The Diagnostic and Statistical Manual of Mental Disorders, Fourth Edition, *Text Revision*.Washington, DC; American Psychiatric Association.

D'souza, Victor S., *Educational Inequalities Among Scheduled Castes: A Case Study in the Punjab*, Chandigarh, Punjab University Press, 1980.

Dubey, S.N. Murdia, *Ratna Administration of Policy and Programmes for Backward Classes in India*, New Delhi, Somaiya, 1976.

Edyburn, D.L., & Gardner, J.E., Integrating Technology into Special Education Teacher Preparation Programs: Creating a Shared Vision. *Journal of Special Education Technology*, 14 (2),. 3-20.

Faraone, S.V., Biederman, J., Neurobiology of Attention-Deficit Hyperactivity Disorder. *Biological Psychiatry*, 1998: 44; 951-958.

Functional Behavioral Assessment of Students with Emotional or Behavioral Problems. Geller, B., Williams, M., Zimerman, B.,

Frazier, J., Beringer, L., Geralis, E. (1998). *Children with Cerebral Palsy: A Parent's Guide*. Rockville, MD: Woodbine Books.

Giangreco, M. Clowenger, C. & Iverson, V. (1996). Choosing options and accommodations for children: A guide to planning inclusive education. Baltimore: Brookes Publishing Co.

Goyal, B.R., *Educating Harijans*, Academic Press, 1981.

Grossman, H., (1995). *Special Education in a Diverse Society*. Boston: Allyn and Bacon. (Product No. H55163)

Hallahan, D.P., & Kauffman, J.M., (1994). *Exceptional Children: Introduction to Special Education* (6th ed.). Boston: Allyn and Bacon. (Product No. H60528)

Holzberg, C.S., (1999). *Special Ed. on the Web. Technology and Learning,* 20 (3), 53.

Holzberg, C.S., Helping all learners succeed: Special Ed. *Success Stories Technology and Learning,* 18 (5), 52-56.

Hoover, D.W., Milich R., Effects of sugar ingestion expectancies on mother-child interaction. *Journal of Abnormal Child Psychology,* 1994; 22; 501-15.

Horner, R., (1994). Functional assessment contributions and future directions. *Journal of Applied Behavior Analysis*, 27, 401-04.

Horner, R. and Carr, E., (1997). Behavioral support for students with severe disabilities: Functional assessment and comprehensive intervention. *Journal of Special Education*, 31, 84-104.

Howell, R. D., (1996). Technological aids for inclusive classrooms. *Theory into Practice*, 35, 58-65.

In *Children and Adults*. Oxford: University Press, 2000, p. 9.

Kaufmann, J.M. (1997). *Characteristics of Emotional and Behavioral Disorders of Children and Youth* (6th ed.). Columbus, OH: Merrill.

Khan, Mumtaj Ali, *Scheduled Castes and their Status in India*, New Delhi, Uppal, 1980.

Khurana G., Educational Facilities for the Scheduled Castes Education, *Quarterly*, 1979-80.

Kimmel, H., Deek, F.P., Farrell, M.L., & O'Shea, M., (1999). *Meeting the Needs of Diverse Student Population.*

Lakshmanna, C., *Depressed Group Students Between Yesterday & Tomorrow.* Trivandrum; 1977.

Langone, J., (1998). Managing inclusive Instructional Settings: Technology, cooperative planning, and team-based organization.

Focus on Exceptional Children, 30 (8), 1-15.

Lewis, R.B., & Doorlag, D.H., (1995). *Teaching special students in the Mainstream* (4th ed.). Englewood Cliffs, NJ: Merrill.

Lewis, T., (1996). Functional assessment of problem behavior: A pilot investigation of the comparative and interactive effects of teacher and peer social attention on students in general education settings. *School Psychology Quarterly*, 11, 1-19.

Lewis, T. and Sugai, G., (1994). Functional-based assessment of social behavior: introduction and overview. *Diagnostique*, 19, 1-4.

Milone, M., (2000). *Special Teachers for Special Needs Technology and Learning*, 20 (9), 40-44.

Mishra, Y.N., Educational Adaptation Social Ambition & Performance of S.C. at Various Levels in Rewa Distt of M.P.,1978, *Unpublished Report.*

Muscott, H., Morgan, D., & Meadows, N., (1996). Planning and implementing effective programs for school-aged children and youth with emotional/behavioral disorders within inclusive schools. In the Council for Children with Behavioral Disorders (Eds.) *Mini-library Series on Emotional/Behavioral Disorders*. Virginia: CCBD.

Naik, J.P., Education of Scheduled Castes, 1965-66. *Occassional Monograph* (6), ICSSR, 1971.

Naik, J.P., Education of Scheduled Tribes 1965-66. *Occassional monograph* (5), ICSSR, 1971.

NCERT Field Studies in Sociology of Education, *All India Report*, NCERT, New Delhi, 1970.

NCERT, *Stagnation and Dropout at Primary Stage Survey and Data Processing Unit*, NCERT, New Delhi, 1977.

Neelsen, John Peter, "Impact of Education on Social Stratification", in *Journal of Social Research*, Vol. XV, Sep. 1972.

Pandit, H.N., Nautiyal, K.L. and Sharma, Y.D., *Implementation of Constitutional Directive on Education: Progress, Problems and Strategies*, NCERT, 1977.

Patwardhan, Sunanda, *Change Among Indian Harijans, Maharashtra: A Case Study*. New Delhi, Orient Longman, 1973.

Pillai, P., (1999). Using technology to Educate Deaf and Hard of Hearing Children in Rural Alaskan General Education Setting. *American Annals of the Deaf*, 144 (5), 373-378.

Pimpley, P.N., 'Social Characteristics of the Scheduled Caste Students in Punjab' in *Indian Journal of Social Work*, 372, 1976 pp. 119-54.

Pimpley, P.N., *Profile of Scheduled Castes Students,* Chandigarh, Punjab University Press, 1980, pp. 120.

Prasad, Anirudha, *Social Engineering and Constitutional Protection of Weaker Sections in India,* New Delhi, Deep & Deep, 1980, p. 279.

Premi, Kusum K., "Educational Opportunities for the Scheduled Castes: Role of Protective Discrimination in Equalisation", *Economic and Political Weekly,* Vol. X, No. 45 & 46, Nov. 9.1974, pp. 1902-10.

Premi, Kusum K.,"Scheduled Castes and Educational Opportunities", *Indian Journal of Social Work,* 1976,37,3, Oct, pp. 251-57.

Premi, Kusum, K., Protective Legislation and Equality of Educational Opportunity: A Study of Scheduled Castes in Punjab, *Ph. D. Thesis,* JNU, 1977, New Delhi.

Rathnaih, B.V., 'Education as an Instrument of Social Change' in *Education Quarterly,* July 1974, Vol. XXVI, No. 2.

Rayappa, P. Hanumantha & Grover, Deepak, *Employment Planning for the Rural Poor: The Case of Scheduled Castes & Scheduled Tribes,* Sterling, 1980.

Sandler, A. & Bedick, P., (2004). *Living with Spina Bifida: A Guide for Families and Professionals.* Chapel Hill, NC: University of North Carolina Press.

Shah, V.P., & Tara Patel, Who goes to Colleges? *Scheduled Caste and Scheduled Tribe Post-Matric Scholarships in Gujarat.* Rachna Pratishthan, Ahmedabad, 1977

Siegel, J., Good, K., & Moore, J., (1996). Integrating Technology into Educating Preservice Special Education Teachers. *Action in Teacher Education,* (17) 4, 53-63.

Silver, L.B., Attention-deficit hyperactivity disorder in adult life. *Child and Adolescent Psychiatric Clinics of North America,* 2000:9; 3:411-523.

Smith, D.D., & Luckasson, R., (1995). *Introduction to special education: Teaching in an age of challenge* (2nd ed.). Boston, MA: Allyn and Bacon.

Still, G.F., *Some abnormal psychical conditions in children; the Goulstonian lectures.* Lancet, 1902; 1;1008-12.

Sugai, George, (1986). Recording classroom events: Maintaining a critical incidents log. *Teaching Exceptional Children,* 18, 98-102.

Taylor, R.L., Sternberg, L., & Richards, S., (1995). *Exceptional children: Integrating research and teaching* (2nd ed.). San Diego, CA: Singular.

The ADHD Molecular Genetics Network. Report from the third international meeting of the attention-deficit hyperactivity disorder molecular genetics network. *American Journal of Medical Genetics*, 2002, 114:272-277.

The MTA Cooperataive Group. A 14-month randomized clinical trial of treatment strategies for attention-deficit hyperactivity disorder (ADHD). *Archives of General Psychiatry*, 1999; 56:1073-1086.

Turnbull, A., Turnbull III, H., Shank, M., & Leal, D., (1995). *Exceptional Lives: Special Education in Today's Schools*. Englewood Cliff, N.J.: Prentice-Hall, Inc.

U.S. Department of Transportation, National Highway Traffic Safety Administration. *State Legislative Fact Sheet*, April 2002.

Vann, R., (1996). Types of youth aggression and violence and implications for prevention and treatment. In the Council for Children with Behavioral Disorders (Eds.). *Mini-library Series on Emotional/Behavioral Disorders*. Virginia: CCBD.

Warner, K.L., Prepubertal and early adolescent bipolarity differentiate from ADHD by manic symptoms, grandiose delusions, ultra-rapid or ultradian cycling. *Journal of Affective Disorders*, 1998, 51:81-91.

Wender, P.H., *ADHD Attention-Deficit Hyperactivity Disorder*.

Wender, P.H., Pharmacotherapy of attention-deficit/hyperactivity in adults. *Journal of Clinical Psychiatry*, 1998; 59 (Supplement 7): 76-79.

Wilens, T.C., Faraone, S.V., Biederman, J., Gunawardene, S., Does stimulant therapy of attention-deficit/hyperactivity disorder beget later substance abuse? *A Meta-Analytic Review of the Literature*. Pediatrics, 2003, 111:1:179-185.

Wilens, T.E., Biederman, J., Spencer, T.J., Attention deficit/hyperactivity disorder across the lifespan. *Annual Review of Medicine*, 2002:53; 113-131.

Wisniewski, L., & Sedlak, R., (1992). Assistive devices for students with disabilities. *Elementary School Journal*, 92(3), 297-314.

Wolraich, M., Milich, R., Stumbo, P. and Schultz, F., The effects of sucrose ingestin on the behavior of hyperactive boys. *Pediatrics*, 1985; 106; 657-682.

Index